gluten-free
BREAKFAST, BRUNCH & BEYOND

gluten-free
BREAKFAST, BRUNCH & BEYOND

BREADS · CAKES · MUFFINS · SCONES
PANCAKES · WAFFLES · FRENCH TOAST
QUICHES AND MORE

LINDA J. AMENDT

The Taunton Press

The Taunton Press, Inc.
63 South Main Street, PO Box 5506
Newtown, CT 06470-5506
e-mail: tp@taunton.com

EDITOR: Carolyn Mandarano
COPY EDITOR: Nina Rynd Whitnah
INDEXER: Heidi Blough
DESIGN AND LAYOUT: carol singer | notice design
PHOTOGRAPHER: Tara Donne
PHOTO EDITOR: Erin Giunta
FOOD STYLIST: Liza Jernow
PROP STYLIST: Amy Wilson
DIGITAL TECH: Kyle Acebo

The following names/manufacturers appearing in
Gluten-Free Breakfast, Brunch & Beyond are trademarks:
Chiquita®, Microplane®, Nutella®, Old Bay®

LIBRARY OF CONGRESS CATALOGING-IN-PUBLICATION DATA IN PROGRESS

ISBN 978-1-60085-712-6

PRINTED IN THE UNITED STATES OF AMERICA
10 9 8 7 6 5 4 3 2 1

To everyone who enjoys breakfast foods
any time of day—for breakfast, brunch, lunch, dinner,
and late-night meals!

acknowledgments

A cookbook is not created by one person; it takes a team of talented individuals coming together to achieve a goal. I want to thank those who all had a hand in making this book come alive.

Special thanks to the team at Taunton Press: my wonderful editor, Carolyn Mandarano, for all your hard work and being a delight to work with; Tara Donne, for your beautiful photography; food stylist Liza Jernow, for your baking skills; prop stylist Amy Wilson, for your creativity; and talented photo editor Erin Giunta, art director Alison Wilkes, copy editor Nina Rynd Whitnah for your attention to detail, and the entire Taunton team.

A big thank you goes out to my amazing agent, Linda Konner. Without you, this book would never have become a reality. I appreciate your professional representation and thoughtful friendship.

And to my friends Sara D'Aquila, Debbie Marshall, Dorothy Reinhold, Eunice Preku, and A. Cooky Oberg, for all your support and encouragement throughout this project.

contents

introduction
welcome back to breakfast

Let me say this up front: I do not have celiac disease nor am I sensitive to gluten, but I do have friends who have varying levels of gluten sensitivity. As an expert home baker, I have been asked for help in understanding and developing gluten-free recipes. I know a thing or two about the challenges of living with food restrictions because I have food allergies, so I understand the difficulties involved in trying to eliminate certain foods from your diet for health reasons.

What am I allergic to? The alkaloids in nightshade, a family of plants that includes tomatoes, sweet and hot peppers (including all chili peppers and bell peppers), tomatillos, potatoes, eggplant, okra, pimentos, paprika, cayenne pepper, gooseberries, huckleberries, Goji berries, belladonna, and the plant containing the highest levels of the nicotine alkaloid—tobacco. Included are any spices or condiments made with nightshade ingredients. Think about how many prepared foods there are that contain red peppers or paprika for color, a dash of hot pepper sauce to add a zing of flavor, or tomato paste used for thickening gravies and sauces, and you'll understand why I am an avid label reader. I am also well aware of the challenges presented when eating out at restaurants, where allergens can hide in any number of seemingly harmless dishes.

In talking with people who are eating gluten-free because of celiac disease, a gluten sensitivity, or as a lifestyle choice, there is one common complaint: the flavor and light texture of their favorite breads and baked goods are missing in gluten-free versions. There is great frustration among gluten-free cooks over the difficulty in replicating the flavor and crumb of breakfast foods made with wheat flour. Many gluten-free baked goods are bland or have "off" flavors from the various substitute grains used to replace wheat flour. Most of these recipes produce baked goods with dry, tough, and gritty textures, making them poor substitutes for foods made with wheat flour.

The biggest challenge in gluten-free baking is to replicate the structure and texture that gluten gives to baked goods, such as yeast breads, quick breads, muffins, biscuits, scones, and even pancakes and waffles. This can be achieved by using a combination of starches, increasing the amount of leaveners, adding extra eggs, and including a few special ingredients to help replace the structural benefits of gluten. Successful gluten-free baking and cooking requires making some changes in the way you prepare foods, such as using smaller or narrower pans, and using some special techniques to get the desired results.

Understanding Gluten

Before venturing into the kitchen, it's important to understand gluten's role in baking.

WHAT IS GLUTEN?

Those of us who do a lot of baking are familiar with gluten and its properties. Gluten is the protein substance found in wheat and wheat flour that, when developed, gives bread dough its elastic texture and the strong structure to trap the gas bubbles released by yeast. It is what gives wheat bread its tender, chewy, light, and airy texture.

In technical terms, gluten is the specific combination of the proteins glutenin and *gliadin*, which is found only in wheat. *Gliadin* is a *prolamin*, a class of proteins found in a variety of grains. In wheat, it is the *gliadin prolamin* that causes problems for people with celiac disease.

But gluten has taken on a broader definition in recent years. Gluten has become a catchall term for all of the *prolamins* that cause problems for people with celiac disease. While technically not gluten, the *prolamins secalin* in rye and *hordein* in barley are also toxic to people with celiac disease or gluten sensitivity. Other grains, such as rice and corn, also contain *prolamins*, but these proteins do not cause a problem for people with celiac disease or gluten sensitivity.

WHERE IS GLUTEN FOUND?

Gluten is found in wheat, rye, and barley as well as in flours made from these grains. It is also found in any products that contain these grains or are derived from any portion of the grain. Gluten has many wonderful traits, including having a high protein content, promoting absorption, and acting as a thickener to bind mixtures. It is used by food manufacturers in a variety of products to add texture and flavor. A surprising number of off-the-shelf products contain gluten.

In addition to fairly obvious grain products, gluten is commonly found in thickeners, seasonings, flavorings, deli meats, licorice, and salad dressings. Soy sauce, malt vinegar, and malted milk contain gluten. Did I mention beer? Brewer's yeast contains gluten, so beer, ale, and lager are all on the gluten list. Gluten is also used to make high-protein imitation meatlike products that are popular among vegetarians. Imitation crab and imitation seafood both have high gluten levels.

Because the term *gluten* is generally used to include rye and barley, a product labeled as wheat-free does not necessarily mean it is gluten-free. Those on a gluten-restricted diet should read labels carefully to ensure they're removing all traces of gluten from their diet. A detailed listing of common foods containing gluten is included on p. 223.

ABOUT THE RECIPES

The gluten-free recipes in this book do not contain wheat, rye, or barley products, but gluten can hide where we least suspect it. When selecting ingredients to use in the recipes, be sure to check the labels and choose gluten-free versions.

If you are allergic to some other ingredients in these recipes, I've given substitution suggestions in the section Convert Your Favorite Recipes to Gluten-Free on p. 224.

Temperature plays a key role in baking foods. Every oven is different, so baking times can vary from kitchen to kitchen. I give a range of baking or cooking times in each recipe and a visual indicator of what to look for when a recipe is done. Your times may vary—it may take a little less time or a little longer for a gluten-free item to bake in your oven. Check the doneness a few minutes earlier than indicated until you learn whether foods bake faster or slower in your oven.

Some ovens heat too hot when set to a specific temperature, while others don't get hot enough. Even if an oven holds temperature accurately, there may be hot or cool spots. I strongly recommend buying a reliable oven thermometer and using it every time you heat your oven. You may be surprised by how far off your oven is, or you may discover that your oven takes a long time to come up to the set temperature. I have had ovens that will heat up to 350°F in 8 minutes and others that take 20 minutes or more to reach that temperature.

As you gain experience working with gluten-free recipes, you'll get a feeling for how these foods cook and bake, how your oven works, and what adjustments, if any, you need to make to achieve the best results in your own kitchen.

Gluten-free cooking and baking takes patience, and it helps if you can maintain a sense of humor. There is no substitution for practice, and there will be a few failures along the way. It takes time to learn what ingredients and techniques work well in your kitchen, and what flavors and textures you and your family like best.

Using quality ingredients—and in the right proportion—can make all the difference in the taste and texture of gluten-free breakfast foods. Understanding, selecting, and measuring those ingredients is the first step to a successful recipe. Many processed and packaged foods are prepared in facilities that also handle wheat, rye, and barley grains and other foods containing gluten. This can result in contamination of an otherwise gluten-free product. If trace amounts of gluten are going to cause you a problem, then you need to do your research by reading labels, looking for gluten-free certified products, and quizzing manufacturers.

ingredients for delicious gluten-free baked goods

Basic Gluten-Free Ingredients

Using quality ingredients can make all the difference in the flavor and texture of the finished dish. Here are the most common gluten-free ingredients used in the recipes in this book.

GLUTEN-FREE FLOURS

A number of flours can be used in gluten-free cooking and baking, though most are heavy and have very strong grain or bean flavors. They tend to create dense baked goods with flavors that are significantly different from items made with wheat flour. I created an all-purpose gluten-free flour for the recipes in this book, and it comes very close to replicating the texture and flavor of wheat flour (see p. 11).

White-rice flour

White-rice flour has a mild flavor and makes a good substitute for wheat flour in gluten-free recipes. It is ground from rice after the bran and germ have been removed. Finely ground or stone-ground white-rice flour produces the best texture in gluten-free baked goods. White-rice flour is relatively inexpensive and has a long shelf life.

Brown-rice flour

Containing the bran, brown-rice flour has more protein, fat, and nutrients than white-rice flour. Considered a whole grain, brown-rice flour is a little heavier than white-rice flour and has a slightly nutty flavor. The higher fat content makes it more perishable than white-rice flour, so it needs to be stored in the refrigerator to preserve freshness. Be sure to bring the flour to room temperature before combining it with other ingredients.

Cornmeal

Ground from dried corn kernels, cornmeal adds great flavor and texture to muffins and breads. Cornmeal is commonly available in yellow and white varieties; yellow cornmeal has a stronger corn flavor.

Buckwheat flour

Buckwheat is in the same botanical family as rhubarb and is not related to wheat. Buckwheat flour makes a good addition to pancake and waffle batters.

STARCHES

Without gluten to support the structure of the dough or batter, gluten-free baked goods can be dense and heavy. Gluten-free flours are also heavier than all-purpose wheat flour, compounding the problem and making baked goods even denser. To counteract this, starches are added to lighten the mixture and replicate the texture of wheat flour.

Tapioca flour, potato starch, and cornstarch all lighten and improve the texture of gluten-free batters and doughs. They also serve as thickeners, help stabilize the structure of baked goods, and produce a lighter and smoother texture.

Tapioca flour

Tapioca flour, also called tapioca starch, is a light powdery starch made from the tuberous root of the cassava plant. Tapioca flour is a key ingredient in gluten-free flour blends because it helps to lighten the texture of baked items while adding a chewy texture and strengthening the structure.

Potato starch (not potato flour)

A finely textured starch made from raw white potatoes, potato starch helps to lighten flours and gives gluten-free breads and other baked goods a more tender texture.

Potato flour is made from cooked potatoes and has a much heavier texture than potato starch. Do not substitute potato flour for potato starch in gluten-free recipes as it will make baked goods very dense and heavy.

Cornstarch

Made from the starchy endosperm of the corn kernel, cornstarch is used to lighten baked goods and thicken sauces. Adding cornstarch to gluten-free biscuits and scones helps give them a more tender texture.

Homemade Gluten-Free All-Purpose Flours

All of the recipes in this book use the homemade gluten-free all-purpose flour on the facing page. I experimented with several different versions before developing this specific blend, which I found to produce the most consistent baking results.

This recipe makes a universal all-purpose flour that can be used as a substitute for wheat flour. Its neutral taste helps replicate the smooth flavor found in baked goods made with wheat flour, and it produces a texture similar to that achieved with all-purpose wheat flour. Comprised of white-rice flour, brown-rice flour, tapioca flour, and potato starch, it is easy to mix together and keep on hand in the pantry for about a month or in the freezer for about 4 months.

Unlike many gluten-free flour blends, this homemade flour has a pleasant, mild flavor that does not alter the taste of the finished product. It works as a great base for building flavors to create delicious gluten-free breads and baked items. This flour blends well with other ingredients and improves the texture of gluten-free baked goods.

Another advantage of this special flour blend is that it eliminates the need to buy and store a large number of bags of different, sometimes difficult to find, and often expensive grains. It can be used in any recipe calling for all-purpose wheat flour.

I also developed a flour blend based on brown-rice flour. It has a texture that is similar to a cross between all-purpose flour and whole-wheat flour. If you prefer to use a more whole-grain flour, choose the Gluten-Free Brown-Rice Flour Blend (see p. 12) in place of the Gluten-Free All-Purpose Flour in any of the recipes in this book. The results will be similar in taste to the all-purpose white-rice blend, but the texture will be slightly denser.

MEASURING FLOUR INGREDIENTS

To measure the flours and starches to make the Gluten-Free All-Purpose Flour or Gluten-Free Brown-Rice Flour Blend, spoon or pour the flour or starch into a dry measuring cup until overflowing and then level off the top by sweeping a straight-edged knife or spatula across the rim of the cup. Do not dip or scoop the flour out of the container with the measuring cup as this will compact the flour into the cup. Also, don't tap the measuring cup on the counter after filling—this will settle the flour and give you an inaccurate measurement. Use this same measuring method to measure the flour in all of the recipes in this book.

XANTHAN GUM AND GUAR GUM

Xanthan gum and guar gum, which may be used interchangeably, give gluten-free doughs and batters more flexibility and stability, helping them to rise and then maintain their shape during and after baking. The addition of gum brings the texture of gluten-free baked goods much closer to the results achieved with wheat flour.

Xanthan gum

Produced from the fermentation of corn sugar, xanthan gum helps improve the viscosity of doughs and batters. It improves the texture of baked goods, giving them a pleasing "mouth feel." Xanthan gum also helps hold baked goods together and gives them more elasticity. Baked goods containing xanthan gum retain more moisture, are less crumbly after they cool, and have a longer shelf life.

Xanthan gum becomes sticky when wet, so always thoroughly blend it into the dry ingredients before combining with the liquid ingredients. I use xanthan gum in my recipes, but you may substitute with an equal amount of guar gum, if you prefer.

Guar gum

Guar gum, made from finely ground guar seeds, works in the same way as xanthan gum in gluten-free baking and may be substituted for xanthan gum in these recipes. Because guar gum contains a lot of fiber, it may be hard for some people to digest.

gluten-free all-purpose flour

MAKES ABOUT 9 CUPS

4 cups finely ground or stone-ground white-rice flour

2 cups stone-ground brown-rice flour

2 cups tapioca flour or tapioca starch

1 cup potato starch (not potato flour)

1. In an extra-large bowl or container, combine the rice flours, tapioca flour, and potato starch. Whisk together until the ingredients are thoroughly blended. Use a large spoon to bring the flour from the bottom of the bowl up to the top and whisk again. Repeat a few times to make sure the flours are evenly distributed throughout the entire mixture.

2. Store the flour in an airtight container or zip-top storage bag at room temperature for up to 1 month. For longer storage, keep the flour in the refrigerator or freezer. Allow the flour to come up to room temperature before using.

3. Lightly stir the flour before measuring. Spoon the flour into the measuring cup and level off the top with a straight-edged utensil, such as the back of a knife.

gluten-free brown-rice flour blend

MAKES ABOUT 9 CUPS

5 cups stone-ground brown-rice flour

2½ cups tapioca flour or tapioca starch

1½ cups potato starch (not potato flour)

1. In an extra-large bowl or container, combine the brown-rice flour, tapioca flour, and potato starch. Whisk together until the ingredients are thoroughly blended. Use a large spoon to bring the flour from the bottom of the bowl up to the top and whisk again. Repeat a few times to make sure the flours are evenly distributed throughout the entire mixture.

2. Store the flour in an airtight container or zip-top storage bag at room temperature for up to 1 month. For longer storage, keep the flour in the refrigerator or freezer. Allow the flour to come up to room temperature before using.

3. Lightly stir the flour before measuring. Spoon the flour into the measuring cup and level off the top with a straight-edged utensil, such as the back of a knife.

LEAVENERS

Leaveners cause baked goods to rise and have a lighter texture. Because gluten-free flours are heavy, the leaveners need to be increased slightly to help raise the weighty dough.

Baking soda

Baking soda is bicarbonate of soda. It interacts with acids, such as buttermilk, citrus, vinegar, brown sugar, and cocoa powder, in a recipe to create carbon dioxide bubbles, which cause doughs and batters to rise. Baking soda starts to activate as soon as it comes in contact with liquid, so plan to get your baked goods in the oven quickly. In gluten-free recipes, the addition of a small amount of baking soda can also help boost the leavening results of baking powder.

Baking powder

Baking powder is a compound leavener containing bicarbonate of soda, an acid, and a starch to prevent caking and to slow down the activation process. Baking powder requires both liquid and heat to activate. Check the label to make sure the baking powder does not contain wheat starch.

Yeast

Yeast is made up of a single-celled organism, *Saccharomyces cerevisiae*. When provided with food, moisture, oxygen, and a warm temperature, yeast begins to grow and ferment. The fermentation process produces carbon dioxide, which expands to make the bread rise. Except for brewer's yeast, all yeast sold in the United States is gluten-free. All of the bread recipes in this book use instant yeast, also known as rapid-rise yeast.

DAIRY INGREDIENTS

The moisture in dairy ingredients works to activate the leavening agents of baking powder and baking soda in quick bread and coffee cake batters as well as to moisten the dry ingredients and to bind them together. Milk sugars in liquid dairy ingredients, called lactose, caramelize when exposed to heat and turn golden brown during baking, adding an additional layer of flavor to baked goods.

Be aware that many nonfat and reduced-fat dairy products, such as sour cream, cream cheese, and cheese, contain thickeners that may not be gluten-free. Check the labels to be sure. While reduced-fat products can usually be substituted for regular dairy ingredients with minimal effect, nonfat products are not designed for cooking and their texture can change significantly when exposed to heat.

Milk

Milk contains both fat and proteins that help to build and support the structure and texture of breads and give them a tender crumb. The higher the fat content in the milk, the more it will enhance the flavor of the bread product. Either whole milk or low-fat 2% milk can be used to prepare the recipes in this book with equally good results. If lower-fat milks are substituted, there will be a noticeable difference in both the flavor and texture of the finished dish.

Milk is an important ingredient in many of the egg-based dishes in this book. It thins the eggs to give the cooked egg mixture a better texture and adds a smoothness to the finished dish. For dietary needs, you can substitute rice milk, soy milk, almond milk, or coconut milk for the cow's milk used in these recipes with minimal changes in the texture. In many beaten egg dishes, water may also be substituted for the milk by slightly reducing the amount of liquid called for in the recipe.

Buttermilk

Buttermilk is a thick and creamy cultured milk, which has been curdled by the addition of an acidic ingredient. This process of adding an acid to fresh milk causes it to separate into liquids and solids. Buttermilk has a tantalizing acidic tang that adds great flavor and gives baked goods a very tender texture. In addition to flavor and texture, buttermilk also provides the acid needed in some recipes to activate the baking soda.

Sour cream

Sour cream is made by souring cream with an acidifier, such as lactic acid. Like buttermilk, it contributes a rich tangy flavor and tender texture, adds moisture to breads and other baked goods, and provides the acid to activate the baking soda. In most cases, a thick, unflavored plain yogurt may be substituted for sour cream with minimal differences in the finished dish.

Butter

Butter adds needed fat and flavor to many gluten-free recipes. It also helps make baked goods tender and provides moisture that is essential during baking. Butter browns as it bakes, helping to improve the color of gluten-free foods.

Butter in stick form is the best choice for cooking and baking. Not only is it easy to measure, but it also has a higher fat content. Butter sold in tubs has a higher percentage of water or air than stick butter and will significantly alter the texture of baked goods and some cooked foods.

Unsalted butter is the best choice for cooking and making all manner of baked goods. It has a fresh flavor that adds to the overall taste of the food. Salt is added to increase the shelf life of butter, and the amount of salt in butters can vary quite a bit from one brand to the next. Using unsalted butter gives you control over the amount of salt in the recipe. Also, unsalted butter has a lower water content and higher fat content than salted butter so gluten-free baked goods have a better texture and are less likely to be dry or crumbly. Always choose a high-quality unsalted butter for baking. Don't use "light" butter as it contains a high percentage of water, which will alter the structure of gluten-free baked goods.

Margarine

If you need to substitute margarine for butter for dietary reasons, buy margarine in stick form only and make sure it contains at least 80% vegetable oil. Never use any product labeled as a "spread"; the higher proportions of air and water alter the texture of gluten-free breads.

COOKING OIL

Like butter, cooking oil provides fat and moisture and makes foods tender. However, oil does not aid in leavening because it cannot be creamed to incorporate air. Always use an oil with a neutral flavor, such as canola, corn, or safflower. Oils labeled simply as "vegetable oil" are usually a blend of neutral-flavored oils and are a good choice for baking.

WHAT TO DO IF YOUR GLUTEN-FREE BAKED GOODS ARE TOO DRY OR CRUMBLY?

If your baked goods are too dry or crumbly, add more butter or oil, not more milk or other liquid.

As a gluten-free item bakes, much of the liquid in the batter evaporates, leaving baked goods dry. Because gluten-free flour blends can absorb a lot of liquid, too much liquid can cause the baked goods to be dense and gummy. Too much liquid also can alter the structural support of the batter and may cause the dish to fall during or after baking.

More butter or oil in the recipe, however, will increase the amount of fat, which will not only moisten the batter but also help to bind the ingredients and add structural support. You'll also find that baked goods will be moister and stay fresh longer.

If the recipe calls for sour cream, which is considered a solid dairy ingredient, you can increase the amount of sour cream rather than the butter or oil. Because the fat content in dairy ingredients adds structure and moisture to gluten-free baked goods, nonfat and reduced-fat sour creams are not recommended for gluten-free baking. No one said gluten-free baking was low-fat baking!

EGGS

Providing proteins, fat, and moisture, eggs contribute important structure and texture to gluten-free foods. They bind the other ingredients together and give strength to batters and doughs. As eggs are beaten, their proteins create a structure that traps air and liquids, which help define the texture of dishes and baked goods. During baking, the trapped air bubbles expand and cause breads and cakes to rise. Eggs also add richness, tenderness, and color to baked goods.

Eggs should be brought to room temperature before beating or adding to other ingredients. Room-temperature eggs beat to a higher volume and incorporate into doughs and batters faster and better than cold eggs. This will produce lighter egg dishes and baked goods.

All of the recipes in this book use large eggs.

SUGARS

Sugars play a far greater role in baking gluten-free foods than just adding sweetness. They provide flavor and structure and make breads and other baked goods tender and enhance their texture and crumb. Sugar also attracts and retains moisture, prolonging freshness and helping gluten-free baked goods maintain their flavor.

Granulated sugar

Granulated sugar is the type of sugar most frequently used in cooking and baking. When creamed with butter, the small sugar grains provide friction and incorporate air into the mixture to create a light and tender texture.

Brown sugar

Brown sugar is basically refined granulated sugar with molasses added. It is made by one of two processes: molasses is boiled down until sugar crystals form, or molasses syrup is combined with granulated sugar crystals. Brown sugar has the same sweetening power as granulated sugar. Dark brown sugar has more molasses in it than light brown sugar, giving it a stronger flavor. Light and dark brown sugars can be used interchangeably in recipes. Be sure to choose a brown sugar that does not list caramel color as an ingredient as many caramel colorings are made from barley and are not gluten-free.

Confectioners' sugar

Confectioners' sugar, also known as powdered sugar, is primarily used for making icings, frostings, and glazes. It can also be dusted on the tops of coffee cakes for decoration and flavor. Confectioners' sugar is made by processing granulated sugar until it is ground ten times finer than regular granulated sugar. A small percentage of cornstarch is then added to absorb moisture from the air and to prevent the sugar from becoming lumpy.

The Gluten-Free Pantry

In addition to gluten-free flours and starches, you will also need some basic ingredients in your pantry, such as salt, pepper, spices, cocoa powder, chocolate, chocolate chips, vanilla extract, almond extract, and any other flavorings or favorite cooking ingredients you like to use. This will require some label reading. While ingredients like baking powder rarely contain gluten, you still need to double-check the labels to make sure that wheat starch is not being used as a thickening or non-caking agent. As you learn which brands are gluten free, you will be able to stock your kitchen with confidence.

Oats do not naturally contain gluten, but they are frequently processed in plants that also package wheat flour. If gluten is a health issue for you, then be sure to use oats that are certified as gluten-free.

ADDING FLAVOR TO GLUTEN-FREE RECIPES

Wheat flour not only adds texture but also flavors foods. To replace that lost flavor, try adding extracts, spices, herbs, and other ingredients, such as vegetables, fruit, dried fruit, coconut, nuts, and seeds, to a variety of gluten-free foods and baked goods. Try out the flavor combinations I've included in the recipes, then experiment and have some fun creating those that appeal to you and your family.

Measuring Ingredients

To accurately measure a variety of ingredients, every kitchen should have a set of liquid measuring cups, dry measuring cups, and measuring spoons. These are all available in graduated sizes to make measuring easier. To get the best results, use the correct type of measuring cup to measure each of the ingredients called for in a recipe.

LIQUID MEASURING CUPS

Use standard glass or plastic measuring cups with pour spouts and graduated measurements marked on the side of the cup to measure liquid ingredients, such as milk, buttermilk, water, and oil, and solid dairy ingredients, such as sour cream and grated cheese. Liquid measuring cups range from 1-cup and 2-cup sizes to 4-cup and even a big 2-quart size. To measure liquid ingredients, place the cup on a level surface and view the measurement markers at eye level to get a precise measurement.

DRY MEASURING CUPS

Flour, sugar, starches, cocoa powder, and other dry ingredients should be measured in cups that are specifically designed for measuring dry ingredients. Made of plastic or metal with a flat rim, dry measuring cups come in sets of graduated sizes ranging from ¼ cup to 1 cup. Spoon dry

MAKING YOUR KITCHEN GLUTEN-FREE

If you or a member of your family has celiac disease or a strong gluten sensitivity, you will need to make some changes in how you set up and organize your kitchen to avoid contamination of your gluten-free ingredients and gluten-free foods. If you're choosing gluten-free as a lifestyle change, then minor contamination is not a health issue.

Bowls, pans, measuring cups and spoons, mixing utensils, and even knives and cutting boards should be set aside and dedicated to gluten-free preparation. Countertops need to be scrubbed clean, or better yet, dedicate a counter to gluten-free only. Even then, you have to be careful of airborne gluten in flour dust and other powdered ingredients. This can present challenges and may require some creative solutions if you are making both gluten-laden and gluten-free foods in your kitchen.

ingredients into the measuring cup to slightly overflowing, then use a straight knife edge or other utensil to level the ingredients even with the top edge of the cup. Don't tap the cup on the counter as this will settle and compact the flour and give you an inaccurate measurement. Other ingredients like chopped chocolate, chocolate chips, nuts, dried fruits, and coconut should also be measured in dry measuring cups.

MEASURING SPOONS

Measuring spoons come in graduated sizes and are used to measure small quantities of dry and liquid ingredients, such as leaveners, gums, spices, and extracts. For dry ingredients, fill the spoon and then scrape off the excess to get a level measure.

CHAPTER TWO

quick breads *and* muffins

Quick bread loaves and muffins are not only a breakfast staple but are also perfect to serve as an accompaniment to a meal or as a snack throughout the day. So called "quick breads" get their name because they are leavened with baking powder and baking soda instead of yeast, so they don't need time for the leavener to work and they will rise quickly in the oven as they bake. They are also quick to assemble and easy to master for bakers of all skill levels.

There are a couple of tricks to getting a great result when making gluten-free quick breads and muffins. Increasing the leaveners will help gluten-free batters rise up better as they bake and produce a lighter texture in the finished bread. Also, adding xanthan gum will improve the structure of the batter and provide support to the loaves and muffins.

Gluten-free quick bread and muffin batters will be thicker than those made with wheat flour. This is because the starches in the gluten-free flour blend will absorb the liquid faster during mixing. Thicker batters rise higher than thin batters because there is a stronger structure to support the bread or muffin. Fruit and nuts are also less likely to sink to the bottom of the loaves or muffins in a thick batter.

Don't make the mistake of adding extra liquid to thin out the batter to the thickness you may be used to with wheat flour. Too much liquid in the batter will produce heavy breads that take a long time to bake and may be soggy or underdone in the center. Also, thin batters will produce muffins with flat tops, and the batter can flow over the rim of the cup, causing the muffin tops to fuse together.

Like other muffins, gluten-free muffins taste best and have a softer, moister texture when eaten still warm from the oven. Quick bread loaves are easier to slice when the loaf is completely cool. But don't worry if you can't wait that long. When the kitchen is filled with the aroma of fresh-baked bread, I also have a hard time keeping my hands off the knife!

Equipment

LOAF PANS

Loaf pans, also referred to as bread pans or tins, are used for baking quick breads and yeast breads. Choose light-colored rectangular metal pans, with plain, flat sides and bottoms and no decorative patterns.

There are two standard sizes for loaf pans: $4\frac{1}{2}$ x $8\frac{1}{2}$ inches and 5 x 9 inches. Gluten-free breads rise up better in narrower pans, so all of the bread recipes in this book are formulated to fit a $4\frac{1}{2}$ x $8\frac{1}{2}$-inch loaf pan. Shiny or light-colored pans produce breads with lighter crusts, while pans with a dark finish result in breads with a dark crust.

MUFFIN PANS

Muffin pans, also called muffin tins or cupcake pans, come in a variety of shapes and sizes. I recommend using regular muffin pans or mini muffin pans for baking gluten-free muffins. Gluten-free batters baked in jumbo muffin pans may not rise up as high and will be heavier than muffins baked in standard pans. Muffin pans made of light-colored aluminum are a good choice for baking muffins. Dark metal pans may cause the muffins to brown too quickly on the bottom and sides before the centers bake.

Muffin cup paper liners

I do not recommend baking gluten-free muffins in paper liners. Gluten-free muffins baked directly in the pan will rise up higher and lighter than muffins baked in paper liners. When the batter is in direct contact with the pan as it heats, the leaveners activate quicker and cause the muffins to rise faster and higher. Paper liners insulate the batter from the heat of the pan, slowing down the leaveners and producing shorter and heavier muffins. Also, gluten-free muffins tend to stick to paper liners more than muffins made with wheat flour.

Mixing Techniques

Unlike with breads containing gluten, you don't have to worry that overmixing will cause your breads to be tough. But you do want to be careful because overmixing gluten-free batters can knock out all the air and result in dense, heavy breads. So use a light hand and don't get too vigorous when mixing up the batter, especially when mixing by hand. There are two basic methods for mixing quick bread and muffin batters: the creaming method and the quick method.

CREAMING METHOD

The creaming method of mixing batters starts with combining the butter and sugar using an electric mixer. It is easier to use a stand mixer for this process, but a hand mixer will do the job as well. Creaming the butter and sugar serves three important purposes:

- To thoroughly combine the butter and sugar before adding the other ingredients
- To incorporate air into the batter to make it lighter
- To start dissolving the sugar into the butter

The butter should be softened before you start creaming. Butter is considered softened when it reaches 65°F. Softened butter creams better and holds more air than room temperature butter (72°F), while butter that is very soft won't hold much air at all. If your butter is too soft, your breads and muffins will be very dense.

After creaming the butter and sugar, the eggs are gradually incorporated into the mixture. The flour mixture is then added along with the liquid ingredients. These are added in small portions and mixed in after each addition to keep from deflating the trapped air in the creamed mixture and to create a smooth batter.

QUICK METHOD

In the quick method, also called the muffin method because it is the common technique used to mix muffin batters, the dry ingredients and liquid ingredients are mixed in different bowls and then quickly combined together.

Place the flour and other dry ingredients in a large bowl and mix them together with a wire whisk until thoroughly blended. It is important to make sure the baking powder and baking soda are evenly distributed throughout the flour.

Even blending of the leaveners within the flour mixture will ensure an even rise and prevent large air bubbles or tunnels from forming in the breads and muffins. Thoroughly whisking the dry ingredients together also means that less mixing is required when they are combined with the liquid ingredients.

In a medium bowl, use a wire whisk to beat eggs until the yolks and whites are thoroughly combined and frothy with no streaks of white remaining. Gradually whisk in the liquid ingredients, one at a time, until thoroughly blended. Then pour the liquid mixture into the bowl containing the flour mixture and stir until combined. Use a light hand when mixing in the flour mixture—stir just until the ingredients are well combined and all of the flour is incorporated into the batter. You don't want any white streaks or lumps to remain, but you also don't want to make the batter heavy by beating out all the air and causing the starches to set up.

Baking Techniques

Because ovens can vary significantly and some reflect more heat down from the top, check the color of the bread after about 30 minutes of baking. If the top is browning too quickly, loosely cover the bread with a piece of foil to prevent it from becoming too dark. Cracked tops and splits down the center of the loaves are normal and characteristic of the appearance of quick breads.

If you find you're consistently having trouble getting your quick breads completely done in the center, try baking the batter in muffin cups instead of in loaf pans. Muffins have more batter surface area exposed to the pan, so they will heat and bake faster. A quick bread recipe that fits a 4½ x 8½-inch loaf pan will make 12 muffins.

TESTING FOR DONENESS

A quick bread loaf is done when there is no sign of wet batter in the cracks and the top looks dry and is lightly firm to the touch. The top will be golden brown, the bread should slightly pull away from the sides of the pan, and a wooden pick inserted in the center will come out clean without any moist batter or crumbs. If the center is still gooey when you test it, bake loaves for another 10 minutes and test again.

Muffins are done when the tops have risen well above the cups, are golden brown, and a wooden pick inserted in the center comes out clean. Over-baking can cause gluten-free muffins to be dry.

When the bread or muffins are done, remove the pan from the oven and immediately turn them out of the pan. Leaving a gluten-free quick bread or muffins in the pan will cause the bottom to become soggy. Cool the bread on a wire rack to allow even air circulation. Gluten-free quick breads and muffins cool best when laid on their sides on the rack. This shifts the weight of the bread and helps the loaves and muffins maintain their shape as they cool.

Quick Tips
QUICK BREADS AND MUFFINS

QUICK BREADS

- Make sure the oven is at the correct temperature before combining the liquid and dry ingredients.

- Position the oven rack in the center of the oven for good air and heat circulation and even baking.

- Quick breads rise better in smaller, narrower pans. All bread recipes in this book call for $4\frac{1}{2}$ x $8\frac{1}{2}$-inch loaf pans.

- Dark-colored bread pans can cause the sides and bottom of the loaf to be too dark.

- Use only the amount of liquid called for in the recipe; too much liquid can cause quick bread loaves to be soggy or sunken in the middle.

- Fill bread pans two-thirds to three-quarters full with batter for a good rise.

- Once the pans are filled, get the bread in the oven quickly.

- It is normal for quick bread loaves to develop cracks and splits in the top as they bake.

- Immediately remove the bread from the pan after baking to keep the bottom of the loaf from becoming soggy.

- Cool quick bread loaves on their sides on a wire rack to help the loaf maintain its shape.

- If you have trouble getting your quick bread loaves done in the middle, try baking the batter in muffin pans.

- Cool quick breads thoroughly to make slicing them easier.

- To help keep quick breads moist and fresh, wrap cooled loaves tightly in plastic wrap.

MUFFINS

- Make sure the oven is at the correct temperature before combining the liquid and dry ingredients.

- Grease the muffin cups well with nonstick cooking spray or unsalted butter to prevent muffins from sticking.

- Thick muffin batters rise up higher and produce taller muffins with better crowns than thin batters.

- A large spoon comes in handy to quickly and easily transfer muffin batter into the muffin pan.

- Fill the muffin cups nearly full and slightly mound the batter in the center.

- Immediately remove the muffins from the pan after baking to prevent the muffins from becoming soggy.

- To easily remove baked muffins from the pan, quickly turn the pan upside-down over a clean towel. Give the pan a light tap on the bottom or a quick shake to remove any that don't fall out.

- Cool muffins on their sides on a wire rack to help them maintain their shape.

- Serve muffins warm for the best flavor and texture.

applesauce bread

Applesauce makes a tender, moist quick bread that is perfect for breakfast and snacking. This bread is lightly spiced with cinnamon, but you can increase the cinnamon or omit it entirely based on your preferences.

MAKES ONE 4½ x 8½-INCH LOAF

Unsalted butter or nonstick cooking spray, for the pan

1½ cups Gluten-Free All-Purpose Flour (see p. 11)

1½ teaspoons baking powder

1 teaspoon ground cinnamon

¾ teaspoon xanthan gum

½ teaspoon baking soda

½ teaspoon table salt

½ cup (1 stick) unsalted butter, softened

1 cup firmly packed brown sugar

2 large eggs

1 teaspoon pure vanilla extract

1 cup applesauce (smooth or chunky)

½ cup chopped walnuts

1. Heat the oven to 350°F. Grease a 4½ x 8½-inch loaf pan with unsalted butter or nonstick cooking spray.

2. In a medium bowl, whisk together the flour, baking powder, cinnamon, xanthan gum, baking soda, and salt until well combined. Set aside.

3. In a large bowl, using an electric mixer on medium speed, cream the butter and brown sugar until light and fluffy, about 2 minutes. Scrape down the sides of bowl. Add the eggs, one at a time, beating well after each addition. Stir in the vanilla. Scrape down the sides of the bowl.

4. Alternately add the flour mixture and the applesauce to the butter-sugar mixture, starting and ending with flour mixture and stirring between each addition until blended. Mix until smooth, about 30 seconds. By hand, gently fold in the walnuts. Spoon the batter evenly into the prepared loaf pan.

5. Bake until golden brown and a wooden pick inserted in the center comes out clean, 50 to 60 minutes. Remove the pan from the oven and immediately remove the bread from the pan. Turn the loaf on its side and let cool on a wire rack.

VARIATION

Add ½ cup finely chopped peeled apples (any variety will do) to the batter along with the walnuts or in place of the walnuts.

apricot bread

I love dried apricots and they make a wonderful addition to quick breads for their flavor and texture. A touch of orange is a great pairing with apricots and enhances their flavor.

MAKES ONE 4½ x 8½-INCH LOAF

Unsalted butter or nonstick cooking spray, for the pan

2 cups Gluten-Free All-Purpose Flour (see p. 11)

2 teaspoons baking powder

¾ teaspoon xanthan gum

½ teaspoon baking soda

¼ teaspoon table salt

⅔ cup chopped dried apricots

2 large eggs

1 cup granulated sugar

¾ cup vegetable oil

3 tablespoons freshly squeezed orange juice

1 teaspoon pure vanilla extract

2 teaspoons grated orange zest

1. Heat the oven to 350°F. Grease a 4½ x 8½-inch loaf pan with unsalted butter or nonstick cooking spray.

2. In a large bowl, whisk together the flour, baking powder, xanthan gum, baking soda, and salt until well combined. Stir in the dried apricots. Make a well in the center and set aside.

3. In a medium bowl, using a wire whisk, lightly beat the eggs. Add the sugar and whisk until smooth. Gradually whisk in the oil until well blended. Whisk in the orange juice and vanilla. Stir in the orange zest.

4. Pour the liquid mixture into the well in the center of the flour mixture and stir until combined. Spoon the batter evenly into the prepared loaf pan.

5. Bake until golden brown and a wooden pick inserted in the center comes out clean, 50 to 60 minutes. Remove the pan from the oven and immediately remove the bread from the pan. Turn the loaf on its side and let cool on a wire rack.

Use moist dried apricots. If your apricots are very dry, soak the chopped fruit in a few tablespoons of orange juice for 30 minutes before making the bread. Drain the apricots well before using.

VARIATION

Add ½ cup chopped almonds or walnuts to the flour mixture before adding the liquid ingredients.

lemon blueberry bread

Lemon with blueberry is a classic combination, and this bread is one of my favorites with its punch of lemon flavor. Make it when blueberries are in season and you've picked too many from your local farm. Stow an extra loaf or two in the freezer to enjoy when fresh blueberries are no longer available.

MAKES ONE 4½ x 8½-INCH LOAF

Unsalted butter or nonstick cooking spray,
   for the pan
2 cups Gluten-Free All-Purpose Flour
   (see p. 11)
1½ teaspoons baking powder
1 teaspoon baking soda
¾ teaspoon xanthan gum
¼ teaspoon table salt
2 large eggs
1 cup granulated sugar
⅔ cup vegetable oil
⅓ cup freshly squeezed lemon juice
2 teaspoons finely grated lemon zest
¾ cup fresh blueberries

1. Heat the oven to 350°F. Grease a 4½ x 8½-inch loaf pan with unsalted butter or nonstick cooking spray.

2. In a large bowl, whisk together the flour, baking powder, baking soda, xanthan gum, and salt until well combined. Make a well in the center and set aside.

3. In a medium bowl, using a wire whisk, lightly beat the eggs. Add the sugar and whisk until smooth. Gradually whisk in the oil until well blended. Whisk in the lemon juice and zest.

4. Pour the liquid mixture into the well in the flour mixture and stir until combined. Fold in the blueberries. Spoon the batter evenly into the prepared loaf pan.

5. Bake until golden brown and a wooden pick inserted in the center comes out clean, 50 to 60 minutes. Remove the pan from the oven and immediately remove the bread from the pan. Turn the loaf on its side and let cool on a wire rack.

Small blueberries work better than large ones in quick breads. The small berries are lighter and will stay suspended in the batter during baking, while large berries tend to sink to the bottom of the loaf.

pumpkin bread

Pumpkin bread is a staple around the fall and winter holidays, but this delicious bread makes a wonderful treat in spring and summer, too. Homemade pumpkin purée from fresh pumpkins in the fall will work well in this recipe. For more depth of spice flavor, use freshly grated nutmeg.

MAKES ONE 4½ X 8½-INCH LOAF

Unsalted butter or nonstick cooking spray, for the pan

1½ cups Gluten-Free All-Purpose Flour (see p. 11)

2 teaspoons baking powder

1½ teaspoons ground cinnamon

¾ teaspoon xanthan gum

½ teaspoon baking soda

½ teaspoon table salt

¼ teaspoon grated nutmeg

⅛ teaspoon ground ginger

½ cup chopped walnuts or pecans

2 large eggs

½ cup granulated sugar

½ cup firmly packed brown sugar

¾ cup canned pumpkin purée

½ cup vegetable oil

1 teaspoon pure vanilla extract

1. Heat the oven to 350°F. Grease a 4½ x 8½-inch loaf pan with unsalted butter or nonstick cooking spray.

2. In a large bowl, whisk together the flour, baking powder, cinnamon, xanthan gum, baking soda, salt, nutmeg, and ginger until well combined. Stir in the walnuts or pecans. Make a well in the center and set aside.

3. In a medium bowl, using a wire whisk, lightly beat the eggs. Add the granulated sugar and brown sugar and whisk until smooth. Add the pumpkin and stir until well combined. Gradually whisk in the oil until well blended. Stir in the vanilla.

4. Pour the liquid mixture into the well in the flour mixture and stir until combined. Spoon the batter evenly into the prepared loaf pan.

5. Bake until golden brown and a wooden pick inserted in the center comes out clean, 50 to 60 minutes. Remove the pan from the oven and immediately remove the bread from the pan. Turn the loaf on its side and let cool on a wire rack.

VARIATIONS

Add ½ cup dark or golden raisins or dried cranberries to the flour mixture before adding the liquid ingredients.

glazed pumpkin bread: In a small bowl, combine ¾ cup confectioners' sugar, 4 to 5 teaspoons whole milk, and ½ teaspoon pure vanilla extract until the glaze is smooth and thin enough to drizzle from a spoon. Drizzle the glaze over the cooled bread.

cinnamon pecan bread

Cinnamon sugar swirled through this pecan bread creates a pretty appearance and ensures delicious flavor in every bite.

MAKES ONE 4½ X 8½-INCH LOAF OR THREE 3 X 5¾-INCH MINI LOAVES

Unsalted butter or nonstick cooking spray, for the pan

For the Filling
3 tablespoons granulated sugar
4½ teaspoons ground cinnamon

For the Bread
2 cups Gluten-Free All-Purpose Flour (see p. 11)
1 teaspoon baking powder
1 teaspoon baking soda
¾ teaspoon xanthan gum
¼ teaspoon table salt
½ cup (1 stick) unsalted butter, softened
1 cup granulated sugar
2 large eggs
1 teaspoon pure vanilla extract
1 cup buttermilk
½ cup chopped pecans

1. Heat the oven to 350°F. Grease a 4½ x 8½-inch loaf pan with unsalted butter or nonstick cooking spray.

2. Make the filling: In a small bowl, whisk together the sugar and the cinnamon until well combined. Set aside.

3. In a medium bowl, whisk together the flour, baking powder, baking soda, xanthan gum, and salt until well combined. Set aside.

4. In a large bowl, using an electric mixer on medium speed, cream the butter and sugar until light and fluffy, about 2 minutes. Scrape down the sides of bowl. Add the eggs, one at a time, beating well after each addition. Stir in the vanilla. Scrape down the sides of bowl.

5. Alternately add the flour mixture and the buttermilk to the sugar-butter mixture, starting and ending with flour mixture and stirring between each addition until blended. Mix until smooth, about 30 seconds. By hand, gently fold in the pecans.

6. Spoon a third of the batter evenly into the prepared loaf pan. Sprinkle half of the cinnamon-sugar filling over top. Spoon another third of the batter into the pan, covering the filling. Sprinkle the remaining filling over the batter. Spoon the remaining batter into the pan and spread smooth with lightly greased fingers or the back of a greased spoon. If making mini loaves, first divide the large bowl of batter into thirds, then fill the mini loaf pans following the directions above.

7. Bake until golden brown and a wooden pick inserted in the center comes out clean, 50 to 60 minutes. Bake mini loaves for 20 minutes. Remove the pan from the oven and immediately remove the bread from the pan. Turn the loaf on its side and let cool on a wire rack.

VARIATION

Iced cinnamon pecan bread: In a small bowl, combine 1 cup confectioners' sugar, 1 tablespoon half-and-half, 2 teaspoons melted unsalted butter, and ½ teaspoon pure vanilla extract until smooth. Pour or spread over the cooled bread.

zucchini bread

Zucchini bread is a great way to use up an abundant harvest from the garden or a fresh bounty from the farmers' market. I like to use small zucchini and grate lots of the dark peel into the measured amount. It gives the bread a good color and more flavor. Avoid using very large zucchini because the center flesh contains a lot of moisture that can make the bread soggy.

MAKES ONE 4½ x 8½-INCH LOAF

Unsalted butter or nonstick cooking spray, for the pan

1½ cups Gluten-Free All-Purpose Flour (see p. 11)

1½ teaspoons baking powder

1 teaspoon ground cinnamon

¾ teaspoon xanthan gum

½ teaspoon baking soda

½ teaspoon table salt

½ teaspoon ground nutmeg

2 large eggs

1 cup granulated sugar

⅔ cup vegetable oil

1 teaspoon pure vanilla extract

1 cup finely grated zucchini

1. Heat the oven to 350°F. Grease a 4½ x 8½-inch loaf pan with unsalted butter or nonstick cooking spray.

2. In a large bowl, whisk together the flour, baking powder, cinnamon, xanthan gum, baking soda, salt, and nutmeg until well combined. Make a well in the center and set aside.

3. In a medium bowl, using a wire whisk, lightly beat the eggs. Add the sugar and whisk until smooth. Gradually whisk in the oil until well blended. Stir in the vanilla and then the zucchini.

4. Pour the liquid mixture into the well in the flour mixture and stir until combined. Spoon the batter evenly into the prepared loaf pan.

5. Bake until golden brown and a wooden pick inserted in the center comes out clean, 50 to 60 minutes. Remove the pan from the oven and immediately remove the bread from the pan. Turn the loaf on its side and let cool on a wire rack.

banana nut bread

I like slightly green bananas for eating, but to get the strongest banana flavor in baked goods, be sure to use ripe bananas. Remember the lyrics in the Chiquita® Banana song? "When they are flecked with brown and have a golden hue, bananas taste the best and are the best for you." That's the exact description of the perfect bananas to use for banana bread.

MAKES ONE 4½ x 8½-INCH LOAF

Unsalted butter or nonstick cooking spray, for the pan

1½ cups Gluten-Free All-Purpose Flour (see p. 11)

1½ teaspoons baking powder

¾ teaspoon xanthan gum

½ teaspoon baking soda

½ teaspoon table salt

½ cup (1 stick) unsalted butter, softened

¾ cup granulated sugar

2 large eggs

1½ teaspoons pure vanilla extract

1¼ cups mashed ripe bananas (2 to 3 medium bananas)

½ cup chopped walnuts

1. Heat the oven to 350°F. Grease a 4½ x 8½-inch loaf pan with unsalted butter or nonstick cooking spray.

2. In a medium bowl, whisk together the flour, baking powder, xanthan gum, baking soda, and salt until well combined. Set aside.

3. In a large bowl, using an electric mixer on medium speed, cream the butter and sugar until light and fluffy, about 2 minutes. Scrape down the sides of the bowl. Add the eggs, one at a time, beating well after each addition. Stir in the vanilla. Scrape down the sides of bowl.

4. Gradually stir the flour mixture into the butter-sugar mixture, mixing until smooth, about 30 seconds. By hand, stir in the bananas and walnuts. Spoon the batter evenly into the prepared loaf pan.

5. Bake until golden brown and a wooden pick inserted in the center comes out clean, 50 to 60 minutes. Remove the pan from the oven and immediately remove the bread from the pan. Turn the loaf on its side and let cool on a wire rack.

VARIATION

Use your favorite nut in this recipe. Try pecans, peanuts, even cashews, or omit the nuts entirely. If you want a bit of nut flavor without the nut crunch, serve a dish of Nutella® or peanut butter on the side.

banana maple muffins

No one will ever suspect that these moist and delicious muffins are actually gluten-free. Maple syrup adds a depth of flavor that enhances the banana. I like to use Grade B maple syrup for baking. It has a stronger maple flavor and darker color than Grade A Amber maple syrup, the type commonly used as a topping for pancakes and waffles. Grade B maple syrup can be found in specialty food markets and some health-food stores.

MAKES 12 MUFFINS

Unsalted butter or nonstick cooking spray, for the pan

1¾ cups Gluten-Free All-Purpose Flour (see p. 11)

2 teaspoons baking powder

¾ teaspoon xanthan gum

½ teaspoon table salt

¼ teaspoon baking soda

½ cup (1 stick) unsalted butter, softened

⅔ cup granulated sugar

⅓ cup firmly packed brown sugar

2 tablespoons maple syrup, preferably Grade B

2 large eggs

1½ cups mashed ripe bananas (about 2 to 3 bananas)

1. Heat the oven to 375°F. Grease a 12-cup muffin pan with unsalted butter or nonstick cooking spray.

2. In a medium bowl, whisk together the flour, baking powder, xanthan gum, salt, and baking soda until well combined. Set aside.

3. In a large bowl, using an electric mixer on medium speed, cream the butter, granulated sugar, and brown sugar until light and fluffy, about 2 minutes. Scrape down the sides of the bowl. Beat in the maple syrup. Add the eggs, one at a time, beating well after each addition. Scrape down the sides of the bowl. Gradually stir in the flour mixture. Mix until smooth, about 30 seconds. By hand, stir in the bananas.

4. Spoon the batter into the prepared muffin pan, filling each cup until nearly full and mounding the batter in the center to the top of the cups, or slightly above.

5. Bake until golden brown and a wooden pick inserted in the center comes out clean, 18 to 20 minutes. Immediately remove the muffins from the pan, transfer to a wire rack, and cool the muffins on their sides. Serve the muffins warm or at room temperature.

VARIATION

banana maple nut muffins: Add ½ cup chopped walnuts or pecans to the muffin batter along with the bananas.

carrot muffins

If you like carrot cake, you'll love these flavorful muffins loaded with carrots, pineapple, and walnuts. If serving for a snack or dessert, add a swipe of homemade cream cheese frosting to the top.

MAKES 12 MUFFINS

Unsalted butter or nonstick cooking spray, for the pan

1¾ cups Gluten-Free All-Purpose Flour (see p. 11)

1½ teaspoons baking powder

¾ teaspoon xanthan gum

½ teaspoon baking soda

½ teaspoon ground cinnamon

½ teaspoon table salt

¼ teaspoon grated nutmeg

½ cup chopped walnuts plus 12 walnut halves

2 large eggs

1 cup granulated sugar

⅔ cup vegetable oil

1 teaspoon pure vanilla extract

¾ cup finely grated peeled carrots (2 to 3 large carrots)

½ cup drained unsweetened crushed pineapple

1. Heat the oven to 375°F. Grease a 12-cup muffin pan with unsalted butter or nonstick cooking spray.

2. In a large bowl, whisk together the flour, baking powder, xanthan gum, baking soda, cinnamon, salt, and nutmeg until well combined. Stir in the chopped walnuts. Make a well in the center and set aside.

3. In a medium bowl, using a wire whisk, lightly beat the eggs. Add the sugar and whisk until smooth. Gradually whisk in the oil until well blended, then whisk in the vanilla. Stir in the carrots and pineapple.

4. Pour the liquid mixture into the well in the flour mixture and stir until combined. Spoon the batter into the prepared muffin pan, filling each cup until nearly full and mounding the batter in the center to the top of the cups, or slightly above. Place a walnut half on top of each.

5. Bake until golden brown and a wooden pick inserted in the center comes out clean, 18 to 20 minutes. Immediately remove the muffins from the pan, transfer to a wire rack, and cool the muffins on their sides. Serve the muffins warm or at room temperature.

I always peel carrots before grating because the peel sometimes has an earthy taste that can affect the flavor of the muffins.

Medium-size carrots have a well-developed flavor and are the best choice for easy grating. Very large carrots can have a woody core, which doesn't have much carrot flavor.

coconut muffins

Flaked coconut pieces can often be rather long and chewy, so I like to give the coconut a quick chop after measuring to improve the finished texture of the muffins. You can use finely flaked unsweetened coconut if you prefer it to sweetened coconut. These muffins are as tasty with scrambled eggs as they are with a cup of tea in the afternoon.

MAKES 12 MUFFINS

For the Muffins

Unsalted butter or nonstick cooking spray, for the pan

2 cups Gluten-Free All-Purpose Flour (see p. 11)

1 tablespoon baking powder

¾ teaspoon xanthan gum

½ teaspoon table salt

⅔ cup sweetened flaked coconut, chopped

2 large eggs

⅔ cup granulated sugar

⅔ cup vegetable oil

⅔ cup whole milk

1 teaspoon pure vanilla extract

½ teaspoon coconut extract

For the Topping

¼ cup sweetened flaked coconut, chopped

1. Heat the oven to 375°F. Grease a 12-cup muffin pan with unsalted butter or nonstick cooking spray.

2. In a large bowl, whisk together the flour, baking powder, xanthan gum, and salt until well combined. Stir in the coconut. Make a well in the center and set aside.

3. In a medium bowl, using a wire whisk, lightly beat the eggs. Add the sugar and whisk until smooth. Gradually whisk in the oil until well blended, then whisk in the milk until well combined. Stir in the vanilla and coconut extracts.

4. Pour the liquid mixture into the well in the flour mixture and stir until combined. Spoon the batter into the prepared muffin pan, filling each cup until nearly full and mounding the batter in the center to the top of the cups, or slightly above. Sprinkle the chopped coconut over top of the batter.

5. Bake until golden brown and a wooden pick inserted in the center comes out clean, 18 to 20 minutes. Immediately remove the muffins from the pan, transfer to a wire rack, and cool the muffins on their sides. Serve the muffins warm or at room temperature.

VARIATION

coconut macadamia nut muffins: **Add ½ cup chopped macadamia nuts to the flour mixture along with the coconut.**

spice muffins

I like the flavor combination of cinnamon, nutmeg, and ginger, but you can vary the spices and the amounts in these tender muffins to suit your taste. Cinnamon, allspice, and ginger make a nice blend, or try cinnamon, star anise, and cloves. Use your imagination and have fun creating your favorite spice combination. If you're using whole spices, be sure to grind them just before using to get the most flavor. Grind them finely in a spice grinder or mortar and pestle so the spices will distribute evenly throughout the batter.

MAKES 12 MUFFINS

Unsalted butter or nonstick cooking spray, for the pan

2 cups Gluten-Free All-Purpose Flour (see p. 11)

2 teaspoons baking powder

1½ teaspoons ground cinnamon

¾ teaspoon xanthan gum

½ teaspoon baking soda

½ teaspoon table salt

½ teaspoon ground nutmeg

¼ teaspoon ground ginger

2 large eggs

1 cup firmly packed brown sugar

⅔ cup vegetable oil

⅓ cup whole milk

1 teaspoon pure vanilla extract

1. Heat the oven to 375°F. Grease a 12-cup muffin pan with unsalted butter or nonstick cooking spray.

2. In a large bowl, whisk together the flour, baking powder, cinnamon, xanthan gum, baking soda, salt, nutmeg, and ginger until well combined. Make a well in the center and set aside.

3. In a medium bowl, using a wire whisk, lightly beat the eggs. Add the brown sugar and whisk until smooth. Gradually whisk in the oil until well blended, then whisk in the milk until well combined. Stir in the vanilla.

4. Pour the liquid mixture into the well in the flour mixture and stir until combined. Spoon the batter into the prepared muffin pan, filling each cup until nearly full and mounding the batter in the center to the top of the cups, or slightly above.

5. Bake until golden brown and a wooden pick inserted in the center comes out clean, 18 to 20 minutes. Immediately remove the muffins from the pan, transfer to a wire rack, and cool the muffins on their sides. Serve the muffins warm or at room temperature.

VARIATIONS

Add ½ cup chopped nuts, dried cranberries, apricots, or raisins to the flour mixture before adding the liquid mixture.

Add ½ cup well-drained crushed pineapple to the liquid mixture before adding to the flour mixture.

Add 1 to 2 teaspoons of minced crystallized ginger for an extra bite of spice.

blueberry muffins

I like to use small blueberries in these muffins because you get blueberries in every bite. For a bit of crunch, sprinkle the tops with turbinado sugar before baking.

MAKES 12 MUFFINS

Unsalted butter or nonstick cooking spray, for the pan

2 cups Gluten-Free All-Purpose Flour (see p. 11)

1 tablespoon baking powder

¾ teaspoon xanthan gum

½ teaspoon table salt

2 large eggs

1 cup granulated sugar

⅔ cup vegetable oil

⅓ cup whole milk

1½ teaspoons pure vanilla extract

¾ cup small fresh blueberries

1. Heat the oven to 375°F. Grease a 12-cup muffin pan with unsalted butter or nonstick cooking spray.

2. In a large bowl, whisk together the flour, baking powder, xanthan gum, and salt until well combined. Make a well in the center and set aside.

3. In a medium bowl, using a wire whisk, lightly beat the eggs. Add the sugar and whisk until smooth. Gradually whisk in the oil until well blended, then whisk in the milk and vanilla.

4. Pour the liquid mixture into the well in the flour mixture and stir until combined. Fold in the blueberries. Spoon the batter into the prepared muffin pan, filling each cup until nearly full and mounding the batter in the center to the top of the cups, or slightly above.

5. Bake until golden brown and a wooden pick inserted in the center comes out clean, 18 to 20 minutes. Immediately remove the muffins from the pan and transfer to a wire rack. Serve the muffins warm or at room temperature.

You can use frozen blueberries if fresh blueberries are not in season or readily available in your area. To keep the batter from turning blue, do not defrost the berries before adding them to the batter. Gently fold the frozen berries into the batter just before filling the muffin cups.

orange cranberry muffins

Not only are these muffins delicious, but they're also very pretty piled on a plate in the middle of the breakfast table. The dried cranberries add texture and a burst of flavor. If you choose to substitute fresh cranberries, be sure to chop them into small pieces so they will bake through quickly.

MAKES 12 MUFFINS

Unsalted butter or nonstick cooking spray, for the pan

1¾ cups Gluten-Free All-Purpose Flour (see p. 11)

2 teaspoons baking powder

¾ teaspoon xanthan gum

½ teaspoon baking soda

½ teaspoon table salt

⅔ cup dried cranberries

2 large eggs

¾ cup granulated sugar

⅔ cup vegetable oil

⅓ cup freshly squeezed orange juice

½ teaspoon pure vanilla extract

2 teaspoons finely grated orange zest

1. Heat the oven to 375°F. Grease a 12-cup muffin pan with unsalted butter or nonstick cooking spray.

2. In a large bowl, whisk together the flour, baking powder, xanthan gum, baking soda, and salt until well combined. Stir in the dried cranberries. Make a well in the center and set aside.

3. In a medium bowl, using a wire whisk, lightly beat the eggs. Add the sugar and whisk until smooth. Gradually whisk in the oil until well blended. Whisk in the orange juice and vanilla, then stir in the orange zest.

4. Pour the liquid mixture into the well in the flour mixture and stir until combined. Spoon the batter into the prepared muffin pan, filling each cup until nearly full and mounding the batter in the center to the top of the cups, or slightly above.

5. Bake until golden brown and a wooden pick inserted in the center comes out clean, 18 to 20 minutes. Immediately remove the muffins from the pan, transfer to a wire rack, and cool the muffins on their sides. Serve the muffins warm or at room temperature.

A Microplane® grater is the perfect tool for finely grating citrus zest.

corn muffins

Serve these golden muffins with a hot bowl of chili or with pork or chicken. For those with a sweet tooth, increase the sugar to ⅔ cup and serve as a healthful snack.

MAKES 12 MUFFINS

Unsalted butter or nonstick cooking spray, for the pan

1 cup Gluten-Free All-Purpose Flour (see p. 11)

1 cup yellow cornmeal

¼ cup granulated sugar

2 teaspoons baking powder

¾ teaspoon xanthan gum

½ teaspoon baking soda

½ teaspoon table salt

2 large eggs

½ cup (1 stick) unsalted butter, melted, or vegetable oil

1 cup buttermilk

1. Heat the oven to 375°F. Grease a 12-cup muffin pan with unsalted butter or nonstick cooking spray.

2. In a large bowl, whisk together the flour, cornmeal, sugar, baking powder, xanthan gum, baking soda, and salt until well combined. Make a well in the center and set aside.

3. In a medium bowl, using a wire whisk, lightly beat the eggs. Gradually whisk in the butter until well blended, then whisk in the buttermilk.

4. Pour the liquid mixture into the well in the flour mixture and stir until combined. Spoon the batter into the prepared muffin pan, filling each cup until nearly full and mounding the batter in the center to the top of the cups, or slightly above.

5. Bake until golden brown and a wooden pick inserted in the center comes out clean, 16 to 18 minutes. Immediately remove the muffins from the pan, transfer to a wire rack, and cool the muffins on their sides. Serve the muffins warm or at room temperature.

VARIATIONS

double corn muffins: **Add ⅔ cup fresh or drained, canned whole corn kernels to the liquid mixture before adding it to the flour mixture.**

jalapeño corn muffins: **Add 2 tablespoons minced fresh red or green jalapeño peppers to the liquid mixture before adding it to the flour mixture.**

cheese muffins

These light and fluffy gems are like a cross between a muffin and a biscuit and have lots of cheese flavor. While you'll get the most Cheddar flavor if you buy a block of cheese and grate it fresh, you can buy prepackaged grated Cheddar to get these muffins in the oven more quickly. They are best when served piping hot from the oven.

MAKES 12 MUFFINS

Unsalted butter or nonstick cooking spray, for the pan

2 cups Gluten-Free All-Purpose Flour (see p. 11)

1 tablespoon baking powder

1 tablespoon granulated sugar

¾ teaspoon xanthan gum

½ teaspoon table salt

1⅓ cups grated sharp Cheddar cheese

2 large eggs

⅔ cup vegetable oil

⅔ cup whole milk

1. Heat the oven to 375°F. Grease a 12-cup muffin pan with unsalted butter or nonstick cooking spray.

2. In a large bowl, whisk together the flour, baking powder, sugar, xanthan gum, and salt until well combined. Stir in the Cheddar cheese. Make a well in the center and set aside.

3. In a medium bowl, using a wire whisk, lightly beat the eggs. Gradually whisk in the oil until well blended, then whisk in the milk.

4. Pour the liquid mixture into the well in the flour mixture and stir until combined. Spoon the batter into the prepared muffin pan, filling each cup until nearly full and mounding the batter in the center to the top of the cups, or slightly above.

5. Bake until golden brown and a wooden pick inserted in the center comes out clean, 18 to 20 minutes. Immediately remove the muffins from the pan, transfer to a wire rack, and cool the muffins on their sides. Serve the muffins warm or at room temperature.

You may need to run a thin-bladed knife around the edge of the muffins to loosen any stuck cheese before turning the muffins out of the pan.

VARIATIONS

garlic cheese muffins: **Add 1 teaspoon garlic powder to the flour mixture.**

cheese and chive muffins: **Add 2 tablespoons finely chopped fresh chives to the liquid mixture before adding it to the flour mixture.**

lorraine muffins: **Use Gruyère instead of Cheddar and add ⅓ cup cooked crumbled gluten-free bacon to the flour mixture.**

herb muffins

You can use any combination of fresh herbs in these versatile muffins. Have fun creating your own favorite blend.

MAKES 12 MUFFINS

Unsalted butter or nonstick cooking spray, for the pan

2 cups Gluten-Free All-Purpose Flour (see p. 11)

1 tablespoon baking powder

1 tablespoon granulated sugar

¾ teaspoon xanthan gum

½ teaspoon table salt

½ teaspoon garlic powder

½ teaspoon onion powder

2 large eggs

⅔ cup vegetable oil

⅓ cup whole milk

2 tablespoons minced fresh flat-leaf parsley

2 tablespoons minced fresh chives

1 tablespoon minced fresh thyme leaves

1. Heat the oven to 375°F. Grease a 12-cup muffin pan with unsalted butter or nonstick cooking spray.

2. In a large bowl, whisk together the flour, baking powder, sugar, xanthan gum, salt, garlic powder, and onion powder until well combined. Make a well in the center and set aside.

3. In a medium bowl, using a wire whisk, lightly beat the eggs. Gradually whisk in the oil until well blended. Whisk in the milk, then stir in the parsley, chives, and thyme.

4. Pour the liquid mixture into the well in the flour mixture and stir until combined. Spoon the batter into the prepared muffin pan, filling each cup until nearly full and mounding the batter in the center to the top of the cups, or slightly above.

5. Bake until golden brown and a wooden pick inserted in the center comes out clean, 18 to 20 minutes. Immediately remove the muffins from the pan, transfer to a wire rack, and cool the muffins on their sides. Serve the muffins warm or at room temperature.

VARIATION

herb cheese muffins: **Add ⅓ cup finely grated Parmesan cheese to the flour mixture.**

CHAPTER THREE

biscuits *and* scones

Biscuits and scones are the easiest to make of all quick breads. They are called quick breads because they are leavened with baking powder and baking soda rather than yeast. Because they are so fast to make, biscuits and scones are a favorite bread to serve hot for breakfast, brunch, or dinner or with a late-morning or afternoon cup of tea or coffee.

Cornstarch is the secret ingredient I add to lighten the texture of gluten-free biscuits and scones, which can otherwise be rather dense. I also add a little extra leavener to the dry ingredients to help give these small breads an additional lift and lightness. Adding xanthan gum helps the biscuits and scones hold their shape as they rise. Guar gum can be substituted for the xanthan gum with similar results.

With the absence of gluten in the flour, you don't have to worry about biscuits and scones becoming tough from handling the dough too much. But overmixing the dough once the liquid and dry ingredients are combined can make these breads heavy and prevent them from rising as much as they should during baking. To create light biscuits and scones, mix the dough just until the liquid and dry ingredients are evenly combined and then handle the dough gently while shaping and transferring it to the baking sheet.

Wheat flour browns naturally during baking, giving baked goods a lovely golden color. Gluten-free flours do not brown as well, but there are a couple of tricks you can use to improve the appearance and texture of the outside of your biscuits and scones. Brushing biscuits with melted butter before baking will help the biscuits brown and give them a buttery flavor. For scones, use an egg wash and an optional dusting of granulated sugar to give a golden top with a touch of crunchy sweetness.

Equipment

BAKING SHEETS

Baking sheets that have a low rim around the edge are known as jellyroll pans because they are designed for baking jellyroll cakes. They also work well for some thin types of bar cookies. While these pans can be used for baking breads like biscuits and scones, the rim can inhibit air circulation around the breads and cause them to bake unevenly. I prefer to use flat cookie sheets, which have a raised edge on only one or two sides of the sheet. These sheets also make it really easy to slide the parchment paper off the pan onto a cooling rack, transferring the whole batch of scones or biscuits to the rack in one quick motion rather than having to transfer each to the rack one at a time.

Heavy-gauge shiny metal sheets are the best choice for baking because they allow biscuits and scones to brown and bake evenly. Dark sheets and those with a darker nonstick finish can cause the

bottoms of the breads to brown too much or even burn before the bread finishes baking. This is because dark baking sheets absorb more heat from the oven while shiny sheets reflect back some of the heat and help the breads bake more evenly.

PASTRY BLENDER

A pastry blender is used to cut butter, shortening, or lard into dry ingredients to create a crumbly mixture and is an essential tool for making great biscuits and scones. It is comprised of a U-shape set of wires attached to a handle that fits snugly into the palm of your hand. If you don't have a pastry blender, two knives drawn together in a scissorlike motion or a large, sturdy fork may be used to cut in the fat. You can also rub it in with your fingertips, but you want to keep the fat cold so be careful that it does not warm up too much from the heat of your fingers.

Shaping Biscuits

The biscuit recipes in this chapter fall into two categories: drop biscuits and cutout biscuits.

Drop biscuits are the fastest to make and are shaped by simply dropping spoonfuls of dough onto the prepared baking sheet. Drop biscuits have a casual, rustic, craggy appearance.

To make cutout biscuits, the dough is turned out onto a lightly floured surface, patted into a flat disk, and cut out with a round or scallop-shape biscuit cutter. To cut out biscuits, make a straight cut using a firm downward motion. Do not twist the biscuit cutter—doing so will cause the edges of the dough to smear together, resulting in uneven rising and lopsided biscuits. A straight cut will yield biscuits with a more uniform shape that rise up evenly on all sides. Cutout biscuits have a more refined appearance than drop biscuits.

Even though the recipes here will specify how to shape the biscuits, you can choose to make drop biscuits or cutout biscuits to suit your personal preference or to fit the style of the meal or occasion.

Shaping Scones

I like to make scones in the traditional wedge shape and have provided these instructions in the recipes. However, you can make cutout scones if you prefer. After patting the dough out into a disk, cut it into wedge shapes or use a floured biscuit cutter to cut out round or scallop-edge scones. For cutout scones, you may need to reduce the baking time by a few minutes, so watch them carefully as they bake.

Quick Tips
BISCUITS AND SCONES

- Use light-colored baking sheets; dark-colored sheets can cause biscuits and scones to darken too much on the bottom.
- Line the baking sheet with parchment paper to prevent biscuits and scones from sticking and to make cleanup a breeze.
- Be sure the oven is fully heated before baking biscuits or scones to get the best rise and a lighter texture.
- Thoroughly combine the dry ingredients to ensure that the leavener is evenly distributed throughout the flour mixture.
- Work quickly to mix the biscuit or scone dough to keep the butter from getting too warm.
- Depending on the weather, humidity, and the moisture content of the flour, you may need to adjust the amount of liquid called for in the recipe.
- Biscuit dough should be moist and a bit sticky, while scone dough should be a little drier.
- Handle the dough with a light touch. Overworking the dough will yield dense, heavy biscuits and scones.
- Adding an egg to gluten-free biscuit doughs helps improve the structure and keep the biscuits from being dense and heavy.

flaky biscuits

Shortening makes flaky biscuits, but you may substitute butter for the shortening, if you prefer.

MAKES ABOUT 8 BISCUITS

1⅓ cups Gluten-Free All-Purpose Flour (see p. 11); more for dusting

⅓ cup cornstarch

1 tablespoon granulated sugar

1 tablespoon baking powder

¾ teaspoon xanthan gum

½ teaspoon table salt

¼ teaspoon baking soda

⅓ cup cold vegetable shortening, cut into pieces

1 large egg

½ cup whole milk

1 tablespoon unsalted butter, melted (optional)

1. Heat the oven to 400°F. Line a baking sheet with parchment paper.

2. In a large bowl, whisk together the flour, cornstarch, sugar, baking powder, xanthan gum, salt, and baking soda until well combined. Add the shortening pieces. Using a pastry blender, a fork, or two knives, cut in the shortening until the mixture resembles coarse crumbs. Make a well in the center and set aside.

3. In a small bowl, using a wire whisk, lightly beat the egg. Gradually whisk in the milk. Pour the liquid mixture into the well in the flour mixture all at once and stir with a fork just until the dry ingredients are moistened and the mixture comes together into a soft dough.

4. Place the dough on a board or other surface lightly dusted with gluten-free all-purpose flour. With lightly floured hands, gently pat into a flat disk about ¾ inch thick. Using a 2-inch biscuit cutter dipped in flour, cut out as many biscuits as possible. Gently gather the scraps into a ball, pat out, and cut out more biscuits. Place the biscuits about 1 inch apart on the prepared baking sheet. Brush the tops of the biscuits with melted butter, if desired.

5. Bake until the biscuits are golden brown, 12 to 15 minutes. Immediately transfer to a wire cooling rack. Serve warm.

buttermilk biscuits

Buttermilk gives biscuits a wonderful flavor and tender texture. Be sure to use a quality buttermilk to get the best flavor. To reheat any leftovers, tightly wrap the biscuits in foil and heat in a 350°F oven for about 10 minutes.

MAKES ABOUT 12 BISCUITS

1¼ cups Gluten-Free All-Purpose Flour (see p. 11)

¾ cup cornstarch

1 tablespoon granulated sugar

2 teaspoons baking powder

1 teaspoon baking soda

¾ teaspoon xanthan gum

½ teaspoon table salt

6 tablespoons (¾ stick) cold unsalted butter, cut into pieces

1 large egg

1 cup buttermilk

1. Heat the oven to 375°F. Line a baking sheet with parchment paper.

2. In a large bowl, whisk together the flour, cornstarch, sugar, baking powder, baking soda, xanthan gum, and salt until well combined. Add the butter pieces. Using a pastry blender, a fork, or two knives, cut in the butter until the mixture resembles coarse crumbs. Make a well in the center and set aside.

3. In a small bowl, using a wire whisk, lightly beat the egg. Gradually whisk in the buttermilk. Pour the liquid mixture into the flour mixture all at once and stir with a fork just until the dry ingredients are moistened and the mixture comes together into a soft dough.

4. Drop heaping tablespoonsful of dough onto the prepared baking sheet, spacing them about 2 inches apart.

5. Bake until the biscuits are golden brown, 12 to 15 minutes. Immediately transfer to a wire cooling rack. Serve warm.

If you don't have buttermilk on hand, you can substitute sour milk. To make sour milk, pour 1 tablespoon of white vinegar or lemon juice into a measuring cup and add enough milk to measure 1 cup. Stir and let rest for 5 minutes before using.

parsley biscuits

Parsley is one of my favorite herbs. It has a universal flavor that makes these biscuits a great accompaniment for most dishes. I like to use Italian parsley, also known as flat-leaf parsley, because it has a more distinctive flavor than the curly variety.

MAKES ABOUT 10 BISCUITS

1 cup Gluten-Free All-Purpose Flour (see p. 11)

⅔ cup cornstarch

2 teaspoons baking powder

1 teaspoon granulated sugar

¾ teaspoon xanthan gum

½ teaspoon baking soda

½ teaspoon table salt

3 tablespoons finely chopped fresh flat-leaf parsley

⅓ cup (5⅓ tablespoons) cold unsalted butter, cut into pieces

1 large egg

¾ cup buttermilk

1. Heat the oven to 375°F. Line a baking sheet with parchment paper.

2. In a large bowl, whisk together the flour, cornstarch, baking powder, sugar, xanthan gum, baking soda, and salt until well combined. Stir in the parsley. Add the butter pieces. Using a pastry blender, a fork, or two knives, cut in the butter until the mixture resembles coarse crumbs. Make a well in the center and set aside.

3. In a small bowl, using a wire whisk, lightly beat the egg. Gradually whisk in the buttermilk. Pour the liquid mixture into the well in the flour mixture all at once and stir with a fork just until the dry ingredients are moistened and the mixture comes together into a soft dough.

4. Drop heaping tablespoonsful of dough onto the prepared baking sheet, spacing them about 2 inches apart.

5. Bake until the biscuits are golden brown, 12 to 15 minutes. Immediately transfer to a wire cooling rack. Serve warm.

VARIATIONS

dill biscuits: **Substitute 1½ tablespoons finely chopped fresh dill for the parsley.**

rosemary biscuits: **Substitute 1½ tablespoons finely chopped fresh rosemary for the parsley.**

lemon thyme biscuits

Lemon and fresh thyme complement each other very well and create a wonderfully flavored biscuit. Strip the thyme leaves from the woody stems before chopping to get the best texture and herb flavor.

MAKES ABOUT 8 BISCUITS

1 cup Gluten-Free All-Purpose Flour
   (see p. 11)

⅔ cup cornstarch

2 teaspoons baking powder

1 teaspoon granulated sugar

¾ teaspoon xanthan gum

½ teaspoon baking soda

½ teaspoon table salt

1½ tablespoons finely chopped fresh
   thyme leaves

1½ tablespoons grated lemon zest

⅓ cup (5⅓ tablespoons) cold unsalted
   butter, cut into pieces

1 large egg

¾ cup buttermilk

1 tablespoon freshly squeezed lemon juice

1. Heat the oven to 375°F. Line a baking sheet with parchment paper.

2. In a large bowl, whisk together the flour, cornstarch, baking powder, sugar, xanthan gum, baking soda, and salt until well combined. Stir in the thyme and lemon zest. Add the butter pieces. Using a pastry blender, a fork, or two knives, cut in the butter until the mixture resembles coarse crumbs. Make a well in the center and set aside.

3. In a small bowl, using a wire whisk, lightly beat the egg. Gradually whisk in the buttermilk, then stir in the lemon juice. Pour the liquid mixture into the well in the flour mixture all at once and stir with a fork just until the dry ingredients are moistened and the mixture comes together into a soft dough.

4. Drop heaping tablespoonsful of dough onto the prepared baking sheet, spacing them about 2 inches apart.

5. Bake until the biscuits are golden brown, 12 to 15 minutes. Immediately transfer to a wire cooling rack. Serve warm.

cheddar cheese biscuits

These cheesy biscuits get an extra zing from a garlicky melted butter topping brushed over the piping-hot biscuits when they come out of the oven. Serve these instead of garlic bread next time you make pasta.

MAKES ABOUT 12 BISCUITS

For the Biscuits

1⅓ cups Gluten-Free All-Purpose Flour (see p. 11)

⅔ cup cornstarch

1 tablespoon granulated sugar

1 tablespoon baking powder

¾ teaspoon xanthan gum

½ teaspoon table salt

¼ teaspoon baking soda

6 tablespoons (¾ stick) cold unsalted butter, cut into pieces

½ cup grated sharp Cheddar cheese

1 large egg

1 cup whole milk

For the Topping

2 tablespoons unsalted butter, melted

½ teaspoon garlic powder

1. Heat the oven to 375°F. Line a baking sheet with parchment paper.

2. In a large bowl, whisk together the flour, cornstarch, sugar, baking powder, xanthan gum, salt, and baking soda until well combined. Add the butter pieces. Using a pastry blender, a fork, or two knives, cut in the butter until the mixture resembles coarse crumbs. Stir in the Cheddar cheese. Make a well in the center and set aside.

3. In a small bowl, using a wire whisk, lightly beat the egg. Gradually whisk in the milk. Pour the liquid mixture into the well in the flour mixture all at once and stir with a fork just until the dry ingredients are moistened and the mixture comes together into a soft dough.

4. Drop heaping tablespoonsful of dough onto the prepared baking sheet, spacing them about 2 inches apart.

5. Bake until the biscuits are golden brown, 12 to 15 minutes.

6. While the biscuits bake, make the topping: In a small bowl, combine the melted butter and garlic powder, stirring until well blended.

7. Immediately transfer the hot biscuits to a wire cooling rack. Brush the tops of the biscuits with the butter mixture. Serve warm.

VARIATION

Vary the flavor of the biscuits by substituting different cheeses. In place of the Cheddar, use Swiss, Gruyère, Colby Jack, or even pepper Jack for a zesty flavor. Add a sprinkling of Parmesan to the top before you bake the biscuits to add an extra zing of cheese.

cream biscuits

The butterfat in heavy cream makes wonderful biscuits with a rich flavor. Serve these with your favorite jam for breakfast or as a teatime treat.

MAKES ABOUT 12 BISCUITS

1½ cups Gluten-Free All-Purpose Flour (see p. 11)

¾ cup cornstarch

1 tablespoon granulated sugar

1 tablespoon baking powder

¾ teaspoon table salt

¾ teaspoon xanthan gum

6 tablespoons (¾ stick) cold unsalted butter, cut into pieces

2 large egg whites

1 cup heavy or whipping cream

1. Heat the oven to 375°F. Line a baking sheet with parchment paper.

2. In a large bowl, whisk together the flour, cornstarch, sugar, baking powder, salt, and xanthan gum until well combined. Add the butter pieces. Using a pastry blender, a fork, or two knives, cut in the butter until the mixture resembles coarse crumbs. Make a well in the center and set aside.

3. In a small bowl, using a wire whisk, lightly beat the egg whites. Gradually whisk in the cream. Pour the liquid mixture into the well in the flour mixture all at once and stir with a fork just until the dry ingredients are moistened and the mixture comes together into a soft dough.

4. Drop heaping tablespoonsful of dough onto the prepared baking sheet, spacing them about 2 inches apart.

5. Bake until the biscuits are golden brown, 12 to 15 minutes. Immediately transfer to a wire cooling rack. Serve warm.

sweet potato biscuits

Since sweet potatoes are available year-round, you can have a taste of fall even on a cool spring day. These have a pretty orange color and a nice touch of spice. Halve and fill with a slice of ham, topped with a scrambled or fried egg and a dash of maple syrup for a hearty breakfast sandwich.

MAKES ABOUT 12 BISCUITS

1½ cups Gluten-Free All-Purpose Flour (see p. 11); more for dusting

½ cup cornstarch

2 tablespoons firmly packed brown sugar

1 tablespoon baking powder

1 teaspoon ground cinnamon

¾ teaspoon xanthan gum

½ teaspoon baking soda

½ teaspoon table salt

½ teaspoon grated nutmeg

⅛ teaspoon ground ginger

6 tablespoons (¾ stick) cold unsalted butter, cut into pieces

1 large egg

1 cup mashed, peeled, cooked sweet potatoes (2 medium)

6 tablespoons whole milk

1 tablespoon unsalted butter, melted (optional)

1. Heat the oven to 400°F. Line a baking sheet with parchment paper.

2. In a large bowl, whisk together the flour, cornstarch, brown sugar, baking powder, cinnamon, xanthan gum, baking soda, salt, nutmeg, and ginger until well combined. Add the butter pieces. Using a pastry blender, a fork, or two knives, cut in the butter until the mixture resembles coarse crumbs. Make a well in the center and set aside.

3. In a small bowl, using a wire whisk, lightly beat the egg. Stir in the mashed sweet potatoes. Gradually whisk in the milk. Pour the liquid mixture into the well in the flour mixture all at once and stir with a fork just until the dry ingredients are moistened and the mixture comes together into a soft dough.

4. Place the dough on a board or other surface lightly dusted with gluten-free all-purpose flour. With lightly floured hands, gently pat into a flat disk about ¾ inch thick. Using a 2-inch biscuit cutter dipped in flour, cut out as many biscuits as possible. Gently gather the scraps into a ball, pat out, and cut out more biscuits. Place the biscuits about 1 inch apart on the prepared baking sheet. Brush the tops of the biscuits with melted butter, if desired.

5. Bake until the biscuits are golden brown, 15 to 20 minutes. Immediately transfer to a wire cooling rack. Serve warm.

cranberry orange scones

For the best flavor and texture, make sure the dried cranberries are moist and fresh. If not, let sit in a cup of warm water for 10 minutes to plump before chopping.

MAKES 12 SCONES

For the Scones

2 cups Gluten-Free All-Purpose Flour (see p. 11); more for dusting

½ cup cornstarch

⅓ cup granulated sugar

1 tablespoon baking powder

¾ teaspoon xanthan gum

½ teaspoon table salt

¼ teaspoon baking soda

½ cup (1 stick) cold unsalted butter, cut into pieces

¾ cup chopped dried cranberries

2 large eggs

¼ cup milk

2 tablespoons freshly squeezed orange juice

½ teaspoon pure vanilla extract

2 tablespoons grated orange zest

For the Egg Wash

1 large egg

1 teaspoon water

Granulated sugar (optional)

VARIATIONS

blueberry orange scones:
Substitute 1 cup fresh blueberries for the dried cranberries.

blueberry lemon scones:
Substitute 1 cup fresh blueberries for the dried cranberries and 2 tablespoons freshly squeezed lemon juice and 2 tablespoons lemon zest for the orange juice and orange zest.

1. Line a baking sheet with parchment paper.

2. In a large bowl, whisk together the flour, cornstarch, sugar, baking powder, xanthan gum, salt, and baking soda until well combined. Add the butter pieces. Using a pastry blender, a fork, or two knives, cut in the butter until the mixture resembles coarse crumbs. Stir in the cranberries. Make a well in the center and set aside.

3. In a small bowl, using a wire whisk, lightly beat the eggs. Gradually whisk in the milk, orange juice, and vanilla until well combined. Stir in the orange zest. Pour the liquid mixture into the well in the flour mixture all at once and stir with a fork just until well blended and the mixture comes together.

4. Divide the dough into two equal portions and shape each into a ball. Place the dough on a board or other surface lightly dusted with gluten-free all-purpose flour. With lightly floured hands, gently pat one ball into a flat disk about ¾ inch thick. Using a sharp knife, cut the disk into 6 equal wedges. Repeat with the remaining ball of dough. Place the wedges on the prepared baking sheet, spacing them about 2 inches apart. Let the scones rest for 15 minutes.

5. Heat the oven to 400°F while the scones rest.

6. Make the egg wash: In a small bowl, combine the egg and water and whisk until well blended. Brush the tops of the scones with the egg wash and sprinkle with sugar, if desired.

7. Bake until the scones are golden brown, 14 to 18 minutes. Immediately transfer to a wire cooling rack. Serve warm.

apricot scones

A touch of almond extract enhances the sweet and tangy flavor of the pretty dried apricots sprinkled through the scones. Perfect for breakfast or brunch topped with butter or sweetened whipped cream, these scones also make an excellent addition to a cheese and fruit platter. They are especially good served warm with Brie and other soft creamy cheeses.

MAKES 12 SCONES

For the Scones

2 cups Gluten-Free All-Purpose Flour (see p. 11); more for dusting

½ cup cornstarch

⅓ cup granulated sugar

1 tablespoon baking powder

¾ teaspoon xanthan gum

½ teaspoon table salt

¼ teaspoon baking soda

¼ teaspoon grated nutmeg

½ cup (1 stick) cold unsalted butter, cut into pieces

1 cup chopped dried apricots

2 large eggs

6 tablespoons milk

1 teaspoon pure vanilla extract

¼ teaspoon pure almond extract

For the Egg Wash

1 large egg

1 teaspoon water

Granulated sugar (optional)

1. Line a baking sheet with parchment paper.

2. In a large bowl, whisk together the flour, cornstarch, sugar, baking powder, xanthan gum, salt, baking soda, and nutmeg until well combined. Add the butter pieces. Using a pastry blender, a fork, or two knives, cut in the butter until the mixture resembles coarse crumbs. Stir in the apricots. Make a well in the center and set aside.

3. In a small bowl, using a wire whisk, lightly beat the eggs. Gradually whisk in the milk, vanilla extract, and almond extract until well combined. Pour the liquid mixture into the well in the flour mixture all at once and stir with a fork just until well blended and the mixture comes together.

4. Divide the dough into two equal portions and shape each into a ball. Place the dough on a board or other surface lightly dusted with gluten-free all-purpose flour. With lightly floured hands, gently pat one ball into a flat disk about ¾ inch thick. Using a sharp knife, cut the disk into 6 equal wedges. Repeat with the remaining ball of dough. Place the wedges on the prepared baking sheet, spacing them about 2 inches apart. Let the scones rest for 15 minutes.

5. Heat the oven to 400°F while the scones rest.

6. Make the egg wash: In a small bowl, combine the egg and water and whisk until well blended. Brush the tops of the scones with the egg wash and sprinkle with sugar, if desired.

7. Bake until the scones are golden brown, 14 to 18 minutes. Immediately transfer to a wire cooling rack. Serve warm.

If the dried apricots stick to your knife as you chop them, spray the knife blade with a light coating of nonstick cooking spray. Respray the knife as needed.

blueberry scones

The classic pairing of blueberries and lemons in these scones gets a tasty twist with a dusting of cinnamon-sugar. Gently combine the flour mixture and liquid ingredients to keep from mashing the blueberries.

MAKES 12 SCONES

For the Scones

2 cups Gluten-Free All-Purpose Flour (see p. 11); more for dusting

½ cup cornstarch

⅓ cup granulated sugar

1 tablespoon baking powder

¾ teaspoon xanthan gum

½ teaspoon table salt

¼ teaspoon baking soda

½ cup (1 stick) cold unsalted butter, cut into pieces

1 cup small fresh blueberries

2 large eggs

6 tablespoons whole milk

2 teaspoons grated lemon zest

½ teaspoon pure vanilla extract

For the Egg Wash

1 large egg

1 teaspoon water

2 tablespoons granulated sugar

½ teaspoon ground cinnamon

1. Line a baking sheet with parchment paper.

2. In a large bowl, whisk together the flour, cornstarch, sugar, baking powder, xanthan gum, salt, and baking soda until well combined. Add the butter pieces. Using a pastry blender, a fork, or two knives, cut in the butter until the mixture resembles coarse crumbs. Stir in the blueberries, combining them gently so as not to smash them. Make a well in the center and set aside.

3. In a small bowl, using a wire whisk, lightly beat the eggs. Gradually whisk in the milk until well combined. Stir in the lemon zest and vanilla extract. Pour the liquid mixture into the well in the flour mixture all at once and stir with a fork just until well blended and the mixture comes together, being careful not to crush the blueberries.

4. Divide the dough into two equal portions and shape each into a ball. Place the dough on a board or other surface lightly dusted with gluten-free all-purpose flour. With lightly floured hands, gently pat one ball into a flat disk about ¾ inch thick. Using a sharp knife, cut the disk into 6 equal wedges. Repeat with the remaining ball of dough. Place the wedges on the prepared baking sheet, spacing them about 2 inches apart. Let the scones rest for 15 minutes.

5. Heat the oven to 400°F while the scones rest.

6. Make the egg wash: In a small bowl, combine the egg and water and whisk until well blended. In another small bowl, combine the sugar and cinnamon until well blended. Brush the tops of the scones with the egg wash and sprinkle with the cinnamon-sugar mixture.

7. Bake until the scones are golden brown, 14 to 18 minutes. Immediately transfer to a wire cooling rack. Serve warm.

currant scones

Dried currants have a distinct, tart flavor and add a nice punch to scones. They can be found in the dried fruit section in most grocery stores but if you have trouble finding them, you can substitute chopped raisins.

MAKES 12 SCONES

For the Scones

2 cups Gluten-Free All-Purpose Flour (see p. 11); more for dusting

½ cup cornstarch

⅓ cup granulated sugar

1 tablespoon baking powder

¾ teaspoon xanthan gum

½ teaspoon baking soda

½ teaspoon table salt

½ cup (1 stick) cold unsalted butter, cut into pieces

1 cup dried currants

2 large eggs

½ cup buttermilk

2 teaspoons pure vanilla extract

For the Egg Wash

1 large egg

1 teaspoon water

Granulated sugar (optional)

VARIATIONS

cinnamon currant scones:

Add 1 teaspoon ground cinnamon to the flour mixture.

currant apple scones:

Reduce the dried currants to ½ cup and add ½ cup finely chopped peeled apples to the liquid mixture before combining with the flour mixture.

1. Line a baking sheet with parchment paper.

2. In a large bowl, whisk together the flour, cornstarch, sugar, baking powder, xanthan gum, baking soda, and salt until well combined. Add the butter pieces. Using a pastry blender, a fork, or two knives, cut in the butter until the mixture resembles coarse crumbs. Stir in the currants. Make a well in the center and set aside.

3. In a small bowl, using a wire whisk, lightly beat the eggs. Gradually whisk in the buttermilk and vanilla extract until well combined. Pour the liquid mixture into the well in the flour mixture all at once and stir with a fork just until well blended and the mixture comes together.

4. Divide the dough into two equal portions and shape each into a ball. Place the dough on a board or other surface lightly dusted with gluten-free all-purpose flour. With lightly floured hands, gently pat one ball into a flat disk about ¾ inch thick. Using a sharp knife, cut the disk into 6 equal wedges. Repeat with the remaining ball of dough. Place the wedges on the prepared baking sheet, spacing them about 2 inches apart. Let the scones rest for 15 minutes.

5. Heat the oven to 400°F while the scones rest.

6. Make the egg wash: In a small bowl, combine the egg and water and whisk until well blended. Brush the tops of the scones with the egg wash and sprinkle with the sugar, if desired.

7. Bake until the scones are golden brown, 14 to 18 minutes. Immediately transfer to a wire cooling rack. Serve warm.

golden raisin scones

Cinnamon both in the scone dough and sprinkled on top gives a warm spice flavor to these tender scones. I like the sweetness of golden raisins in these scones, but you can use dark raisins, if you prefer.

MAKES 12 SCONES

For the Scones

2 cups Gluten-Free All-Purpose Flour (see p. 11); more for dusting

½ cup cornstarch

⅓ cup granulated sugar

1 tablespoon baking powder

1 teaspoon ground cinnamon

¾ teaspoon xanthan gum

½ teaspoon table salt

¼ teaspoon baking soda

½ cup (1 stick) cold unsalted butter, cut into pieces

1 cup golden raisins

2 large eggs

6 tablespoons whole milk

1 teaspoon pure vanilla extract

For the Egg Wash

1 large egg

1 teaspoon water

2 tablespoons granulated sugar

½ teaspoon ground cinnamon

1. Line a baking sheet with parchment paper.

2. In a large bowl, whisk together the flour, cornstarch, sugar, baking powder, cinnamon, xanthan gum, salt, and baking soda until well combined. Add the butter pieces. Using a pastry blender, a fork, or two knives, cut in the butter until the mixture resembles coarse crumbs. Stir in the raisins. Make a well in the center and set aside.

3. In a small bowl, using a wire whisk, lightly beat the eggs. Gradually whisk in the milk and vanilla extract until well combined. Pour the liquid mixture into the well in the flour mixture all at once and stir with a fork just until well blended and the mixture comes together.

4. Divide the dough into two equal portions and shape each into a ball. Place the dough on a board or other surface lightly dusted with gluten-free all-purpose flour. With lightly floured hands, gently pat one ball into a flat disk about ¾ inch thick. Using a sharp knife, cut the disk into 6 equal wedges. Repeat with the remaining ball of dough. Place the wedges on the prepared baking sheet, spacing them about 2 inches apart. Let the scones rest for 15 minutes.

5. Heat the oven to 400°F while the scones rest.

6. Make the egg wash: In a small bowl, combine the egg and water and whisk until well blended. In another small bowl, combine the sugar and cinnamon until well blended. Brush the tops of the scones with the egg wash, then sprinkle with the cinnamon-sugar mixture.

7. Bake until the scones are golden brown, 14 to 18 minutes. Immediately transfer to a wire cooling rack. Serve warm.

cherry almond scones

You can use either sweet or sour dried cherries in these scones—both work equally well. I like to use a blend of sweet and sour when I have them on hand.

MAKES 12 SCONES

For the Scones

2 cups Gluten-Free All-Purpose Flour (see p. 11); more for dusting

½ cup cornstarch

⅓ cup granulated sugar

1 tablespoon baking powder

¾ teaspoon xanthan gum

½ teaspoon table salt

¼ teaspoon baking soda

½ cup (1 stick) cold unsalted butter, cut into pieces

¾ cup chopped dried cherries, sweet or sour

⅓ cup chopped sliced almonds

2 large eggs

6 tablespoons whole milk

½ teaspoon pure vanilla extract

½ teaspoon pure almond extract

For the Egg Wash

1 large egg

1 teaspoon water

Granulated sugar (optional)

1. Line a baking sheet with parchment paper.

2. In a large bowl, whisk together the flour, cornstarch, sugar, baking powder, xanthan gum, salt, and baking soda until well combined. Add the butter pieces. Using a pastry blender, a fork, or two knives, cut in the butter until the mixture resembles coarse crumbs. Stir in the cherries and almonds. Make a well in the center and set aside.

3. In a small bowl, using a wire whisk, lightly beat the eggs. Gradually whisk in the milk, vanilla extract, and almond extract until well combined. Pour the liquid mixture into the well in the flour mixture all at once and stir with a fork just until well blended and the mixture comes together.

4. Divide the dough into two equal portions and shape each into a ball. Place the dough on a board or other surface lightly dusted with gluten-free all-purpose flour. With lightly floured hands, gently pat one ball into a flat disk about ¾ inch thick. Using a sharp knife, cut the disk into 6 equal wedges. Repeat with the remaining ball of dough. Place the wedges on the prepared baking sheet, spacing them about 2 inches apart. Let the scones rest for 15 minutes.

5. Heat the oven to 400°F while the scones rest.

6. Make the egg wash: In a small bowl, combine the egg and water and whisk until well blended. Brush the tops of the scones with the egg wash and sprinkle with sugar, if desired.

7. Bake until the scones are golden brown, 14 to 18 minutes. Immediately transfer to a wire cooling rack. Serve warm.

walnut scones

Scones loaded with nuts have many fans, including me. These make a wonderful accompaniment to a piping-shot cup of tea or coffee. Toast the nuts to bring out their natural oils and intensify the nutty flavor.

MAKES 12 SCONES

For the Scones

2 cups Gluten-Free All-Purpose Flour (see p. 11); more for dusting

⅔ cup cornstarch

⅓ cup granulated sugar

2 teaspoons baking powder

1 teaspoon ground cinnamon

¾ teaspoon xanthan gum

½ teaspoon baking soda

½ teaspoon table salt

½ cup (1 stick) cold unsalted butter, cut into pieces

1⅓ cups chopped walnuts

2 large eggs

½ cup buttermilk

1 teaspoon pure vanilla extract

For the Egg Wash

1 large egg

1 teaspoon water

Granulated sugar (optional)

3 tablespoons finely chopped walnuts (optional)

VARIATIONS

pecan scones: **Substitute chopped pecans for the chopped walnuts.**

walnut apple scones: **Reduce the walnuts to ⅔ cup and add ½ cup finely chopped peeled apples to the liquid mixture before combining with the flour mixture.**

1. Line a baking sheet with parchment paper.

2. In a large bowl, whisk together the flour, cornstarch, sugar, baking powder, cinnamon, xanthan gum, baking soda, and salt until well combined. Add the butter pieces. Using a pastry blender, a fork, or two knives, cut in the butter until the mixture resembles coarse crumbs. Stir in the walnuts. Make a well in the center and set aside.

3. In a small bowl, using a wire whisk, lightly beat the eggs. Gradually whisk in the buttermilk and vanilla extract until well combined. Pour the liquid mixture into the well in the flour mixture all at once and stir with a fork just until well blended and the mixture comes together.

4. Divide the dough into two equal portions and shape each into a ball. Place the dough on a board or other surface lightly dusted with gluten-free all-purpose flour. With lightly floured hands, gently pat one ball into a flat disk about ¾ inch thick. Using a sharp knife, cut the disk into 6 equal wedges. Repeat with the remaining ball of dough. Place the wedges on the prepared baking sheet, spacing them about 2 inches apart. Let the scones rest for 15 minutes.

5. Heat the oven to 400°F while the scones rest.

6. Make the egg wash: In a small bowl, combine the egg and water and whisk until well blended. Brush the tops of the scones with the egg wash and sprinkle with the sugar or finely chopped walnuts, if desired.

7. Bake until the scones are golden brown, 14 to 18 minutes. Immediately transfer to a wire cooling rack. Serve warm.

Nuts can turn rancid quickly, so always taste them before adding to baked goods. To store nuts, seal in a zip-top bag and keep them in the freezer to preserve their flavor.

CHAPTER FOUR

pancakes
and
crêpes

Homemade gluten-free pancakes and crêpes are quick to prepare and can be served for breakfast, brunch, lunch, or dinner. Both are very versatile. Pancakes can be adorned simply with syrup or a fruit topping or loaded with your favorite ingredients. Crêpes make a perfect wrap for a variety of savory and sweet fillings. Meat, poultry, seafood, vegetables, fruit, jam, and even ice cream all make wonderful fillings for these delicate pancakes.

Crêpes—simply very thin, tender pancakes—have a reputation of being hard to make, but they're actually very easy to prepare. If you can tilt and turn a small frying pan, you can make delicious crêpes.

Pancakes

CHOOSING A GRIDDLE

While you can make pancakes in a large frying pan, a griddle is the ideal pan for cooking them. Stovetop griddles are specialty pans that come in round, square, or rectangular shapes. A rectangular griddle is designed to sit over two burners and can hold a lot of pancakes at one time, making it a good choice for large families or when entertaining.

The bottom of a griddle is completely flat, with a low raised ridge around the outside of the pan. The low sides provide good air circulation around the pancakes so they cook evenly on all edges. Griddles can be made from both lightweight and heavy materials. It is worth investing in a sturdy, heavyweight griddle as it will conduct and hold heat more evenly than a thin griddle. Even though most griddles have a nonstick coating, it is always a good idea to grease the griddle with a little unsalted butter or nonstick cooking spray before making a batch of pancakes.

Another good choice is to use an electric griddle that sits on the countertop. Electric griddles keep a steady temperature so pancakes cook evenly. They also have room for lots of pancakes, making them a great tool for feeding a hungry crowd.

MAKING THE BATTER

I like thick, light pancakes that rise up high. These recipes are designed to create fluffy pancakes. If you prefer thin pancakes, add a little extra milk or buttermilk to the batter until you reach the preferred consistency. You can always thin a thick batter, but it's much harder to thicken a batter that's too thin.

Use a light touch when mixing pancake batters. After adding the liquid ingredients to the dry, you want to mix the batter just until they are combined—don't beat it smooth. The less mixing you do, the better. Some small lumps in the batter are just fine. For fluffier pancakes, let the batter rest for 5 minutes before making the pancakes.

COOKING THE PANCAKES

Heat a stovetop griddle over medium heat or an electric griddle to 350°F. When hot, grease the griddle with a small amount of unsalted butter or nonstick cooking spray. The pan should be hot enough to quickly melt the butter but not brown it. You may also want to add a little butter to the griddle between each batch of pancakes. Spoon or ladle about ⅓ cup batter per pancake onto the greased griddle, leaving 1 to 2 inches of space between each pancake.

Cook the pancakes on the first side for about 3 minutes. The pancakes will be ready to turn when the bottoms are lightly browned and small bubbles start to form on the top. Gently lift the edge of one pancake to check the doneness on the underside. If not quite ready, let the pancakes cook for another 30 seconds to 1 minute and then check again.

You may need to adjust the heat up or down a bit to find the best temperature for your griddle. Generally, medium heat is the best temperature for cooking gluten-free pancakes on a stovetop griddle, but you might need to adjust it to medium-low or medium-high depending on the amount of heat your burners put out. As you gain experience cooking gluten-free pancakes on your stove, you will learn what setting works best to give you the results you want. For electric griddles, a setting of 350°F is usually ideal for cooking pancakes.

Crêpes

CHOOSING A CRÊPE PAN

Use a small (8-inch) nonstick frying pan or a crêpe pan to shape and cook crêpes. A crêpe pan is specifically designed for making crêpes, with its flat bottom and very shallow sides. The right size pan is important when making crêpes. Crêpes made in a pan larger than 8 inches may not cook all the way through in the center by the time the outer edges start to brown, resulting in undercooked crêpes.

MIXING THE BATTER

The key to making crêpes is a smooth, thin batter. A blender works well to remove even the smallest of lumps and to emulsify and aerate the batter. If you don't want to use a blender, you can mix the batter with an electric mixer or even by hand using a wire whisk. Just make sure the batter is perfectly smooth. After mixing, if there are any lumps remaining, strain the batter through a sieve to remove them. Refrigerate the batter for at least 1 hour to let it rest before cooking the crêpes. This will allow the flour to absorb the liquid, which will produce more tender crêpes. The finished batter should be about the thickness of heavy cream.

COOKING CRÊPES

Remove the crêpe batter from the refrigerator and give the batter a vigorous stir to make sure it is well blended after resting.

Heat the frying pan or crêpe pan over medium heat. Before cooking the first crêpe, add a small amount of unsalted butter to the pan or spray it with nonstick cooking spray. The pan should be hot enough that the butter melts quickly but does not brown. Tilt and turn the pan to coat the bottom with the melted butter.

Add 3 tablespoons of batter to the hot pan. Lift the pan off the heat and immediately tilt and turn it, swirling the batter until it evenly coats the bottom of the pan in a thin layer. If necessary, adjust the amount of batter needed to evenly coat the pan you are using.

Return the pan to the heat and let the first side of the crêpe cook; it should be done in about 1 minute. Use a knife or a spatula to gently loosen the edges of the crêpe from the pan—the underside will be pale with light brown flecks of color and the edges will start to look dry or crisp when it's ready to flip. Using a spatula, carefully turn the crêpe over. Alternatively, you can lift the edge of the crêpe with a knife, pick it up with your fingers, and quickly flip it over. If the edges do not easily release from the pan or if the crêpe starts to tear when you try to turn it, the first side of the crêpe is not done enough. Let it cook for another 10 to 15 seconds and try again.

The second side of the crêpe will cook faster than the first, taking only about 30 seconds. When it is done (follow the doneness clues noted above), simply slide the crêpe out of the pan and onto a plate. If the crêpes will be used warm, cover the plate with a piece of foil. You can also keep crêpes warm in a 200°F oven.

It may take a crêpe or two to get the pan at the right temperature so that the batter spreads evenly and does not brown too fast or cook too slow. Consider the first crêpe a test and adjust the heat as needed. After making the first crêpe it is not necessary to butter or spray the pan again unless the crêpes start to stick. Continue cooking crêpes until you have used up the batter.

STORING CRÊPES

Crêpes are always best eaten when freshly made, but they can be placed in a zip-top bag and stored in the refrigerator for a few days or tightly wrapped in foil and kept in the freezer for a few weeks. Before storing, separate each crêpe with wax paper to ensure they don't stick together and tear when you try to separate them. Or you can stack them directly on top of each other before refrigerating or freezing and then warm the entire stack before separating the crêpes.

Quick Tips
PANCAKES AND CRÊPES

PANCAKES

- Be careful not to overmix the batter as this will result in dense, flat pancakes.
- Cook pancakes on a nonstick stove-top griddle or electric griddle and give the griddle enough time to heat. Otherwise, the pancakes will be pale, won't rise well, and will take a long time to cook.
- Grease the griddle with a bit of unsalted butter or nonstick cooking spray to prevent pancakes from sticking.
- Pour the batter from a low height to make pancakes of uniform shape.
- For even cooking, make sure the pancakes do not touch each other.
- Turn the pancakes when bubbles form on the surface.
- Use a wide nonstick spatula to easily turn pancakes.

CRÊPES

- Crêpe batter should be the consistency of heavy cream. If it is too thick, thin the batter with a little milk.
- Add a bit of unsalted butter or nonstick cooking spray to the pan before adding batter for the first crêpe. You shouldn't need to add any more as you cook the crêpes, unless you find the crêpes sticking to the pan.
- Immediately after adding the batter to the pan, turn and tilt the pan to distribute the batter in an even layer.
- Adjust the amount of batter per crêpe up or down depending on the size of the pan you are using and the thickness of the batter.
- Keep a close eye on the crêpes as they cook so they don't brown too much.
- Flip the crêpe once the edges look dry and crisp, using a spatula to loosen the edges and your fingers or spatula to lift and help flip the crêpe.
- Crêpes should be uniformly thin without holes or tears.
- It's common for the first crêpe to be a little misshapen, and it may be underdone or overcooked. Think of it as a test crêpe to check the batter thickness and the temperature of the pan.
- For a quick elegant dessert, fill crêpes with ice cream and top with fresh seasonal fruit.

traditional pancakes

This basic recipe makes delicious pancakes that can be dressed up in many ways by serving them with fruit toppings or flavored syrups or by adding chopped fruit in the batter.

MAKES 10 TO 12 PANCAKES

2 cups Gluten-Free All-Purpose Flour (see p. 11)

2 tablespoons granulated sugar

4 teaspoons baking powder

½ teaspoon table salt

½ teaspoon xanthan gum

2 large eggs

4 tablespoons (½ stick) unsalted butter, melted, or ¼ cup vegetable oil

1⅔ cups whole milk

1 teaspoon pure vanilla extract

Nonstick cooking spray or unsalted butter, for the pan

Maple syrup, for serving (optional)

Mixed diced fresh fruit, for serving (optional)

1. Heat a griddle or large nonstick frying pan over medium heat, or heat an electric griddle to 350°F.

2. In a medium bowl, using a wire whisk, combine the flour, sugar, baking powder, salt, and xanthan gum until well blended. Make a well in the center and set aside.

3. In a medium bowl, using a wire whisk, lightly beat the eggs. Gradually whisk in the melted butter until evenly combined. Whisk in the milk until well blended, then stir in the vanilla extract. Pour the liquid mixture into the well in the flour mixture all at once. Stir just until combined and the flour mixture is moistened. There may be a few small lumps; do not overmix.

4. Lightly grease the griddle with nonstick cooking spray or unsalted butter. Ladle or spoon about ⅓ cup of batter per pancake onto the griddle. Cook until the pancakes rise, bubbles start to come to the surface, and the underside is golden brown, 3 to 4 minutes. Turn over and cook until golden brown, 1½ to 2 minutes more, adjusting the heat if needed to prevent overbrowning. Serve hot with your favorite syrup or fruit topping, if desired.

buttermilk pancakes

Buttermilk adds a lot of flavor to these tasty pancakes and makes them rise up light and fluffy. The addition of a bit of baking soda works with the acid in the buttermilk to give an additional leavening "lift" that makes these rise up higher than pancakes made with milk.

MAKES 10 TO 12 PANCAKES

1¾ cups Gluten-Free All-Purpose Flour (see p. 11)

2 tablespoons granulated sugar

2 teaspoons baking powder

½ teaspoon baking soda

½ teaspoon table salt

½ teaspoon xanthan gum

2 large eggs

2 tablespoons unsalted butter, melted, or vegetable oil

1¾ cups buttermilk

1½ teaspoons pure vanilla extract

Nonstick cooking spray or unsalted butter, for the pan

Maple syrup, for serving (optional)

Mixed diced fresh fruit, for serving (optional)

1. Heat a griddle or large nonstick frying pan over medium heat, or heat an electric griddle to 350°F.

2. In a medium bowl, using a wire whisk, combine the flour, sugar, baking powder, baking soda, salt, and xanthan gum until well blended. Make a well in the center and set aside.

3. In a medium bowl, using a wire whisk, lightly beat the eggs. Gradually whisk in the melted butter until evenly combined. Whisk in the buttermilk until well blended, then stir in the vanilla extract. Pour the liquid mixture into the well in the flour mixture all at once. Stir just until combined and the flour mixture is moistened. There may be a few small lumps; do not overmix.

4. Lightly grease the griddle with nonstick cooking spray or unsalted butter. Ladle or spoon about ⅓ cup of batter per pancake onto the griddle. Cook until the pancakes rise, bubbles start to come to the surface, and the underside is golden brown, 3 to 4 minutes. Turn over and cook until golden brown, 1½ to 2 minutes more, adjusting the heat if needed to prevent overbrowning. Serve hot with your favorite syrup or fruit topping, if desired.

blueberry pancakes

Nothing can beat the flavor of fresh blueberry pancakes hot off the griddle. In fact, buy or pick extra blueberries and freeze them for use when they aren't in season (see the tip below for more on this). I love to serve these pancakes for dinner topped with a mixture of fresh berries or melted butter and warm maple syrup.

MAKES 12 TO 14 PANCAKES

1¾ cups Gluten-Free All-Purpose Flour (see p. 11)

2 tablespoons granulated sugar

2 teaspoons baking powder

½ teaspoon baking soda

½ teaspoon table salt

½ teaspoon xanthan gum

2 large eggs

¼ cup (4 tablespoons) unsalted butter, melted, or vegetable oil

1¾ cups buttermilk

1 tablespoon grated orange zest

½ teaspoon pure vanilla extract

1 cup fresh blueberries

Nonstick cooking spray or unsalted butter, for the pan

Maple or blueberry syrup, for serving (optional)

Additional fresh blueberries, for serving (optional)

VARIATION

cinnamon blueberry pancakes:
Omit the orange zest and add 1 teaspoon ground cinnamon to the flour mixture before combining with the liquid ingredients.

1. Heat a griddle or large nonstick frying pan over medium heat, or heat an electric griddle to 350°F.

2. In a medium bowl, using a wire whisk, combine the flour, sugar, baking powder, baking soda, salt, and xanthan gum until well blended. Make a well in the center and set aside.

3. In a medium bowl, using a wire whisk, lightly beat the eggs. Gradually whisk in the melted butter until evenly combined. Whisk in the buttermilk until well blended. Stir in the orange zest and vanilla extract. Pour the liquid mixture into the flour mixture all at once. Stir just until combined and the flour mixture is moistened. There may be a few small lumps; do not overmix. Gently stir in the blueberries just until evenly distributed.

4. Lightly grease the griddle with nonstick cooking spray or unsalted butter. Ladle or spoon about ⅓ cup of batter per pancake onto the griddle. Cook until the pancakes rise, bubbles start to come to the surface, and the underside is golden brown, 3 to 4 minutes. Turn over and cook until golden brown, 1½ to 2 minutes more, adjusting the heat if needed to prevent overbrowning. Serve hot with maple or blueberry syrup, and fresh blueberries, if desired.

If blueberries are not in season, you may use frozen blueberries instead. Don't defrost the blueberries. Just toss the frozen berries into the batter and stir just enough to distribute them. Defrosting the berries or overstirring the batter after adding the frozen berries will cause the batter to turn blue.

apple pancakes

Containing both applesauce and apple pieces, these lightly spiced pancakes are reminiscent of warm apple pie. Applesauce adds a nice moistness to the pancakes and increases the apple flavor. I like to use smooth applesauce in this recipe because it gives the pancakes a velvety texture. Any good cooking apple, such as Gala, Fuji, Jonagold, Golden Delicious, or Granny Smith, will work well. Be sure to peel the apple before grating as the peel can be tough when cooked.

If you like a little sweetness with your breakfast, serve these with a dollop of whipped cream or sprinkling of confectioners' sugar. If serving for a special breakfast or brunch, sauté some peeled diced apples in a little butter and cinnamon and serve on top of the warm pancakes.

MAKES 8 TO 10 PANCAKES

1½ cups Gluten-Free All-Purpose Flour (see p. 11)

3 tablespoons firmly packed brown sugar

2 teaspoons baking powder

1 teaspoon ground cinnamon

½ teaspoon table salt

½ teaspoon xanthan gum

¼ teaspoon grated nutmeg

2 large eggs

2 tablespoons unsalted butter, melted, or vegetable oil

½ cup unsweetened applesauce

1 cup whole milk

¾ cup grated or finely chopped peeled apple

Nonstick cooking spray or unsalted butter, for the pan

Maple syrup, for serving (optional)

1. Heat a griddle or large nonstick frying pan over medium heat, or heat an electric griddle to 350°F.

2. In a medium bowl, using a wire whisk, combine the flour, brown sugar, baking powder, cinnamon, salt, xanthan gum, and nutmeg until well blended. Make a well in the center and set aside.

3. In a medium bowl, using a wire whisk, lightly beat the eggs. Gradually whisk in the melted butter until evenly combined, then stir in the applesauce. Whisk in the milk until well blended. Pour the liquid mixture into the well in the flour mixture all at once. Stir just until combined and the flour mixture is moistened. There may be a few small lumps; do not overmix. Gently stir in the apples just until evenly distributed.

4. Lightly grease the griddle with nonstick cooking spray or unsalted butter. Ladle or spoon about ⅓ cup of batter per pancake onto the griddle. Cook until the pancakes rise, bubbles start to come to the surface, and the underside is golden brown, 3 to 4 minutes. Turn over and cook until golden brown, 1½ to 2 minutes more, adjusting the heat if needed to prevent overbrowning. Serve hot with maple syrup, if desired.

～◦◦◎ ◎◦◦～

Individual serving-size containers of applesauce hold ½ cup of applesauce and are the perfect premeasured amount to use in this recipe.

banana nut pancakes

This recipe makes good use of both ripe and overripe bananas. Mashing the bananas and mixing them into the batter ensures that every bite is loaded with banana flavor. You may omit the nuts, if you prefer. Top with sliced bananas or with fresh strawberries for a strawberry-banana treat.

MAKES 12 TO 14 PANCAKES

2 cups Gluten-Free All-Purpose Flour (see p. 11)

2 tablespoons granulated sugar

1 tablespoon baking powder

½ teaspoon table salt

½ teaspoon xanthan gum

2 large eggs

3 tablespoons unsalted butter, melted, or vegetable oil

1¼ cups whole milk

2½ medium-size ripe bananas, mashed

1 teaspoon pure vanilla extract

¾ cup chopped walnuts or pecans

Nonstick cooking spray or unsalted butter, for the pan

Maple syrup, for serving (optional)

VARIATIONS

banana blueberry pancakes: Substitute ¾ cup fresh blueberries for the nuts.

banana spice pancakes: Add 1 teaspoon ground cinnamon, ¼ teaspoon grated nutmeg, and ⅛ teaspoon ground ginger to the flour mixture before combining with the liquid ingredients.

tropical pancakes: Omit the nuts and stir ¾ cup chopped shredded or flaked coconut into the dry ingredients. Top the pancakes with drained crushed pineapple and serve with coconut syrup, if desired.

1. Heat a griddle or large nonstick frying pan over medium heat, or heat an electric griddle to 350°F.

2. In a medium bowl, using a wire whisk, combine the flour, sugar, baking powder, salt, and xanthan gum until well blended. Make a well in the center and set aside.

3. In a medium bowl, using a wire whisk, lightly beat the eggs. Gradually whisk in the melted butter until evenly combined. Whisk in the milk until well blended. Stir in the bananas and vanilla extract. Pour the liquid mixture into the well in the flour mixture all at once. Stir just until combined and the flour mixture is moistened. There may be a few small lumps; do not overmix. Gently stir in the nuts just until evenly distributed.

4. Lightly grease the griddle with nonstick cooking spray or unsalted butter. Ladle or spoon about ⅓ cup of batter per pancake onto the griddle. Cook until the pancakes rise, bubbles start to come to the surface, and the underside is golden brown, about 3 to 4 minutes. Turn over and cook until golden brown, 1½ to 2 minutes more, adjusting the heat if needed to prevent overbrowning. Serve hot with maple syrup, if desired.

For the best texture, do not purée or completely mash the bananas. Leave some small pieces of banana when you mash them.

Bananas that are golden in color with small brown flecks have the strongest banana flavor and will give you the best results.

buckwheat pancakes

The addition of buckwheat flour makes delicious multigrain pancakes. Topped with maple syrup, these tender pancakes are a great way to start the day on a cold winter morning. Or top them with plain or vanilla yogurt, diced fresh fruit, raisins, and dried cranberries or blueberries.

MAKES 10 TO 12 PANCAKES

1 cup Gluten-Free All-Purpose Flour (see p. 11)

¾ cup buckwheat flour

3 tablespoons firmly packed brown sugar

1 tablespoon baking powder

1 teaspoon ground cinnamon

½ teaspoon baking soda

½ teaspoon table salt

½ teaspoon xanthan gum

3 large eggs

3 tablespoons unsalted butter, melted, or vegetable oil

2 cups buttermilk

2 teaspoons pure vanilla extract

Nonstick cooking spray or unsalted butter, for the pan

Maple syrup, for serving (optional)

Mixed diced fresh fruit, for serving (optional)

1. Heat a griddle or large nonstick frying pan over medium heat, or heat an electric griddle to 350°F.

2. In a medium bowl, using a wire whisk, combine the all-purpose and buckwheat flours, brown sugar, baking powder, cinnamon, baking soda, salt, and xanthan gum until well blended. Make a well in the center and set aside.

3. In a medium bowl, using a wire whisk, lightly beat the eggs. Gradually whisk in the melted butter until evenly combined. Whisk in the buttermilk until well blended, then stir in the vanilla extract. Pour the liquid mixture into the well in the flour mixture all at once. Stir just until combined and the flour mixture is moistened. There may be a few small lumps; do not overmix.

4. Lightly grease the griddle with nonstick cooking spray or unsalted butter. Ladle or spoon about ⅓ cup of batter per pancake onto the griddle. Cook until the pancakes rise, bubbles start to come to the surface, and the underside is golden brown, 3 to 4 minutes. Turn over and cook until golden brown, 1½ to 2 minutes more, adjusting the heat if needed to prevent overbrowning. Serve hot with your favorite syrup or fruit topping.

VARIATION

Add ¾ cup walnuts or pecans to the pancake batter.

double corn pancakes

These pancakes are wonderful made with fresh corn kernels at the peak of the summer and fall corn season. During the winter and spring months or on busy days, drained canned whole corn kernels or thawed frozen corn kernels will make a good substitution.

MAKES 10 TO 12 PANCAKES

1¼ cups Gluten-Free All-Purpose Flour (see p. 11)

1 cup cornmeal

2 tablespoons granulated sugar

2 teaspoons baking powder

½ teaspoon baking soda

½ teaspoon table salt

½ teaspoon xanthan gum

2 large eggs

3 tablespoons unsalted butter, melted, or vegetable oil

1⅓ cups whole milk

½ teaspoon pure vanilla extract

1 cup fresh corn kernels, or canned whole kernel corn, drained

Nonstick cooking spray or unsalted butter, for the pan

1. Heat a griddle or large nonstick frying pan over medium heat, or heat an electric griddle to 350°F.

2. In a medium bowl, using a wire whisk, combine the flour, cornmeal, sugar, baking powder, baking soda, salt, and xanthan gum until well blended. Make a well in the center and set aside.

3. In a medium bowl, using a wire whisk, lightly beat the eggs. Gradually whisk in the melted butter until evenly combined. Whisk in the milk until well blended, then stir in the vanilla extract. Pour the liquid mixture into the well in the flour mixture all at once. Stir just until combined and the flour mixture is moistened. There may be a few small lumps; do not overmix. Gently stir in the corn just until it's evenly distributed.

4. Lightly grease the griddle with nonstick cooking spray or butter. Ladle or spoon about ⅓ cup of batter per pancake onto the griddle. Cook until the pancakes rise, bubbles start to come to the surface, and the underside is golden brown, 3 to 4 minutes. Turn over and cook until golden brown, 1½ to 2 minutes more, adjusting the heat if needed to prevent overbrowning. Serve hot.

VARIATION

mexican corn pancakes: **Add ⅔ cup peeled, seeded, and drained finely chopped tomatoes and 1 to 2 tablespoons finely chopped, seeded jalapeño peppers.**

pumpkin pancakes

The aroma of pumpkin pie fills the house as these yummy pancakes cook. Be sure to use canned puréed pumpkin, not pumpkin pie filling, which contains spices and other ingredients.

MAKES 12 TO 14 PANCAKES

2 cups Gluten-Free All-Purpose Flour (see p. 11)

1 tablespoon baking powder

1½ teaspoons ground cinnamon

½ teaspoon grated nutmeg

½ teaspoon baking soda

½ teaspoon table salt

½ teaspoon xanthan gum

¼ teaspoon ground ginger

3 large eggs

3 tablespoons unsalted butter, melted, or vegetable oil

One 15-ounce can (1¼ cups) puréed pumpkin

⅓ cup firmly packed brown sugar

1¼ cups whole milk

1 teaspoon pure vanilla extract

Unsalted butter or nonstick cooking spray, for the pan

Maple syrup, for serving (optional)

1. Heat a griddle or large nonstick frying pan over medium heat, or heat an electric griddle to 350°F.

2. In a medium bowl, using a wire whisk, combine the flour, baking powder, cinnamon, nutmeg, baking soda, salt, xanthan gum, and ginger until well blended. Make a well in the center and set aside.

3. In a medium bowl, using a wire whisk, lightly beat the eggs. Gradually whisk in the melted butter until evenly combined. Add the pumpkin and brown sugar and stir until smooth. Whisk in the milk until well blended. Stir in the vanilla extract. Pour the liquid mixture into the well in the flour mixture all at once. Stir just until combined and the flour mixture is moistened. There may be a few small lumps; do not overmix.

4. Lightly grease the griddle with nonstick cooking spray or unsalted butter. Ladle or spoon about ⅓ cup of batter per pancake onto the griddle. Cook until the pancakes rise and the underside is golden brown, 3 to 4 minutes. Turn over and cook until golden brown, 1½ to 2 minutes more, adjusting the heat if needed to prevent over-browning. Serve hot with maple syrup, if desired.

VARIATION

pumpkin nut pancakes: Gently stir 1 cup chopped pecans or walnuts into the pancake batter.

crêpe batter

This is a very versatile crêpe batter that can be used with any type of filling, from fruits and chocolate to vegetables and meats. You can mix the batter in a blender, with an electric mixer, or by hand. All will give you good results.

MAKES 10 TO 12 CRÊPES

Unsalted butter or nonstick cooking spray, for the pan

1 cup Gluten-Free All-Purpose Flour (see p. 11)

½ teaspoon table salt

⅛ teaspoon baking powder

⅛ teaspoon xanthan gum

2 large eggs

1 cup whole milk

2 tablespoons unsalted butter, melted, or vegetable oil

1. In a small bowl, whisk together the flour, salt, baking powder, and xanthan gum until well combined.

2. **TO MIX THE BATTER IN A BLENDER:** Place the eggs in the blender jar. Add the flour mixture, milk, butter. Cover the jar and blend on medium until the batter is smooth, about 30 seconds. Scrape down the sides of the jar and blend for another 10 to 15 seconds. Cover and chill for at least 1 hour before making the crêpes.

TO MIX THE BATTER WITH AN ELECTRIC MIXER: In a large bowl, using an electric mixer fitted with the wire whip beater attachment, beat the eggs on medium speed. Gradually beat in the flour mixture, alternating with the milk, in three portions each, beating well after each addition. Gradually beat in the melted butter. Scrape down the sides of the bowl and beat until the batter is smooth, about 30 seconds. Cover and chill for at least 1 hour before making the crêpes.

TO MIX THE BATTER BY HAND: In a medium bowl, using a wire whisk, lightly beat the eggs. Gradually beat in the flour mixture, alternating with the milk, in three portions each, beating well after each addition. Gradually beat in the melted butter. Whisk vigorously until the batter is very smooth. Cover and chill for at least 1 hour before making the crêpes.

3. Heat an 8-inch nonstick frying pan or crêpe pan over medium heat. Lightly whisk the crêpe batter until smooth. Grease the pan with a small amount of butter or nonstick cooking spray. Lift the pan off the heat and pour in 3 tablespoons of crêpe batter. Immediately tilt and swirl the pan to evenly coat the bottom with a thin layer of batter. Keep swirling the pan just until the batter is set. Return the pan to the heat and cook until the edges of the crêpe are dry and the underside is pale with light brown flecks, 1 to 1½ minutes. Using a spatula or knife, gently loosen the edges of the crêpe and then use a spatula or your fingers to help turn the crêpe over. Cook until the bottom has light brown flecks, about 30 seconds. Slide the crêpe onto a plate, cover with foil, and keep warm while making the remaining crêpes.

sweet vanilla crêpe batter

Vanilla extract and a touch of sugar add extra flavor and special interest to sweet crêpes. These crêpes are perfect to use with dessert fillings, such as ice cream or fruit drizzled with chocolate or caramel sauce.

MAKES 10 TO 12 CRÊPES

1 cup Gluten-Free All-Purpose Flour (see p. 11)

2 teaspoons granulated sugar

½ teaspoon table salt

⅛ teaspoon baking powder

⅛ teaspoon xanthan gum

2 large eggs

1 cup whole milk

2 tablespoons unsalted butter, melted, or vegetable oil

½ teaspoon pure vanilla extract

Unsalted butter or nonstick cooking spray, for the pan

1. In a small bowl, whisk together the flour, sugar, salt, baking powder, and xanthan gum until well combined.

2. **TO MIX THE BATTER IN A BLENDER:** Place the eggs in the blender jar. Add the flour mixture, milk, butter, and vanilla. Cover the jar and blend on medium speed until the batter is smooth, about 30 seconds. Scrape down the sides of the jar and blend for another 10 to 15 seconds. Cover and chill for at least 1 hour before making the crêpes.

TO MIX THE BATTER WITH AN ELECTRIC MIXER: In a large bowl, using an electric mixer fitted with the wire whip beater attachment, lightly beat the eggs on medium speed. Gradually beat in the flour mixture, alternating with the milk, in three portions each, beating well after each addition. Gradually beat in the melted butter. Stir in the vanilla extract. Scrape down the sides of the bowl and beat until the batter is very smooth, about 30 seconds. Cover and chill for at least 1 hour before making the crêpes.

TO MIX THE BATTER BY HAND: In a medium bowl, using a wire whisk, lightly beat the eggs. Gradually beat in the flour mixture, alternating with the milk, in three portions each, beating well after each addition. Gradually beat in the melted butter. Stir in the vanilla extract. Whisk vigorously until the batter is very smooth. Cover and chill for at least 1 hour before making the crêpes.

3. Heat an 8-inch nonstick frying pan or crêpe pan over medium. Lightly whisk the crêpe batter until smooth. Grease the pan with butter or nonstick spray. Lift the pan off the heat and pour in 3 tablespoons of batter. Immediately tilt and swirl the pan to evenly coat the bottom with a thin layer of batter. Keep swirling the pan just until the batter is set. Return the pan to the heat and cook until the edges are dry and the underside is pale with light brown flecks, 1 to 1½ minutes. Using a spatula or knife, gently loosen the edges, then use a spatula or your fingers to turn the crêpe over. Cook until the bottom has light brown flecks, about 30 seconds. Slide the crêpe onto a plate, cover with foil, and keep warm while making the remaining crêpes.

orange crêpe batter

Fresh orange juice and orange zest give these crêpes a lovely flavor, making them a perfect complement to fresh fruit or sweet fillings.

MAKES 10 TO 12 CRÊPES

1 cup Gluten-Free All-Purpose Flour (see p. 11)

2 teaspoons granulated sugar

½ teaspoon table salt

⅛ teaspoon baking powder

⅛ teaspoon xanthan gum

2 large eggs

1 cup milk

2 tablespoons unsalted butter, melted, or vegetable oil

1 tablespoon freshly squeezed orange juice

2 teaspoons grated orange zest

Unsalted butter or nonstick cooking spray, for the pan

1. In a small bowl, whisk together the flour, sugar, salt, baking powder, and xanthan gum until well combined.

2. **TO MIX THE BATTER IN A BLENDER:** Place the eggs in the blender jar. Add the flour mixture, milk, butter, orange juice, and orange zest. Cover the jar and blend on medium speed until the batter is smooth, about 30 seconds. Scrape down the sides of the jar and blend for another 10 to 15 seconds. Cover and chill for at least 1 hour before making the crêpes.

TO MIX THE BATTER WITH AN ELECTRIC MIXER: In a large bowl, using an electric mixer fitted with the wire whip beater attachment, lightly beat the eggs on medium speed. Gradually beat in the flour mixture, alternating with the milk, in three portions each, beating well after each addition. Gradually beat in the melted butter, then stir in the orange juice and orange zest. Scrape down the sides of the bowl and beat until the batter is very smooth, about 30 seconds. Cover and chill for at least 1 hour before making the crêpes.

TO MIX THE BATTER BY HAND: In a medium bowl, using a wire whisk, lightly beat the eggs. Gradually beat in the flour mixture, alternating with the milk, in three portions each, beating well after each addition. Gradually beat in the melted butter, then stir in the orange juice and orange zest. Whisk vigorously until the batter is very smooth. Cover and chill for at least 1 hour before making the crêpes.

3. Heat an 8-inch nonstick frying pan or crêpe pan over medium. Lightly whisk the crêpe batter until smooth. Grease the pan with butter or nonstick spray. Lift the pan off the heat and pour in 3 table-spoons of batter. Immediately tilt and swirl the pan to evenly coat the bottom with a thin layer of batter. Keep swirling the pan just until the batter is set. Return the pan to the heat and cook until the edges are dry and the underside is pale with light brown flecks, 1 to 1½ minutes. Using a spatula or knife, gently loosen the edges, then use a spatula or your fingers to turn the crêpe over. Cook until the bottom has light brown flecks, about 30 seconds. Slide the crêpe onto a plate, cover with foil, and keep warm while making the remaining crêpes.

parmesan crêpe batter

These crêpes are wonderful stuffed with a variety of savory fillings. Watch the crêpes carefully as they cook because the cheese can cause them to brown more quickly than regular crêpes.

MAKES 10 TO 12 CRÊPES

1 cup Gluten-Free All-Purpose Flour (see p. 11)

½ teaspoon table salt

⅛ teaspoon baking powder

⅛ teaspoon xanthan gum

3 tablespoons freshly grated Parmesan cheese

2 large eggs

1¼ cups whole milk

2 tablespoons unsalted butter, melted, or vegetable oil

Unsalted butter or nonstick cooking spray, for the pan

1. In a small bowl, whisk together the flour, salt, baking powder, and xanthan gum until well combined. Stir in the cheese.

2. **TO MIX THE BATTER IN A BLENDER:** Place the eggs in the blender jar. Add the flour mixture, milk, and butter. Cover the jar and blend on medium speed until the batter is smooth, about 30 seconds. Scrape down the sides of the jar and blend for another 10 to 15 seconds. Cover and chill for at least 1 hour before making the crêpes.

TO MIX THE BATTER WITH AN ELECTRIC MIXER: In a large bowl, using an electric mixer fitted with the wire whip beater attachment, lightly beat the eggs on medium speed. Gradually beat in the flour mixture, alternating with the milk, in three portions each, beating well after each addition. Gradually beat in the melted butter. Scrape down the sides of the bowl and beat until the batter is very smooth, about 30 seconds. Cover and chill for at least 1 hour before making the crêpes.

TO MIX THE BATTER BY HAND: In a medium bowl, using a wire whisk, lightly beat the eggs. Gradually beat in the flour mixture, alternating with the milk, in three portions each, beating well after each addition. Gradually beat in the melted butter. Whisk vigorously until the batter is very smooth. Cover and chill for at least 1 hour before making the crêpes.

3. Heat an 8-inch nonstick frying pan or crêpe pan over medium. Lightly whisk the crêpe batter until smooth. Grease the pan with butter or nonstick spray. Lift the pan off the heat and pour in 3 tablespoons of batter. Immediately tilt and swirl the pan to evenly coat the bottom with a thin layer of batter. Keep swirling the pan just until the batter is set. Return the pan to the heat and cook until the edges are dry and the underside is pale with light brown flecks, 1 to 1½ minutes. Using a spatula or knife, gently loosen the edges, then use a spatula or your fingers to turn the crêpe over. Cook until the bottom has light brown flecks, about 30 seconds. Slide the crêpe onto a plate, cover with foil, and keep warm while making the remaining crêpes.

spinach mushroom crêpes

You can use your favorite variety of mushrooms in this recipe. These crêpes are also delicious made with 1 cup of feta cheese in the filling in place of the Monterey Jack and sprinkled with just the Parmesan over the top.

SERVES 4

8 warm Crêpes (see p. 80) or Parmesan Crêpes (see p. 83)

Nonstick cooking spray, for the pan

2 tablespoons unsalted butter

1 pound mushrooms, sliced

2 tablespoons finely chopped shallots or onions

1 tablespoon minced garlic

4 cups stemmed and chopped fresh spinach leaves

Pinch of table salt

Pinch of ground black pepper

1½ cups grated Monterey Jack cheese

½ cup freshly grated Parmesan cheese

1. Prepare the crêpes and keep warm.

2. Heat the oven to 350°F. Grease a 13 x 9 x 2-inch baking pan with nonstick cooking spray. Set aside.

3. In a large frying pan over medium heat, melt the butter. Stir in the mushrooms, shallots, and garlic and sauté, stirring frequently, until tender, 3 to 5 minutes. Add the spinach and stir to combine. Cover the pan and cook just until the spinach is wilted, about 1 minute. Uncover and stir in the salt and pepper. Remove the pan from the heat.

4. Evenly divide the spinach mixture between the warm crêpes, spooning the mixture down the center of each. Sprinkle 1 cup of Monterey Jack over the top of the filling in the crêpes. Roll up the crêpes and arrange in a single layer in the prepared pan, seam side down. Sprinkle the remaining Monterey Jack and Parmesan evenly over the top of the crêpes. Cover the pan with foil.

5. Bake until the crêpes are hot and the cheeses are melted, 15 to 20 minutes. Serve hot.

egg and cheese crêpes

These crêpes, which are filled with scrambled eggs and cheese, are a substantial entrée to serve for breakfast or dinner.

SERVES 4

For the Crêpes

8 warm Crêpes (see p. 80) or Parmesan
    Crêpes (see p. 83)

8 large eggs

⅓ cup whole milk

1½ teaspoons finely chopped fresh
    thyme leaves

¼ teaspoon table salt

⅛ teaspoon ground black pepper

1 tablespoon unsalted butter

1 cup grated Monterey Jack cheese

For the Topping (optional)

⅔ cup sour cream

1 large avocado, peeled, pitted, and sliced

½ cup halved cherry tomatoes

1. Prepare the crêpes and keep warm.

2. In a medium bowl, using a wire whisk, beat the eggs until foamy. Gradually whisk in the milk until well blended. Stir in the thyme, salt, and pepper.

3. In a large frying pan, over medium heat, melt the butter. Add the egg mixture and stir gently, scraping the bottom of the pan, until the eggs are almost cooked through. Sprinkle the cheese over the eggs. Gently stir and cook just until the eggs are done.

4. Evenly divide the egg mixture between the warm crêpes, spooning the mixture down the center of each. Roll up the crêpes and place 2 on each serving plate, seam side down. Top with a spoonful of sour cream and garnish with avocado slices and cherry tomato halves, if desired.

cinnamon apple crêpes

Sweet, spicy, and tender sautéed apples wrapped in a light vanilla-flavored crêpe. Need I say anything more? For dessert, top the crêpes with vanilla ice cream or whipped cream.

SERVES 4

For the Crêpes

8 warm Sweet Vanilla Crêpes (see p. 81)
   or Crêpes (see p. 80)

3 tablespoons unsalted butter

5 medium cooking apples, peeled, cored,
and thinly sliced

¼ cup firmly packed brown sugar

1 teaspoon ground cinnamon

¼ teaspoon grated nutmeg

For the Topping

1 teaspoon granulated sugar

¼ teaspoon ground cinnamon

Vanilla ice cream or whipped cream
   (optional)

1. Prepare the crêpes and keep warm.

2. In a large frying pan, over medium heat, melt the butter. Add the apples and sauté, stirring frequently, for 10 minutes. Add the brown sugar and stir until it's completely dissolved. Stir in the cinnamon and nutmeg. Sauté, stirring frequently, until the apples are tender, about 5 to 7 minutes.

3. Combine the granulated sugar and ground cinnamon.

4. Evenly divide the apple mixture between the warm crêpes, spooning the mixture down the center of each. Fold the edges of the crêpes to the middle, overlapping them in the center. Place 2 crêpes on each plate and sprinkle with cinnamon-sugar. Serve with ice cream or whipped cream, if desired.

～∘⌒◉⌒∘～

I like to use Granny Smith apples for these crêpes, but any variety that holds its shape when cooked will work well. Other recommended types include Gala, Fuji, and Jonagold.

mixed berry crêpes

I like to make these easy and delicious crêpes when fresh berries are in season. The sugar and orange juice give the berries a touch of sweetness and combine with the berry juices to create a bit of a citrus sauce. Use the orange crêpe batter to amp up the citrus flavor.

SERVES 4

8 Crêpes (see p. 80), Sweet Vanilla Crêpes (see p. 81), or Orange Crêpes (see p. 82)

¾ cup sliced fresh strawberries

¾ cup fresh raspberries

¾ cup fresh blackberries or boysenberries

¾ cup fresh blueberries

⅓ cup freshly squeezed orange juice

¼ cup granulated sugar

Vanilla ice cream or whipped cream (optional)

1. Prepare the crêpes.

2. In a large bowl, combine all the berries, the orange juice, and sugar and toss gently until the berries are coated.

3. Evenly divide the berry mixture between the crêpes, spooning the mixture down the center of each. Fold the edges of the crêpes to the middle, overlapping them in the center. Place 2 crêpes on each plate and spoon the remaining fruit juices over the top. Serve with ice cream or whipped cream, if desired.

⚬⚬⚬

Use any combination of fresh berries you like or that are available in your area.

blueberry cheese crêpes

With a lightly spiced blueberry sauce over tender crêpes filled with a slightly sweet cheese filling, these make a perfect dish to serve for brunch or a luscious dessert for family and company meals. Add a spoonful of ice cream on top to take the dessert over the edge.

SERVES 4

8 Crêpes (see p. 80), Sweet Vanilla
    Crêpes (see p. 81), or Orange Crêpes
    (see p. 82)
¼ cup granulated sugar
1 teaspoon cornstarch
¼ teaspoon ground cinnamon
¼ cup water
2 cups fresh blueberries
1 cup ricotta cheese
1 cup sour cream
⅓ cup confectioners' sugar
¼ teaspoon pure vanilla extract

1. Prepare the crêpes.

2. In a medium saucepan, combine the sugar, cornstarch, and cinnamon until well blended. Whisk in the water until smooth. Over medium heat, cook and stir until the sugar is completely dissolved. Add the blueberries. Bring to a gentle boil and cook, stirring constantly, until the sauce thickens. Remove the pan from the heat and set aside.

3. In a medium bowl, combine the ricotta cheese, sour cream, confectioners' sugar, and vanilla until smooth.

4. Evenly divide the cheese mixture between the crêpes, spooning the mixture down the center of each. Roll up the crêpes and place 2 on each plate, seam side down. Spoon the blueberry topping over the filled crêpes.

If fresh blueberries are not available, you can substitute frozen blueberries in this recipe. Do not defrost the berries. Simply measure out 2 cups and add them to the pan for the topping.

jam crêpes

Use your favorite flavor of jam, preserves, or marmalade to make these sweet crêpes. Don't use jellies, which are smooth; the fruit in preserves or marmalades will add texture and a burst of flavor when you bite into it.

SERVES 4

8 Crêpes (see p. 80) or Sweet Vanilla Crêpes (see p. 81)

1 cup seedless jam, preserves, or marmalade

1½ tablespoons confectioners' sugar

1. Prepare the crêpes.

2. Spread each crêpe with 2 tablespoons of jam. Fold the crêpes in half, and then in half again to form triangles. Lightly dust the top with confectioners' sugar.

To dust the crêpes with a fine layer of lump-free confectioners' sugar, place the sugar in a small sieve and gently press it through the mesh with the back of a small spoon as you move the sieve over the crêpes.

CHAPTER FIVE

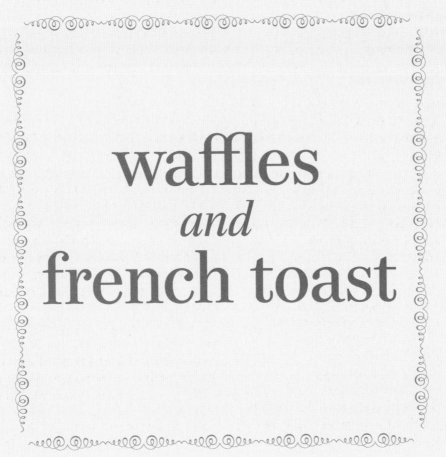

waffles
and
french toast

Waffles and French toast are family favorites and are great served for breakfast or dinner, but that's where the similarities end—at least in the recipes in this chapter. Waffles bake up with a light fluffy texture; they can contain sweet or savory ingredients or be served as a base for a variety of toppings, including fresh fruit and fruit sauces, eggs, creamed chicken, or sautéed fresh vegetables (or the classic—butter and maple syrup). The French toast recipes I've developed are more casserole-like, making them convenient for serving a crowd or family on a busy morning or for a stress-free dinner. These also are assembled in advance and then refrigerated for at least 8 hours, so they're a great make-ahead dish.

Making Waffles

The honeycombed surface of waffles adds its own texture as well as pockets for whatever topping is being used. The right mouth-feel of the cooked waffle mainly comes down to the batter being just right. Waffle batter is similar to a pancake batter with a couple of differences. Waffle batters contain more butter. This added fat gives waffles their rich flavor and helps them brown while baking. Also, to give waffles their light, fluffy texture, most recipes call for separating the eggs. The egg yolks are combined with the liquid ingredients and mixed into the dry ingredients, while the egg whites are beaten until stiff and then gently folded into the batter at the end of the mixing process. The air incorporated into the beaten egg whites helps waffles bake up with a delicate interior texture.

WAFFLE IRONS

Modern waffle irons have nonstick surfaces and come in a variety of shapes and sizes. Many have adjustable temperature settings that allow you to cook waffles to different doneness levels. I strongly recommend purchasing an iron that has an adjustable temperature setting.

The waffle recipes in this chapter will work with any nonstick waffle iron; however, you may need to adjust the amount of batter as well as the temperature setting to achieve the best results. It may take some experimentation with your specific waffle iron.

Waffle irons can vary, so be sure to follow the manufacturer's care, preparation, baking, and cleaning instructions. And follow the manufacturer's instructions to season your waffle iron before the first use to prevent sticking.

MIXING THE BATTER

The eggs and milk or buttermilk should be brought to room temperature before making the waffle batter. Eggs are easier to separate when they are

cold, but egg whites will beat up to a higher volume when at room temperature. This will make lighter waffles. If the milk is too cold when it is combined with the egg yolk and melted butter mixture, the butter will resolidify.

When combining ingredients in waffle batters, you want to use a gentle touch. Overmixing the batter will result in dense waffles. After adding the liquid ingredients, stir the batter just until the ingredients are combined with a few small lumps remaining. Add part of the beaten egg whites to the batter and gently fold them in. This will lighten the weight of the batter and keep it from deflating the remaining beaten egg whites. Add the rest of the egg whites and carefully fold them in. The finished batter should be light and airy.

BAKING WAFFLES

Set the waffle iron to the desired temperature and heat it until the light indicates the iron is ready for use. Using a heat-resistant brush, grease the waffle iron with vegetable oil, following the manufacturer's recommendation.

Pour the batter into the center of the waffle iron and carefully spread it out to the edges with a nonmetal heatproof spatula. If the batter is too thick, gently fold in a little more milk or buttermilk before baking the next waffle. Be careful not to deflate the batter.

The amount of batter needed to fill a waffle iron will vary depending on the size, shape, and type of iron being used. Small waffle irons may need only ½ cup of batter per waffle, while large irons or Belgian waffle irons may take 1 cup or more of batter to fill. Follow the manufacturer's recommendation for the amount of batter to use, making any adjustments needed to achieve the results you want.

Shut the lid tightly and close the latch on the waffle iron. Bake until the steam stops and the light indicates the waffle is done. Slowly open the lid; the waffle should be lightly browned and crisp on the outside and, when fully cooked, easily release from the iron. If the lid does not open easily, close the lid and bake for another 1 to 2 minutes. Remove the waffle from the iron and keep hot in a 200°F oven until ready to serve.

CLEANING AND STORING THE WAFFLE IRON

After all the waffles are baked, unplug the waffle iron and allow it to cool completely. Before putting the waffle iron away, remove any crumbs and wipe down the inside with a dry paper towel. Do not clean the iron with soap or submerge it in water. This can cause the plates to rust or leave a soapy residue on the nonstick surface. It will also remove any seasoning and require the iron to be seasoned again before use.

Making Oven-Baked French Toast

French toast casseroles, as oven-baked French toast is known, are easy to make, but there are a few things to keep in mind to ensure they come out perfectly. Once the French toast is assembled, it needs to be refrigerated for at least 8 hours or overnight to allow the bread to soak up the egg mixture. Remove the French toast from the refrigerator, place it on a wire rack to provide air circulation all around the dish, and let it come up to room temperature before baking. Unless your kitchen temperature is cold, the French toast will be warm enough to bake after about 30 minutes.

French toast is best made with day-old bread, meaning the bread has started to dry out. This enables the bread to absorb more of the egg custard and give the baked French toast its fluffy,

creamy, soufflé-like texture. Fresh bread or moist bread will produce a soggy French toast. If the gluten-free bread you are using is fresh baked or on the moist side, set the slices out on a wire rack for an hour or two to let it dry out a bit before assembling the casserole. Store-bought packaged bread is generally considered day-old bread.

While typically made with a white French type of bread, a variety of standard or specialty gluten-free breads can be used. Feel free to experiment with your favorite gluten-free breads—multigrain, raisin, cinnamon, or even challah bread will add extra interest to your French toast.

Thick slices of bread—about 1 inch is ideal—make the best oven-baked French toast. This size will absorb the egg mixture to produce a custardy texture. If you can't find thick gluten-free bread, you can stack two thin slices on top of each other.

Gluten-free bread loaves can vary significantly in size, so you may need to use a slice or two more than indicated in the recipe. You want to arrange the bread in the pan so that the slices fit snugly with the edges touching but not so tight that the bread is compacted, which will prevent the egg mixture from being absorbed evenly.

French toast stratas are made with cubed bread instead of slices. The bread is cut into ½-inch to 1-inch cubes, spread in the bottom of the pan, and then covered with the egg custard. Gently press the bread cubes down into the egg custard to ensure that each piece is moistened. Like French toast casseroles, French toast stratas are very versatile and can be flavored with a variety of ingredients.

SERVING THE FRENCH TOAST

Some French toast recipes have a topping and are designed to be turned out of the pan like an upside-down cake. If you don't have a heatproof serving platter large enough to hold the inverted French toast, you can serve individual portions directly from the pan. Cut the French toast into serving pieces, then use a wide spatula to remove the servings from the pan, and flip each portion over onto a serving plate so that the glazed side is facing up. Be careful flipping the pieces as the topping will be hot.

Quick Tips
WAFFLES AND OVEN FRENCH TOAST

WAFFLES

- Follow the manufacturer's instructions included with your waffle iron for seasoning, heating, and cleaning your waffle iron.

- Gently fold in the beaten egg whites to keep them from deflating.

- If the batter is too thick, gently fold in a little more milk or buttermilk.

- Melted butter in the batter gives waffles a rich flavor and helps the waffles brown. Vegetable oil may be substituted for the melted butter if you need to make dairy-free waffles.

- Heat the waffle iron before adding the batter.

- Spoon the batter into the center of the waffle iron and carefully spread it to the edges with a nonmetal heatproof spatula.

- The first waffle is usually considered a test waffle to determine if the waffle iron is hot enough. The next waffle will be better.

- Bake until the steam stops and the light on the waffle iron says "ready."

- When the waffle is done, the top plate of the waffle iron should lift easily and the waffle should be lightly browned.

- Create cool waffle shapes by only partially filling the waffle iron with batter.

- Cut large waffles into smaller pieces and use as a base for savory toppings to make appetizers.

- Allow the waffle iron to cool completely before cleaning and storing.

- The number of waffles a recipe makes will vary depending on the size and depth of your waffle iron.

FRENCH TOAST

- Use thick-sliced bread or double-stack thin slices of bread for a casserole. For French toast strata, cut bread into $1/2$- to 1-inch cubes.

- For a custardy texture, refrigerate the French toast overnight.

- Remove the French toast from the refrigerator 30 minutes before baking to allow it to come to room temperature.

- If the French toast starts to brown too much while baking, loosely cover it with a piece of foil.

- Serve entrée portions of French toast with fresh fruit or as an accompaniment for eggs or meat. For a special dessert treat, top French toast with ice cream or whipped cream.

easy waffles

Quick to mix together, this batter makes tender waffles that are perfect for busy mornings or fast dinners.

MAKES 5 TO 6 LARGE WAFFLES

1¾ cups Gluten-Free All-Purpose Flour (see p. 11)

1 tablespoon granulated sugar

1 tablespoon baking powder

½ teaspoon table salt

¼ teaspoon xanthan gum

2 large eggs

½ cup (1 stick) unsalted butter, melted, or vegetable oil

2 cups whole milk

1 teaspoon pure vanilla extract

Maple syrup, for serving (optional)

1. Heat a waffle iron according to the manufacturer's instructions.

2. In a large bowl, using a wire whisk, combine the flour, sugar, baking powder, salt, and xanthan gum until well blended. Make a well in the center and set aside.

3. In a medium bowl, using a wire whisk, beat the eggs until frothy. Gradually whisk in the melted butter until evenly combined. Whisk in the milk until well blended. Stir in the vanilla extract. Pour the liquid mixture into the well in the flour mixture all at once. Stir just until combined and the flour mixture is moistened. There may be a few small lumps; do not overmix.

4. Grease the heated waffle iron according to the manufacturer's instructions. Spoon ¾ cup to 1 cup of batter, or the amount recommended by the manufacturer, into the waffle iron. Use a heatproof spatula to spread the batter all the way to the edges. Close the lid and bake until the indicator light signals the waffle is done or until the waffle is golden brown. Repeat with the remaining batter. Serve hot with your favorite syrup or topping, if desired.

buttermilk waffles

Buttermilk gives these waffles a wonderful flavor and a light, fluffy texture. The crispy golden pockets are perfect for holding melted butter and maple syrup, or your favorite syrup flavor.

MAKES 5 TO 6 LARGE WAFFLES

1½ cups Gluten-Free All-Purpose Flour (see p. 11)

2 tablespoons granulated sugar

2 teaspoons baking powder

½ teaspoon baking soda

½ teaspoon table salt

¼ teaspoon xanthan gum

3 large eggs, separated

½ cup (1 stick) unsalted butter, melted, or vegetable oil

1⅔ cups buttermilk

1 teaspoon pure vanilla extract

Maple syrup, for serving (optional)

1. Heat a waffle iron according to the manufacturer's instructions.

2. In a large bowl, using a wire whisk, combine the flour, sugar, baking powder, baking soda, salt, and xanthan gum until well blended. Make a well in the center and set aside.

3. In a medium bowl, using a wire whisk, lightly beat the egg yolks. Gradually whisk in the melted butter until evenly combined. Whisk in the buttermilk until well blended. Stir in the vanilla extract. Set aside.

4. In a large bowl, using an electric mixer fitted with the whisk attachment or by hand using a wire balloon whisk, beat the egg whites just until stiff and the peaks hold their shape when the beater or whisk is lifted from the bowl.

5. Pour the liquid mixture into the well in the flour mixture all at once. Stir just until combined and the flour mixture is moistened. There may be a few small lumps; do not overmix. Add about 1 cup of the beaten egg whites to the batter and fold in to lighten the batter. Add the remaining egg whites and gently fold in just until blended.

6. Grease the heated waffle iron according to the manufacturer's instructions. Spoon ¾ cup to 1 cup of batter, or the amount recommended by the manufacturer, into the waffle iron. Use a heatproof spatula to spread the batter all the way to the edges. Bake until the indicator light signals the waffle is done or until the waffle is golden brown. Repeat with the remaining batter. Serve hot with your favorite syrup or topping.

VARIATIONS

buttermilk spice waffles: **Add 1 teaspoon ground cinnamon, ¼ teaspoon grated nutmeg, and ¼ teaspoon ground ginger into the flour mixture.**

nut waffles: **Stir 1 cup chopped walnuts or pecans into the batter before folding in the egg whites.**

sour cream waffles

Thanks to the sour cream in the batter, these waffles have a mild tangy flavor, making them perfect as a base for savory entrées, such as grilled chicken or beef stew. You can also cut them into small pieces and add a sweet or savory topping to serve for party appetizers.

MAKES 5 TO 6 LARGE WAFFLES

1½ cups Gluten-Free All-Purpose Flour (see p. 11)

3 tablespoons granulated sugar

2 teaspoons baking powder

1 teaspoon baking soda

½ teaspoon table salt

¼ teaspoon xanthan gum

3 large eggs, separated

½ cup (1 stick) unsalted butter, melted, or vegetable oil

1½ cups regular sour cream

¾ cup whole milk

2 teaspoons pure vanilla extract

Maple syrup, for serving (optional)

1. Heat a waffle iron according to the manufacturer's instructions.

2. In a large bowl, using a wire whisk, combine the flour, sugar, baking powder, baking soda, salt, and xanthan gum until well blended. Make a well in the center and set aside.

3. In a medium bowl, using a wire whisk, lightly beat the egg yolks. Gradually whisk in the melted butter until evenly combined. Whisk in the sour cream until well blended, then stir in the milk and vanilla extract. Set aside.

4. In a large bowl, using an electric mixer fitted with the whisk attachment or by hand using a wire balloon whisk, beat the egg whites just until stiff and the peaks hold their shape when the beater or whisk is lifted from the bowl.

5. Pour the liquid mixture into the well in the flour mixture all at once. Stir just until combined and the flour mixture is moistened. There may be a few small lumps; do not overmix. Add about 1 cup of the beaten egg whites to the batter and fold in to lighten the batter. Add the remaining egg whites and gently fold in just until blended.

6. Grease the heated waffle iron according to the manufacturer's instructions. Spoon ¾ cup to 1 cup of batter, or the amount recommended by the manufacturer, into the waffle iron. Use a heatproof spatula to spread the batter all the way to the edges. Bake until the indicator light signals the waffle is done or until the waffle is golden brown. Repeat with the remaining batter. Serve hot with your favorite syrup or topping.

VARIATION

sour cream maple walnut waffles: **Reduce the vanilla extract to ½ teaspoon and add 1½ teaspoons maple flavoring to the liquid ingredients. Add 1 cup chopped walnuts to the batter before folding in the egg whites.**

coconut waffles

You can almost imagine yourself in the Caribbean when you taste these waffles. For an extra punch of tropical flavor, stir ¾ cup drained crushed pineapple into the batter before folding in the egg whites. You can also serve these topped with diced tropical fruits, like mangoes, papayas, and more pineapple.

MAKES 5 TO 6 LARGE WAFFLES

1 cup Gluten-Free All-Purpose Flour (see p. 11)

⅓ cup coconut flour

1 tablespoon baking powder

½ teaspoon table salt

¼ teaspoon xanthan gum

3 large eggs, separated

½ cup (1 stick) unsalted butter, melted, or vegetable oil

1½ cups whole milk

½ teaspoon pure vanilla extract

½ teaspoon coconut extract

Maple syrup, for serving (optional)

1. Heat a waffle iron according to the manufacturer's instructions.

2. In a large bowl, using a wire whisk, combine the flours, baking powder, salt, and xanthan gum until well blended. Make a well in the center and set aside.

3. In a medium bowl, using a wire whisk, lightly beat the egg yolks. Gradually whisk in the melted butter until evenly combined. Whisk in the milk until well blended. Stir in the vanilla and coconut extracts. Set aside.

4. In a large bowl, using an electric mixer fitted with the whisk attachment or by hand using a wire balloon whisk, beat the egg whites just until stiff and the peaks hold their shape when the beater or whisk is lifted from the bowl.

5. Pour the liquid mixture into the well in the flour mixture all at once. Stir just until combined and the flour mixture is moistened. There may be a few small lumps; do not overmix. Add about 1 cup of the beaten egg whites to the batter and fold in to lighten the batter. Add the remaining egg whites and gently fold in just until blended.

6. Grease the heated waffle iron according to the manufacturer's instructions. Spoon ¾ cup to 1 cup of batter, or the amount recommended by the manufacturer, into the waffle iron. Use a heatproof spatula to spread the batter all the way to the edges. Bake until the indicator light signals the waffle is done or until the waffle is golden brown. Repeat with the remaining batter. Serve hot with your favorite syrup or topping.

blueberry waffles

Juicy blueberries and a touch of cinnamon baked into a fluffy waffle start the day off right. Top these waffles with more fresh blueberries, a mixture of fresh berries, or blueberry syrup. You can also add a little cornstarch, granulated sugar, and lemon zest to undrained, thawed frozen blueberries and cook for a few minutes to make a blueberry topping.

MAKES 5 TO 6 LARGE WAFFLES

1½ cups Gluten-Free All-Purpose Flour (see p. 11)

2 tablespoons granulated sugar

2 teaspoons baking powder

1 teaspoon ground cinnamon

½ teaspoon baking soda

½ teaspoon table salt

¼ teaspoon xanthan gum

3 large eggs, separated

½ cup (1 stick) unsalted butter, melted, or vegetable oil

1⅔ cups buttermilk

1 teaspoon pure vanilla extract

1 cup fresh small blueberries

Maple syrup, for serving (optional)

1. Heat a waffle iron according to the manufacturer's instructions.

2. In a large bowl, using a wire whisk, combine the flour, sugar, baking powder, cinnamon, baking soda, salt, and xanthan gum until well blended. Make a well in the center and set aside.

3. In a medium bowl, using a wire whisk, lightly beat the egg yolks. Gradually whisk in the melted butter until evenly combined. Whisk in the buttermilk until well blended. Stir in the vanilla extract. Set aside.

4. In a large bowl, using an electric mixer fitted with the whisk attachment or by hand using a wire balloon whisk, beat the egg whites just until stiff and the peaks hold their shape when the beater or whisk is lifted from the bowl.

5. Pour the liquid mixture into the well in the flour mixture all at once. Stir just until combined and the flour mixture is moistened. There may be a few small lumps; do not overmix. Stir in the blueberries. Add about 1 cup of the beaten egg whites to the batter and fold in to lighten the batter. Add the remaining egg whites and gently fold in just until blended.

6. Grease the heated waffle iron according to the manufacturer's instructions. Spoon ¾ cup to 1 cup of batter, or the amount recommended by the manufacturer, into the waffle iron. Use a heatproof spatula to spread the batter all the way to the edges. Bake until the indicator light signals the waffle is done or until the waffle is golden brown. Repeat with the remaining batter. Serve hot with your favorite syrup or topping.

orange waffles

Add a delightful citrus note to your morning or evening meal with these tender orange-scented waffles. Serve with a dollop of plain or vanilla yogurt, with orange or lemon zest on top, if desired. Or, top the waffles with whipped cream and drizzle with chocolate syrup for a tempting dessert.

MAKES 5 TO 6 LARGE WAFFLES

1⅔ cups Gluten-Free All-Purpose Flour (see p. 11)

3 tablespoons granulated sugar

2 teaspoons baking powder

1 teaspoon baking soda

½ teaspoon table salt

¼ teaspoon xanthan gum

3 large eggs, separated

½ cup (1 stick) unsalted butter, melted, or vegetable oil

1⅓ cups regular sour cream

¾ cup whole milk

¼ cup freshly squeezed orange juice

2 tablespoons orange zest

Maple syrup, for serving (optional)

1. Heat a waffle iron according to the manufacturer's instructions.

2. In a large bowl, using a wire whisk, combine the flour, sugar, baking powder, baking soda, salt, and xanthan gum until well blended. Make a well in the center and set aside.

3. In a medium bowl, using a wire whisk, lightly beat the egg yolks. Gradually whisk in the melted butter until evenly combined. Whisk in the sour cream until well blended, then stir in the milk, orange juice, and orange zest. Set aside.

4. In a large bowl, using an electric mixer fitted with the whisk attachment or by hand using a wire balloon whisk, beat the egg whites just until stiff and the peaks hold their shape when the beater or whisk is lifted from the bowl.

5. Pour the liquid mixture into the well in the flour mixture all at once. Stir just until combined and the flour mixture is moistened. There may be a few small lumps; do not overmix. Add about 1 cup of the beaten egg whites to the batter and fold in to lighten the batter. Add the remaining egg whites and gently fold in just until blended.

6. Grease the heated waffle iron according to the manufacturer's instructions. Spoon ¾ cup to 1 cup of batter, or the amount recommended by the manufacturer, into the waffle iron. Use a heatproof spatula to spread the batter all the way to the edges. Bake until the indicator light signals the waffle is done or until the waffle is golden brown. Repeat with the remaining batter. Serve hot with your favorite syrup or topping.

VARIATION

lemon waffles: Increase the granulated sugar to ¼ cup. Use 3 tablespoons freshly squeezed lemon juice and 2 tablespoons lemon zest in place of the orange juice and orange zest.

chocolate waffles

Chocolate and sour cream make a great flavor combination for waffles. You can top these with fresh berries to serve for breakfast. Or top with whipped cream and strawberries for brunch, or ice cream and chocolate sauce or caramel sauce for dessert. Make fun shapes for special occasions or smaller waffles for the kids by partially filling the waffle iron with batter.

MAKES 5 TO 6 LARGE WAFFLES

1½ cups Gluten-Free All-Purpose Flour (see p. 11)

¼ cup cocoa powder

⅓ cup granulated sugar

2 teaspoons baking powder

1 teaspoon baking soda

½ teaspoon table salt

¼ teaspoon xanthan gum

1 cup finely chopped semisweet chocolate or mini chocolate chips

3 large eggs, separated

½ cup (1 stick) unsalted butter, melted, or vegetable oil

1½ cups regular sour cream

1⅓ cups whole milk

2 teaspoons pure vanilla extract

Maple syrup, for serving (optional)

1. Heat a waffle iron according to the manufacturer's instructions.

2. In a large bowl, using a wire whisk, combine the flour, cocoa powder, sugar, baking powder, baking soda, salt, and xanthan gum until well blended. Stir in the chocolate. Make a well in the center and set aside.

3. In a medium bowl, using a wire whisk, lightly beat the egg yolks. Gradually whisk in the melted butter until evenly combined. Whisk in the sour cream until well blended, then stir in the milk and vanilla extract. Set aside.

4. In a large bowl, using an electric mixer fitted with the whisk attachment or by hand using a wire balloon whisk, beat the egg whites just until stiff and the peaks hold their shape when the beater or whisk is lifted from the bowl.

5. Pour the liquid mixture into the well in the flour mixture all at once. Stir just until combined and the flour mixture is moistened. There may be a few small lumps; do not overmix. Add about 1 cup of the beaten egg whites to the batter and fold in to lighten the batter. Add the remaining egg whites and gently fold in just until blended.

6. Grease the heated waffle iron according to the manufacturer's instructions. Spoon ¾ cup to 1 cup of batter, or the amount recommended by the manufacturer, into the waffle iron. Use a heatproof spatula to spread the batter all the way to the edges. Bake until the indicator light signals the waffle is done or until the waffle is golden brown. Repeat with the remaining batter. Serve hot with your favorite syrup or topping.

chocolate chip waffles

Kids of all ages will flip for these waffles. Be sure to serve them hot, so that the chocolate chips are just melting and gooey. For those with a sweet tooth, sprinkle additional chocolate chips on top before serving. If serving these for someone special, top with chocolate curls instead of chocolate chips.

MAKES 5 TO 6 LARGE WAFFLES

1½ cups Gluten-Free All-Purpose Flour (see p. 11)

2 tablespoons granulated sugar

2 teaspoons baking powder

½ teaspoon baking soda

½ teaspoon table salt

¼ teaspoon xanthan gum

3 large eggs, separated

⅔ cup (1 stick plus 2⅔ tablespoons) unsalted butter, melted, or vegetable oil

1½ cups buttermilk

2 teaspoons pure vanilla extract

1 cup mini chocolate chips or finely chopped semisweet chocolate

Maple syrup, for serving (optional)

Mixed diced fresh fruit, for serving (optional)

1. Heat a waffle iron according to the manufacturer's instructions.

2. In a large bowl, using a wire whisk, combine the flour, sugar, baking powder, baking soda, salt, and xanthan gum until well blended. Make a well in the center and set aside.

3. In a medium bowl, using a wire whisk, lightly beat the egg yolks. Gradually whisk in the melted butter until evenly combined. Whisk in the buttermilk until well blended, then stir in the vanilla extract. Set aside.

4. In a large bowl, using an electric mixer fitted with the whisk attachment or by hand using a wire balloon whisk, beat the egg whites just until stiff and the peaks hold their shape when the beater or whisk is lifted from the bowl.

5. Pour the liquid mixture into the well in the flour mixture all at once. Stir just until combined and the flour mixture is moistened. There may be a few small lumps; do not overmix. Stir in the mini chocolate chips. Add about 1 cup of the beaten egg whites to the batter and fold in to lighten the batter. Add the remaining egg whites and gently fold in just until blended.

6. Grease the heated waffle iron according to the manufacturer's instructions. Spoon ¾ cup to 1 cup of batter, or the amount recommended by the manufacturer, into the waffle iron. Use a heatproof spatula to spread the batter all the way to the edges. Bake until the indicator light signals the waffle is done or until the waffle is golden brown. Repeat with the remaining batter. Serve hot with your favorite syrup or fruit topping or with ice cream or whipped cream and additional chocolate chips.

carrot waffles

If you like carrot bread or carrot cake, then you'll love these warmly spiced carrot waffles. You can increase or decrease the amount of spices to suit your family's taste. Make some of these waffles in the morning, then save them in a zip-top bag, cut them into large pieces, and give to the kids for an after-school snack.

I like the ribbons of carrot from shredding on the large holes of a box grater, but you can use smaller holes or finely dice the grated carrots for less texture in the finished waffles.

MAKES 5 TO 6 LARGE WAFFLES

1½ cups Gluten-Free All-Purpose Flour (see p. 11)

½ cup granulated sugar

1½ tablespoons baking powder

1 teaspoon ground cinnamon

½ teaspoon grated nutmeg

½ teaspoon table salt

¼ teaspoon xanthan gum

4 large eggs, separated

½ cup (1 stick) unsalted butter, melted, or vegetable oil

1½ cups whole milk

½ teaspoon pure vanilla extract

1 cup grated carrots

Maple syrup, for serving (optional)

VARIATIONS

carrot pineapple waffles:
Stir ⅔ cup drained crushed pineapple into the batter along with the carrots.

carrot raisin waffles:
Stir ⅔ cup chopped golden or dark raisins into the batter along with the carrots.

1. Heat a waffle iron according to the manufacturer's instructions.

2. In a large bowl, using a wire whisk, combine the flour, sugar, baking powder, cinnamon, nutmeg, salt, and xanthan gum until well blended. Make a well in the center and set aside.

3. In a medium bowl, using a wire whisk, lightly beat the egg yolks. Gradually whisk in the melted butter until evenly combined. Whisk in the milk until well blended. Stir in the vanilla extract. Set aside.

4. In a large bowl, using an electric mixer fitted with the whisk attachment or by hand using a wire balloon whisk, beat the egg whites just until stiff and the peaks hold their shape when the beater or whisk is lifted from the bowl.

5. Pour the liquid mixture into the well in the flour mixture all at once. Stir just until combined and the flour mixture is moistened. There may be a few small lumps; do not overmix. Stir in the carrots. Add about 1 cup of the beaten egg whites to the batter and fold in to lighten the batter. Add the remaining egg whites and gently fold in just until blended.

6. Grease the heated waffle iron according to the manufacturer's instructions. Spoon ¾ cup to 1 cup of batter, or the amount recommended by the manufacturer, into the waffle iron. Use a heatproof spatula to spread the batter all the way to the edges. Bake until the indicator light signals the waffle is done or until the waffle is golden brown. Repeat with the remaining batter. Serve hot with your favorite syrup.

cheddar waffles

I love Cheddar waffles for dinner. While you can serve them unadorned, they also make a wonderful base for a variety of toppings. Try Cheddar waffles with fresh steamed vegetables topped with cheese sauce, meats in a cream sauce, or a meat or vegetable stew.

The intensity of Cheddar flavor will be based on the cheese you use. Choose an aged block and freshly grate the cheese. Don't use pregrated cheese for these waffles, as the flavor of the cooked waffles will suffer.

MAKES 5 TO 6 LARGE WAFFLES

1⅔ cups Gluten-Free All-Purpose Flour (see p. 11)

1 tablespoon baking powder

½ teaspoon table salt

¼ teaspoon xanthan gum

3 large eggs, separated

½ cup (1 stick) unsalted butter, melted, or vegetable oil

1½ cups whole milk

⅔ cup finely grated Cheddar cheese

VARIATIONS

apple cheddar waffles:
Add ⅔ cup finely chopped peeled apples to the batter before folding in the egg whites. Or sauté diced peeled apples and serve on top.

broccoli cheddar waffles:
Make a Cheddar cheese sauce by melting 1½ tablespoons butter, stirring in 1½ tablespoons gluten-free flour, and adding salt and pepper to taste. Gradually add ¾ cup milk, stirring constantly until thick and smooth, then add ½ cup grated Cheddar and stir until smooth. Sauté 1½ cups broccoli florets, add to the cheese sauce, and serve over the top of the waffles.

1. Heat a waffle iron according to the manufacturer's instructions.

2. In a large bowl, using a wire whisk, combine the flour, baking powder, salt, and xanthan gum until well blended. Make a well in the center and set aside.

3. In a medium bowl, using a wire whisk, lightly beat the egg yolks. Gradually whisk in the melted butter until evenly combined. Whisk in the milk until well blended. Set aside.

4. In a large bowl, using an electric mixer fitted with the whisk attachment or by hand using a wire balloon whisk, beat the egg whites just until stiff and the peaks hold their shape when the beater or whisk is lifted from the bowl.

5. Pour the liquid mixture into the well in the flour mixture all at once. Stir just until combined and the flour mixture is moistened. There may be a few small lumps; do not overmix. Gently stir in the cheese. Add about 1 cup of the beaten egg whites to the batter and fold in to lighten the batter. Add the remaining egg whites and gently fold in just until blended.

6. Grease the heated waffle iron according to the manufacturer's instructions. Spoon ¾ cup to 1 cup of batter, or the amount recommended by the manufacturer, into the waffle iron. Use a heatproof spatula to spread the batter all the way to the edges. Bake until the indicator light signals the waffle is done or until the waffle is golden brown. Repeat with the remaining batter.

cornmeal waffles

These delicious waffles taste like corn muffins. Serve them with maple syrup for a sweet treat or top with salsa for a savory sensation. For dinner, top with shredded chicken, grated cheese, and salsa to make savory tostada waffles.

MAKES 5 TO 6 LARGE WAFFLES

1 cup Gluten-Free All-Purpose Flour
   (see p. 11)

1 cup yellow cornmeal

3 tablespoons granulated sugar

2 teaspoons baking powder

1 teaspoon baking soda

½ teaspoon table salt

¼ teaspoon xanthan gum

3 large eggs, separated

½ cup (1 stick) unsalted butter, melted,
   or vegetable oil

1¾ cups buttermilk

Maple syrup, for serving (optional)

Mixed diced fresh fruit, for serving
   (optional)

1. Heat a waffle iron according to the manufacturer's instructions.

2. In a large bowl, using a wire whisk, combine the flour, cornmeal, sugar, baking powder, baking soda, salt, and xanthan gum until well blended. Make a well in the center and set aside.

3. In a medium bowl, using a wire whisk, lightly beat the egg yolks. Gradually whisk in the melted butter until evenly combined. Whisk in the buttermilk until well blended. Set aside.

4. In a large bowl, using an electric mixer fitted with the whisk attachment or by hand using a wire balloon whisk, beat the egg whites just until stiff and the peaks hold their shape when the beater or whisk is lifted from the bowl.

5. Pour the liquid mixture into the well in the flour mixture all at once. Stir just until combined and the flour mixture is moistened. There may be a few small lumps; do not overmix. Add about 1 cup of the beaten egg whites to the batter and fold in to lighten the batter. Add the remaining egg whites and gently fold in just until blended.

6. Grease the heated waffle iron according to the manufacturer's instructions. Spoon ¾ cup to 1 cup of batter, or the amount recommended by the manufacturer, into the waffle iron. Use a heatproof spatula to spread the batter all the way to the edges. Bake until the indicator light signals the waffle is done or until the waffle is golden brown. Repeat with the remaining batter. Serve hot with your favorite syrup or topping.

VARIATION

mexican corn waffles: **Add ¾ cup fresh or thawed frozen corn kernels, 1 to 2 teaspoons finely chopped seeded jalapeño peppers, and 2 teaspoons minced cilantro to the batter before folding in the beaten egg whites.**

spinach waffles

Enjoy these savory waffles by themselves or top with hard-cooked eggs and a cream or cheese sauce for a satisfying supper. These are also delicious with a slice of ham and soft-cooked egg on top.

MAKES 5 TO 6 LARGE WAFFLES

1½ cups Gluten-Free All-Purpose Flour (see p. 11)

1 tablespoon baking powder

½ teaspoon table salt

¼ teaspoon xanthan gum

⅓ cup finely grated Parmesan cheese

4 large eggs, separated

½ cup (1 stick) unsalted butter, melted, or vegetable oil

1½ cups whole milk

¾ cup chopped fresh spinach leaves (½ bunch)

1. Heat a waffle iron according to the manufacturer's instructions.

2. In a large bowl, using a wire whisk, combine the flour, baking powder, salt, and xanthan gum until well blended. Stir in the Parmesan. Make a well in the center and set aside.

3. In a medium bowl, using a wire whisk, lightly beat the egg yolks. Gradually whisk in the melted butter until evenly combined. Whisk in the milk until well blended. Set aside.

4. In a large bowl, using an electric mixer fitted with the whisk attachment or by hand using a wire balloon whisk, beat the egg whites just until stiff and the peaks hold their shape when the beater or whisk is lifted from the bowl.

5. Pour the liquid mixture into the well in the flour mixture all at once. Stir just until combined and the flour mixture is moistened. There may be a few small lumps; do not overmix. Gently stir in the spinach. Add about 1 cup of the beaten egg whites to the batter and fold in to lighten the batter. Add the remaining egg whites and gently fold in just until blended.

6. Grease the heated waffle iron according to the manufacturer's instructions. Spoon ¾ cup to 1 cup of batter, or the amount recommended by the manufacturer, into the waffle iron. Use a heatproof spatula to spread the batter all the way to the edges. Bake until the indicator light signals the waffle is done or until the waffle is golden brown. Repeat with the remaining batter.

multigrain waffles

You can make these waffles extra special by adding nuts, spices, or even fruit to the batter. If you add fruit, be sure it's fresh (not canned) and cut into ½-inch dice. I like adding these waffles to a cheese and fruit plate.

MAKES 5 TO 6 LARGE WAFFLES

¾ cup Gluten-Free All-Purpose Flour (see p. 11)

⅓ cup buckwheat flour

⅓ cup sorghum flour

2 tablespoons coconut flour

1 tablespoon granulated sugar

2½ teaspoons baking powder

½ teaspoon baking soda

½ teaspoon table salt

¼ teaspoon xanthan gum

3 large eggs, separated

⅔ cup (1 stick plus 2⅔ tablespoons) unsalted butter, melted, or vegetable oil

1⅔ cups buttermilk

1 teaspoon pure vanilla extract

Maple syrup, for serving (optional)

Mixed diced fresh fruit, for serving (optional)

1. Heat a waffle iron according to the manufacturer's instructions.

2. In a large bowl, using a wire whisk, combine all of the flours, the sugar, baking powder, baking soda, salt, and xanthan gum until well blended. Make a well in the center and set aside.

3. In a medium bowl, using a wire whisk, lightly beat the egg yolks. Gradually whisk in the melted butter until evenly combined. Whisk in the buttermilk until well blended, then stir in the vanilla extract. Set aside.

4. In a large bowl, using an electric mixer fitted with the whisk attachment or by hand using a wire balloon whisk, beat the egg whites just until stiff and the peaks hold their shape when the beater or whisk is lifted from the bowl.

5. Pour the liquid mixture into the well in the flour mixture all at once. Stir just until combined and the flour mixture is moistened. There may be a few small lumps; do not overmix. Add about 1 cup of the beaten egg whites to the batter and fold in to lighten the batter. Add the remaining egg whites and gently fold in just until blended.

6. Grease the heated waffle iron according to the manufacturer's instructions. Spoon ¾ cup to 1 cup of batter, or the amount recommended by the manufacturer, into the waffle iron. Use a heatproof spatula to spread the batter all the way to the edges. Bake until the indicator light signals the waffle is done or until the waffle is golden brown. Repeat with the remaining batter. Serve hot with your favorite syrup or topping.

french toast strata

Scented with vanilla and almond extracts, this French toast is a comforting dish served hot from the oven and drizzled with pure maple syrup. This basic French toast would also be good with blueberry, boysenberry, or strawberry syrup.

SERVES 6 TO 8

Nonstick cooking spray, for the pan
8 cups cubed day-old gluten-free bread
8 large eggs
3 tablespoons granulated sugar
2 cups whole milk
2 teaspoons pure vanilla extract
½ teaspoon pure almond extract
Syrup, for serving (optional)

1. Grease a 13 x 9 x 2-inch baking pan with nonstick cooking spray.

2. Spread the bread cubes evenly in the bottom of the prepared pan. Set aside.

3. In a large bowl, using a wire whisk, beat the eggs until foamy. Add the sugar and beat until evenly combined. Gradually whisk in the milk until well blended, then stir in the vanilla and almond extracts. Pour the custard evenly over top of the bread mixture. Gently press the bread cubes into the custard. Cover the pan with plastic wrap and refrigerate overnight.

4. Remove the pan from the refrigerator and let stand at room temperature for 30 minutes. Meanwhile, position a rack in the middle of the oven and heat the oven to 350°F.

5. Bake the strata, uncovered, until the top is puffed and golden brown and a wooden pick inserted in the center comes out with a few moist crumbs, 35 to 45 minutes. If the top starts to brown too quickly, cover loosely with a piece of foil. Remove the pan from the oven and place on a wire rack. Let cool for 5 minutes before serving hot with your favorite syrup.

VARIATION

Toss 1½ cups chopped dried fruit—apricots, cherries, blueberries, dates, or a combination—with the bread cubes before spreading in the pan.

cranberry french toast strata

Cranberries and pecans baked into a fluffy French toast casserole will brighten any day. The dried cranberries will absorb some of the orange-flavored liquid during soaking, giving them an added flavor dimension. Use chopped fresh or frozen cranberries in place of the dried cranberries, if you prefer. Leftovers make a great afternoon snack.

SERVES 6 TO 8

Nonstick cooking spray, for the pan

8 cups cubed day-old gluten-free bread

1²⁄₃ cups dried cranberries

1 cup chopped pecans

8 large eggs

3 tablespoons granulated sugar

1½ cups whole milk

²⁄₃ cup freshly squeezed orange juice

1½ tablespoons finely grated orange zest

1 teaspoon pure vanilla extract

Maple syrup, for serving (optional)

1. Grease a 13 x 9 x 2-inch baking pan with nonstick cooking spray. Set aside.

2. In a large bowl, combine the bread, dried cranberries, and pecans and toss until evenly blended. Spread evenly in the bottom of the prepared pan.

3. In a large bowl, using a wire whisk, beat the eggs until foamy. Add the sugar and beat until well combined. Gradually whisk in the milk until well blended, then stir in the orange juice, orange zest, and vanilla extract. Pour the custard evenly over the top of the bread mixture. Gently press the bread cubes into the custard. Cover the pan with plastic wrap and refrigerate overnight.

4. Remove the pan from the refrigerator and let stand at room temperature for 30 minutes. Meanwhile, position a rack in the middle of the oven and heat the oven to 350°F.

5. Bake the strata, uncovered, until the top is puffed and golden brown and a wooden pick inserted in the center comes out with a few moist crumbs, 35 to 45 minutes. If the top starts to brown too quickly, cover loosely with a piece of foil. Remove the pan from the oven and place on a wire rack. Let cool for 5 minutes before serving while hot.

blueberry french toast strata

Make this strata next time you're having overnight guests and are thinking about making blueberry pancakes for breakfast. The best part—you'll assemble the dish the night before and simply bake it in the morning. Serve with warm maple syrup and additional fresh blueberries.

SERVES 6 TO 8

Nonstick cooking spray, for the pan

5 cups cubed day-old gluten-free bread

2 cups fresh blueberries

One 8-ounce package cream cheese, at room temperature

3 tablespoons granulated sugar

1 teaspoon ground cinnamon

5 large eggs

1¼ cups whole milk

2 teaspoons pure vanilla extract

Maple syrup, for serving (optional)

1. Grease a 13 x 9 x 2-inch baking pan with nonstick cooking spray. Set aside.

2. In a large bowl, combine the bread and blueberries and toss gently until evenly blended; try not to break up the blueberries. Spread evenly in the bottom of the prepared pan.

3. In a large bowl, using an electric mixer, beat the cream cheese until smooth. Add the sugar and cinnamon and beat until well combined. Add the eggs, one at a time, beating well after each addition. Gradually stir in the milk until well blended, then stir in the vanilla extract. Pour the custard evenly over the top of the bread mixture. Gently press the bread cubes into the custard. Cover the pan with plastic wrap and refrigerate overnight.

4. Remove the pan from the refrigerator and let stand at room temperature for 30 minutes. Meanwhile, position the rack in the middle of the oven and heat the oven to 350°F.

5. Bake the strata, uncovered, until the top is puffed and golden brown and a wooden pick inserted in the center comes out with a few moist crumbs, 35 to 45 minutes. If the top starts to brown too quickly, cover loosely with a piece of foil. Remove the pan from the oven and place on a wire rack. Let cool for 5 minutes before serving while hot.

walnut raisin french toast strata

You can use dark raisins or golden raisins in this dish. Or try some of each for a pretty presentation. Chopped pecans or almonds can be substituted if you're not a walnut fan.

SERVES 6 TO 8

Nonstick cooking spray, for the pan
8 cups cubed day-old gluten-free bread
1½ cups chopped walnuts
1 cup raisins
8 large eggs
3 tablespoons granulated sugar
2 teaspoons ground cinnamon
½ teaspoon grated nutmeg
2 cups whole milk
1 teaspoon pure vanilla extract
Maple syrup, for serving (optional)
Mixed diced fresh fruit, for serving (optional)

1. Grease a 13 x 9 x 2-inch baking pan with nonstick cooking spray. Set aside.

2. In a large bowl, combine the bread, walnuts, and raisins and toss until well blended. Spread evenly in the bottom of the prepared pan.

3. In a large bowl, using a wire whisk, beat the eggs until foamy. Add the sugar, cinnamon, and nutmeg and beat until well combined. Gradually whisk in the milk until well blended, then stir in the vanilla extract. Pour the custard evenly over the top of the bread mixture. Gently press the bread cubes into the custard. Cover the pan with plastic wrap and refrigerate overnight.

4. Remove the pan from the refrigerator and let stand at room temperature for 30 minutes. Meanwhile, position a rack in the middle of the oven and heat the oven to 350°F.

5. Bake the strata, uncovered, until the top is puffed and golden brown and a wooden pick inserted in the center comes out with a few moist crumbs, 35 to 45 minutes. If the top starts to brown too quickly, cover loosely with a piece of foil. Remove the pan from the oven and place on a wire rack. Let cool for 5 minutes before serving while hot with your favorite topping, if desired.

pecan oven french toast

Crunchy pecans and a brown sugar caramel topping make this French toast an everyday or special occasion treat. You can use walnuts, almonds, macadamias, or your favorite nut in place of the pecans.

SERVES 6 TO 8

Nonstick cooking spray, for the pan

6 tablespoons (¾ stick) unsalted butter, cut into pieces

1 cup firmly packed dark brown sugar

2 tablespoons light corn syrup

½ teaspoon pure almond extract

1¼ cups chopped pecans

Eight to ten 1-inch-thick slices day-old gluten-free bread

4 large eggs

1¾ cups whole milk

1 teaspoon pure vanilla extract

Maple syrup, for serving (optional)

Mixed diced fresh fruit, for serving (optional)

1. Grease a 13 x 9 x 2-inch baking pan with nonstick cooking spray. Set aside.

2. In a small saucepan, over low heat, melt the butter. Add the brown sugar and corn syrup and heat, stirring constantly, until the mixture is smooth. Remove the pan from the heat and stir in the almond extract. Immediately pour the hot sugar mixture into the prepared baking pan and spread evenly. Sprinkle the pecans evenly over the top of the sugar mixture.

3. Arrange the bread slices in a single layer on top of the pecans. Set aside.

4. In a large bowl, using a wire whisk, beat the eggs until foamy. Gradually whisk in the milk until well blended, then stir in the vanilla extract. Pour the custard evenly over the top of the bread slices, making sure each slice is well saturated. Cover the pan with plastic wrap and refrigerate overnight.

5. Remove the pan from the refrigerator and let stand at room temperature for 30 minutes. Meanwhile, position a rack in the middle of the oven and heat the oven to 375°F.

6. Bake the French toast casserole, uncovered, until the top is puffed and golden brown, 35 to 40 minutes. Remove the pan from the oven and immediately invert it onto a large heatproof serving platter or rimmed baking sheet. Carefully remove the pan. Be cautious when inverting and handling the pan as the topping will be very hot. Let sit for 5 minutes for the caramel to set. Serve hot with your favorite topping, if desired.

cinnamon oven french toast

Pop this fragrant French toast in the oven on a crisp fall morning and let the aroma of cinnamon warm the kitchen. For even more flavor, use thick slices of the Cinnamon Swirl Bread on p. 148 or Raisin Bread on p. 151. This French toast is delicious served with orange slices warmed in a frying pan with a bit of butter and a dash of ground cinnamon.

SERVES 6 TO 8

Nonstick cooking spray, for the pan

Eight to ten 1-inch-thick slices day-old gluten-free bread

4 large eggs

¼ cup granulated sugar

1 tablespoon ground cinnamon

1¾ cups whole milk

1 teaspoon pure vanilla extract

Maple syrup, for serving (optional)

1. Grease a 13 x 9 x 2-inch baking pan with nonstick cooking spray. Arrange the bread slices in a single layer in the pan. Set aside.

2. In a large bowl, using a wire whisk, beat the eggs until foamy. Add the sugar and cinnamon and beat until well combined. Gradually whisk in the milk until well blended, then stir in the vanilla extract. Pour the custard evenly over the top of the bread slices, making sure each slice is well saturated. Cover the pan with plastic wrap and refrigerate overnight.

3. Remove the pan from the refrigerator and let stand at room temperature for 30 minutes. Meanwhile, position a rack in the middle of the oven and heat the oven to 375°F.

4. Bake the French toast, uncovered, until the top is puffed and golden brown, 35 to 40 minutes. Remove the pan from the oven and place on a wire rack. Let cool for 5 minutes before serving with syrup, if desired.

orange oven french toast

Bright fresh orange flavor makes this French toast a winner with citrus lovers. I like the flavor of almonds with orange, but you could also use walnuts, pecans, macadamias, or even unsalted cashews.

SERVES 6 TO 8

Nonstick cooking spray, for the pan

6 tablespoons (¾ stick) unsalted butter, cut into pieces

1 cup firmly packed dark brown sugar

2 tablespoons light corn syrup

2 teaspoons grated orange zest

⅔ cup sliced almonds

Eight to ten 1-inch-thick slices day-old gluten-free bread

4 large eggs

3 tablespoons granulated sugar

1 cup freshly squeezed orange juice

¾ cup whole milk

3 tablespoons grated orange zest

1 teaspoon pure vanilla extract

Maple syrup, for serving (optional)

1. Grease a 13 x 9 x 2-inch baking pan with nonstick cooking spray. Set aside.

2. In a small saucepan, over low heat, melt the butter. Add the brown sugar and corn syrup and heat, stirring constantly, until the mixture is smooth. Remove the pan from the heat and stir in the 2 teaspoons of the orange zest. Immediately pour the hot sugar mixture into the prepared baking pan and spread evenly. Sprinkle the almonds evenly over the top of the sugar mixture.

3. Arrange the bread slices in a single layer on top of the almonds. Set aside.

4. In a large bowl, using a wire whisk, beat the eggs until foamy. Add the granulated sugar and beat until well combined. Gradually whisk in the orange juice and milk until well blended. Stir in the remaining 3 tablespoons orange zest and the vanilla extract. Pour the custard evenly over the top of the bread slices, making sure each slice is well saturated. Cover the pan with plastic wrap and refrigerate overnight.

5. Remove the pan from the refrigerator and let stand at room temperature for 30 minutes. Meanwhile, position the rack in the middle of the oven. Heat the oven to 375°F.

6. Bake the French toast casserole, uncovered, until the top is puffed and golden brown, 35 to 40 minutes. Remove the pan from the oven and immediately invert it onto a large heatproof serving platter or rimmed baking sheet. Carefully remove the pan. Be cautious when inverting and handling the pan as the topping will be very hot. Let sit for 5 minutes for the caramel to set. Serve hot with your favorite syrup.

CHAPTER SIX

coffee cakes

Whether served as a family treat or for a special occasion, a tantalizing coffee cake on the breakfast table is always a welcome sight. A simple type of cake made from a quick batter leavened with baking powder and baking soda, coffee cakes are quick to prepare and easy to serve. These wonderful cakes can be served for breakfast, for brunch, as a snack with coffee, and even as a delightful dessert. You can serve them unadorned or dress them up with a simple icing.

The batter for gluten-free coffee cakes will be thicker than those made with wheat flour because the starches in the gluten-free flour blend will absorb the liquid faster during mixing. A thick gluten-free batter will rise much higher than thinner batter from wheat flour because the structure of the batter will be stronger and better able to support the coffee cake as it bakes. This is especially important if the cake has a filling or contains heavy ingredients, such as fruit, nuts, or chocolate.

As with other gluten-free baked goods, gluten-free coffee cakes taste best and have a moister texture when eaten the same day they are baked.

Equipment

BAKING PANS

Many gluten-free coffee cakes, especially crumb cakes, can be baked in square pans. Sturdy, shiny, single-walled metal baking pans, preferably made of aluminum, are my favorite choice. Shiny metal pans reflect heat, which slows down the browning process and allows coffee cakes to bake all the way through without overbrowning on the outside. Metal pans with a dark or dull finish absorb more heat than shiny pans. If you only have a dark metal pan, reduce the oven temperature by 25°F to help keep the edges of the coffee cake from becoming too dark. You may also need to extend the baking time a bit to bake the coffee cake all the way through in the center.

For the best results, always use the size and shape of pan that is indicated in the recipe. Changing the pan size can produce different results. The recipes in this book prepared in square pans use a standard 9-inch baking pan.

SPRINGFORM PANS

A springform pan is a two-piece round baking pan with a removable bottom. A spring latch on the side of the pan allows the outer pan ring to expand and tighten. When tightened, the sides hold the bottom of the pan in place. When the latch is loosened, the sides can be easily removed from the baked cake. This is the type of pan used to make cheesecakes. As with other baking pans, springform pans made from shiny metal produce more even baking and browning than dark pans.

The bottom of the springform pan has an indentation that is designed to hold the crumb

crust of cheesecake. This indentation makes it difficult to get cakes and other baked goods out of the pan in one piece. However, with most springform pans, you can turn the bottom piece upside down and bake on the flat surface. This makes it much easier to remove cakes from the pan and is the way I use my springform pans for baking cakes of all kinds. A round cake pan with high sides and a removable bottom may be used in place of a springform pan.

TUBE PANS

A tube pan, also known as an angel food cake pan, is a deep, smooth-sided baking pan with a hollow tube in the middle. The hollow tube allows heat to reach the center of the cake, baking a large cake from the middle as well as from the outside. The tube also prevents the outside of the cake from drying out before the inside is cooked through. Tube pans are great for baking tall cakes to ensure that the cake will rise and bake evenly, avoiding the problem of a dense cake that is overdone on the outside while still underbaked and gooey on the inside. These pans are especially helpful when baking cakes that contain a large amount of batter, those with heavier batters, and cakes containing a filling.

Usually constructed of aluminum, tube pans can be made as a single-piece pan or as a two-piece pan with a removable bottom, which makes it much easier to remove the cake from the pan after baking. I use a two-piece tube pan that used to be my mother's and that I have been baking with since I was a child. I always think of my mom when I use that pan and it brings back happy memories.

BUNDT PANS

A Bundt pan is a decorative one-piece tube pan with a fixed center tube. Typically made of cast aluminum, these pans are usually 10 inches in diameter and up to 5 inches deep. Bundt pans have fluted or ridged designs that give the finished cake an impressive appearance. Bundt pans are not just for looks though. The center tube also helps coffee cakes bake faster and more evenly by providing more surface area to cook the batter. It allows heavier cake batters to rise up and bake uniformly without leaving a soggy center.

Be sure to grease a Bundt pan well to prevent the cake from sticking and to make it easy to unmold after baking.

Mixing Coffee Cake Batters

Most coffee cake batters are made using the creaming method. Creaming is a very important technique in making any type of cake and is especially helpful in lightening the texture of gluten-free coffee cakes.

As the butter and sugar are beaten together, the sugar crystals cut into the butter and create air bubbles. These air bubbles become trapped and the butter and sugar mixture expands. This process takes about 3 minutes of constant beating. When the butter and sugar are properly creamed, the mixture is referred to as being light and fluffy. Light means that the butter has turned pale in color and is lighter in texture. Fluffy means that the butter and sugar mixture contains lots of trapped air and has increased in volume.

To get a nicely creamed mixture, butter should be softened, but not too warm. Butter is considered softened at 65°F. Butter warms up as it is beaten, so starting with it at this temperature prevents it from getting too warm and soft during mixing. If the butter is too warm during creaming, it won't hold as many trapped air bubbles and the cake will be denser and heavier.

Once the butter-sugar mixture is light and fluffy, eggs are incorporated gradually to retain the light texture that has been created. The eggs should be at room temperature. If the eggs are too cold when you add them to the butter and sugar, the mixture may "break," meaning it will appear curdled. Adding the eggs one at a time and beating well between each addition will help keep the mixture

from breaking. Should the mixture break, scrape down the bowl and keep beating until the mixture comes back together before adding more eggs. If the mixture does not smooth out, beat in the eggs and then gradually start adding the flour mixture. The flour will help bind the ingredients into a smooth batter.

The flour mixture is added to the creamed mixture along with the milk, sour cream, or other liquid ingredients. To help create a smooth batter, the flour mixture and the liquid ingredients are alternately blended in, starting and ending with the flour. This is done in portions to gradually incorporate the ingredients into the batter and to prevent the weight of the flour from deflating the air bubbles trapped in the creamed mixture. If you were to dump everything in at once, the flour would quickly absorb the liquid and become a lumpy mess.

Baking Coffee Cakes

For even baking, position the oven rack one notch below the center of the oven before preheating the oven. This will help the cake rise and bake evenly. When baking a cake in a tube pan or Bundt pan, position the oven rack in the lower third of the oven.

If the top of a coffee cake starts browning too quickly, loosely cover the cake with a piece of foil partway through baking to prevent it from becoming too dark. A coffee cake is done when the top looks dry and a wooden pick or cake tester inserted in the center comes out clean without any wet batter or moist crumbs. The top will be golden brown and the cake will start to pull away slightly from the sides of the pan.

Quick Tips
COFFEE CAKES

- Kitchen temperatures can vary significantly, so don't let the butter get too warm as it softens.
- Butter that is too soft won't hold air well and will result in dense, heavy coffee cakes.
- Cut the butter into several pieces before combining with the sugar to get a fluffier creamed mixture.
- Thoroughly cream the butter and sugar until light and fluffy to incorporate lots of air into the batter. This will help the coffee cake rise up higher and have a lighter, more tender texture.
- Do not reduce the amount of sugar in a coffee cake batter. Sugar adds structure, tenderness, and moisture to gluten-free cakes.
- Do not reduce the number of eggs in a gluten-free coffee cake recipe. Eggs help bind all of the ingredients together and give the cake more support and structure during baking.
- Scrape down the sides of the bowl several times during the mixing process to make sure the ingredients are combined in the batter evenly.
- Grease pans well with unsalted butter or nonstick cooking spray to prevent coffee cakes from sticking to the pan.
- Make sure the oven is at the correct temperature before combining the liquid and dry ingredients. After mixing, coffee cake batters should go into a hot oven quickly to get the best rise.
- Remove the coffee cake from the pan soon after baking to keep the cake from becoming soggy.

apple walnut crumb cake

Entertaining overnight guests? Serve this impressive coffee cake for breakfast, brunch, or dessert. You can use Gala, Fuji, or your favorite variety of apple to make this cake. I don't recommend using Golden Delicious apples because they tend to fall apart during baking.

MAKES ONE 10-INCH COFFEE CAKE

Unsalted butter or nonstick cooking spray, for the pan

For the Streusel

1 cup firmly packed brown sugar

⅓ cup Gluten-Free All-Purpose Flour (see p. 11)

1 teaspoon ground cinnamon

1⅓ cups finely chopped, peeled, and cored apples

1 cup finely chopped walnuts

¼ cup (4 tablespoons) unsalted butter, melted

For the Cake

3 cups Gluten-Free All-Purpose Flour (see p. 11)

2½ teaspoons baking powder

¾ teaspoon baking soda

¾ teaspoon xanthan gum

½ teaspoon ground cinnamon

½ teaspoon table salt

1 cup (2 sticks) unsalted butter, softened

1 cup granulated sugar

4 large eggs

1 teaspoon pure vanilla extract

1 cup sour cream

Heat the oven to 350°F. Grease a 10-inch tube pan with unsalted butter or nonstick cooking spray.

MAKE THE STREUSEL

In a small bowl, whisk together the brown sugar, flour, and cinnamon until well blended. Stir in the apples and walnuts. Add the melted butter and, using a fork or your fingers, mix until evenly combined and the mixture starts to come together. Set aside.

MAKE THE CAKE

1. In a medium bowl, whisk together the flour, baking powder, baking soda, xanthan gum, cinnamon, and salt until well combined. Set aside.

2. In a large bowl, using an electric mixer on medium speed, cream the butter and granulated sugar until light and fluffy, about 3 minutes. Scrape down the sides of the bowl. Add the eggs, one at a time, beating well after each addition. Scrape down the sides of the bowl. Stir in the vanilla.

3. Alternately add the flour mixture and the sour cream to the butter-sugar mixture, starting and ending with the flour mixture, stirring between each addition until blended. Mix until smooth, about 30 seconds.

4. Spoon half of the batter into the prepared pan. Sprinkle two-thirds of the streusel mixture over the batter. Top with the remaining batter and spread smooth. Crumble the remaining streusel over the top of the batter.

5. Bake until golden brown and a wooden pick inserted in the center comes out clean, 50 to 60 minutes. Let the cake cool in the pan on a wire rack for 5 minutes. If necessary, gently run a knife blade between the cake and the edge of the pan to loosen. Remove the sides and center of the pan and transfer the coffee cake onto a wire rack. Serve the coffee cake warm or at room temperature.

cinnamon crumb cake

This crumb cake is reminiscent of an old-fashioned crumb cake with lots of cinnamon flavor.

MAKES ONE 9-INCH COFFEE CAKE

Unsalted butter or nonstick cooking spray, for the pan

For the Topping

⅔ cup Gluten-Free All-Purpose Flour (see p. 11)

⅔ cup granulated sugar

¾ teaspoon ground cinnamon

3½ tablespoons unsalted butter, cut into pieces

For the Filling

⅓ cup granulated sugar

2½ teaspoons ground cinnamon

For the Cake

2 cups Gluten-Free All-Purpose Flour (see p. 11)

2 teaspoons baking powder

½ teaspoon baking soda

½ teaspoon table salt

½ teaspoon xanthan gum

2 large eggs

¾ cup granulated sugar

⅔ cup vegetable oil

⅔ cup whole milk

1 teaspoon pure vanilla extract

Heat the oven to 350°F. Grease a 9-inch square baking pan with unsalted butter or nonstick cooking spray.

MAKE THE TOPPING

In a small bowl, whisk together the flour, sugar, and cinnamon until well blended. Using a fork or your fingers, work in the butter until evenly combined and the mixture starts to come together. Set aside.

MAKE THE FILLING

In a small bowl, whisk together the sugar and cinnamon until well blended. Set aside.

MAKE THE CAKE

1. In a large bowl, whisk together the flour, baking powder, baking soda, salt, and xanthan gum until well combined. Make a well in the center and set aside.

2. In a medium bowl, using a wire whisk, lightly beat the eggs. Add the sugar and whisk until smooth. Gradually whisk in the oil until well blended. Whisk in the milk and vanilla. Pour the liquid mixture into the well in the flour mixture and stir until well combined.

3. Spoon two-thirds of the batter evenly into the prepared pan. Sprinkle the filling mixture over the batter. Spoon the remaining batter over the filling and spread smooth with lightly greased fingers or the back of a greased spoon. Crumble the topping over the top of the batter.

4. Bake until golden brown and a wooden pick inserted in the center comes out clean, 40 to 50 minutes. Let the cake cool in the pan on a wire rack for 10 minutes. Invert the cake onto a plate or wire rack lined with waxed paper. Place a wire rack on the bottom of the cake and turn the cake right side up. Serve the coffee cake warm or at room temperature.

almond coffee cake

Baked in a tube pan, this pretty coffee cake has lots of almond flavor. Top with a drizzle of vanilla icing and chopped almonds to make it special.

MAKES ONE 10-INCH COFFEE CAKE

Unsalted butter or nonstick cooking spray, for the pan

For the Streusel

½ cup granulated sugar

½ cup firmly packed brown sugar

⅓ cup Gluten-Free All-Purpose Flour (see p. 11)

1½ cups coarsely chopped sliced almonds

¼ cup (4 tablespoons) unsalted butter, melted

For the Cake

3 cups Gluten-Free All-Purpose Flour (see p. 11)

2½ teaspoons baking powder

¾ teaspoon baking soda

¾ teaspoon xanthan gum

½ teaspoon table salt

1 cup (2 sticks) unsalted butter, softened

1 cup granulated sugar

4 large eggs

1½ teaspoons almond extract

1 cup sour cream

For the Icing

1 cup confectioners' sugar

1 tablespoon half-and-half or light cream

1½ teaspoons unsalted butter, melted

¼ teaspoon almond extract

Heat the oven to 350°F. Grease a 10-inch tube pan with unsalted butter or nonstick cooking spray.

MAKE THE STREUSEL
In a small bowl, whisk together the granulated sugar, brown sugar, and flour until well blended. Stir in the almonds. Add the melted butter and, using a fork or your fingers, mix until evenly combined and the mixture starts to come together. Set aside.

MAKE THE CAKE
1. In a medium bowl, whisk together the flour, baking powder, baking soda, xanthan gum, and salt until well combined. Set aside.

2. In a large bowl, using an electric mixer on medium speed, cream the butter and granulated sugar until light and fluffy, about 3 minutes. Scrape down the sides of the bowl. Add the eggs, one at a time, beating well after each addition. Scrape down the sides of the bowl. Stir in the almond extract.

3. Alternately add the flour mixture and the sour cream to the butter-sugar mixture, starting and ending with the flour mixture, stirring between each addition until blended. Mix until smooth, about 30 seconds.

4. Spoon half of the batter into the prepared pan. Sprinkle two-thirds of the streusel mixture over the batter. Top with the remaining batter; spread smooth. Crumble the remaining streusel over the top of the batter.

5. Bake until golden brown and a wooden pick inserted in the center comes out clean, 50 to 60 minutes. Let the cake cool in the pan on a wire rack for 5 minutes. If necessary, gently run a knife blade between the cake and the edge of the pan to loosen. Remove the sides and center of the pan and transfer the coffee cake onto a wire rack to cool.

MAKE THE ICING
In a medium bowl, combine the confectioners' sugar, half-and-half, butter, and almond extract. Beat with a whisk until smooth and spreadable. Spread or drizzle the icing over the cake.

cherry coffee cake

With a layer of cherry filling hiding inside and almonds on top, this coffee cake makes an eye-catching presentation when sliced and served.

MAKES ONE 9-INCH COFFEE CAKE

Unsalted butter or nonstick cooking spray, for the pan

For the Filling
1 can (21 ounces) cherry pie filling
¼ teaspoon almond extract

For the Cake
1½ cups Gluten-Free All-Purpose Flour (see p. 11)
1½ teaspoons baking powder
½ teaspoon baking soda
½ teaspoon table salt
¼ teaspoon xanthan gum
½ cup (1 stick) unsalted butter, softened
¾ cup granulated sugar
3 large eggs
1 teaspoon pure vanilla extract
½ teaspoon almond extract
½ cup sour cream
3 tablespoons sliced almonds

For the Icing
¾ cup confectioners' sugar
1 tablespoon half-and-half or light cream
¼ teaspoon almond extract

VARIATION

You can vary the filling by using apple, blueberry, or peach pie filling and omitting the almond extract in the filling mixture.

Heat the oven to 350°F. Grease a 9-inch springform pan or a deep 9-inch round cake pan with a removable bottom with unsalted butter or nonstick cooking spray.

MAKE THE FILLING
In a small bowl, combine the cherry pie filling and the almond extract until well blended. Set aside.

MAKE THE CAKE
1. In a medium bowl, whisk together the flour, baking powder, baking soda, salt, and xanthan gum until well combined. Set aside.

2. In a large bowl, using an electric mixer on medium speed, cream the butter and granulated sugar until light and fluffy, about 3 minutes. Scrape down the sides of the bowl. Add the eggs, one at a time, beating well after each addition. Scrape down the sides of the bowl. Stir in the vanilla and almond extracts.

3. Alternately add the flour mixture and the sour cream to the butter-sugar mixture, starting and ending with the flour mixture, stirring between each addition until blended.

4. Spoon half of the batter into the prepared pan. Spoon the cherry filling over the batter. Top with the remaining batter and spread smooth. Sprinkle the almonds over the top of the batter.

5. Bake until golden brown and a wooden pick inserted in the center comes out clean, 40 to 50 minutes. Let the cake cool in the pan on a wire rack for 5 minutes. If necessary, gently run a knife blade between the cake and the edge of the pan to loosen. Remove the sides of the pan and transfer the coffee cake onto a wire rack. Serve the coffee cake warm or at room temperature.

MAKE THE ICING
In a small bowl, combine the confectioners' sugar, half-and-half, and almond extract. Beat until smooth. Drizzle the icing over the cake.

peach coffee cake

This is a great coffee cake to make during the summer when local peaches are at their peak of ripeness. When fresh peaches are not available, you can use canned peaches instead.

MAKES ONE 9-INCH COFFEE CAKE

Unsalted butter or nonstick cooking spray, for the pan

For the Filling

2 tablespoons freshly squeezed orange juice

2 teaspoons granulated sugar

2 medium peaches, peeled, pitted, and cut into ½-inch slices

For the Topping

½ cup Gluten-Free All-Purpose Flour (see p. 11)

½ cup granulated sugar

3 tablespoons unsalted butter, cut into pieces

For the Cake

1¼ cups Gluten-Free All-Purpose Flour (see p. 11)

1½ teaspoons baking powder

¼ teaspoon baking soda

¼ teaspoon table salt

¼ teaspoon xanthan gum

½ cup (1 stick) unsalted butter, softened

¾ cup granulated sugar

2 large eggs

2 teaspoons grated orange zest

1 teaspoon pure vanilla extract

½ cup whole milk

Heat the oven to 350°F. Grease a 9-inch springform pan or a deep 9-inch round cake pan with a removable bottom with unsalted butter or nonstick cooking spray.

MAKE THE FILLING
In a medium bowl, combine the orange juice and sugar until well blended. Add the peach slices and toss to coat.

MAKE THE TOPPING
In a small bowl, whisk together the flour and sugar until well blended. Using a fork or your fingers, work in the butter until evenly combined and the mixture starts to come together. Set aside.

MAKE THE CAKE
1. In a medium bowl, whisk together the flour, baking powder, baking soda, salt, and xanthan gum until well combined. Set aside.

2. In a large bowl, using an electric mixer on medium speed, cream the butter and sugar until light and fluffy, about 3 minutes. Scrape down the sides of the bowl. Add the eggs, one at a time, beating well after each addition. Scrape down the sides of the bowl. Stir in the orange zest and vanilla.

3. Alternately add the flour mixture and the milk to the butter-sugar mixture, starting and ending with the flour mixture, stirring between each addition until blended. Spoon the batter into the prepared pan and spread evenly. Arrange the peach slices over the top of the batter. Crumble the topping over the peaches.

4. Bake until golden brown and a wooden pick inserted in the center comes out clean, 40 to 50 minutes. Let the cake cool in the pan on a wire rack for 5 minutes. If necessary, gently run a knife blade between the cake and the edge of the pan to loosen. Remove the sides of the pan and transfer the coffee cake onto a wire rack. Serve warm or at room temperature.

blueberry coffee cake

Small blueberries work best in this cake because they will spread evenly through the batter and give you berries in every bite. If you would like a little extra crunch, sprinkle some turbinado sugar over the top of the batter before popping the cake into the oven.

MAKES ONE 9-INCH COFFEE CAKE

Unsalted butter or nonstick cooking spray, for the pan

For the Topping

⅓ cup Gluten-Free All-Purpose Flour (see p. 11)

¼ cup granulated sugar

½ teaspoon ground cinnamon

1½ tablespoons unsalted butter, cut into pieces

For the Cake

1½ cups Gluten-Free All-Purpose Flour (see p. 11)

2 teaspoons baking powder

1 teaspoon ground cinnamon

½ teaspoon baking soda

½ teaspoon table salt

¼ teaspoon xanthan gum

⅔ cup (1 stick plus 2⅔ tablespoons) unsalted butter, softened

¾ cup granulated sugar

2 large eggs

1 teaspoon pure vanilla extract

¾ cup sour cream

1 cup fresh blueberries

Heat the oven to 350°F. Grease a 9-inch springform pan or a deep 9-inch round cake pan with a removable bottom with unsalted butter or nonstick cooking spray.

MAKE THE TOPPING

In a small bowl, whisk together the flour, sugar, and cinnamon until well blended. Using a fork or your fingers, work in the butter until evenly combined and the mixture starts to come together. Set aside.

MAKE THE CAKE

1. In a medium bowl, whisk together the flour, baking powder, cinnamon, baking soda, salt, and xanthan gum until well combined. Set aside.

2. In a large bowl, using an electric mixer on medium speed, cream the butter and sugar until light and fluffy, about 3 minutes. Scrape down the sides of the bowl. Add the eggs, one at a time, beating well after each addition. Scrape down the sides of the bowl. Stir in the vanilla.

3. Alternately add the flour mixture and the sour cream to the butter-sugar mixture, starting and ending with the flour mixture, stirring between each addition until blended. Gently fold in the blueberries. Spoon the batter into the prepared pan and spread evenly. Sprinkle the topping over the top of the batter.

4. Bake until golden brown and a wooden pick inserted in the center comes out clean, 45 to 55 minutes. Let the cake cool in the pan on a wire rack for 5 minutes. If necessary, gently run a knife blade between the cake and the edge of the pan to loosen. Remove the sides of the pan and transfer the coffee cake onto a wire rack. Serve the coffee cake warm or at room temperature.

chocolate chip crumb cake

Although this coffee cake is intended to be a sweet morning treat, it also makes a great snacking cake or dessert, particularly if you increase the amount of chopped chocolate to 1 cup. If you want even more chocolate, sprinkle extra chopped chocolate or mini chocolate chips over the top of the cake after it comes out of the oven.

MAKES ONE 9-INCH COFFEE CAKE

Unsalted butter or nonstick cooking spray, for the pan

For the Topping

½ cup Gluten-Free All-Purpose Flour (see p. 11)

¼ cup granulated sugar

¼ cup firmly packed brown sugar

3 tablespoons unsalted butter, cut into pieces

For the Cake

2 cups Gluten-Free All-Purpose Flour (see p. 11)

1½ teaspoons baking powder

½ teaspoon baking soda

½ teaspoon table salt

½ teaspoon xanthan gum

1 cup (2 sticks) unsalted butter, softened

½ cup granulated sugar

½ cup firmly packed brown sugar

2 large eggs

2 teaspoons pure vanilla extract

⅔ cup buttermilk

¾ cup finely chopped chocolate or mini chocolate chips

VARIATIONS

chocolate-cinnamon: If you like a touch of cinnamon with your chocolate, add ½ teaspoon ground cinnamon to the flour mixture.

Heat the oven to 350°F. Grease a 9-inch square baking pan with unsalted butter or nonstick cooking spray.

MAKE THE TOPPING

In a small bowl, whisk together the flour, granulated sugar, and brown sugar until well blended. Using a fork or your fingers, work in the butter until evenly combined and the mixture starts to come together. Set aside.

MAKE THE CAKE

1. In a medium bowl, whisk together the flour, baking powder, baking soda, salt, and xanthan gum until well combined. Set aside.

2. In a large bowl, using an electric mixer on medium speed, cream the butter, granulated sugar, and brown sugar until light and fluffy, about 3 minutes. Scrape down the sides of the bowl. Add the eggs, one at a time, beating well after each addition. Scrape down the sides of the bowl. Stir in the vanilla.

3. Alternately add the flour mixture and the buttermilk to the butter-sugar mixture, starting and ending with the flour mixture, stirring between each addition until blended. Gently fold in the chopped chocolate. Spoon the batter into the prepared pan and spread evenly. Crumble the topping over the top of the batter.

4. Bake until golden brown and a wooden pick inserted in the center comes out clean, 45 to 55 minutes. Let the cake cool in the pan on a wire rack for 10 minutes, then invert the cake onto a plate or wire rack lined with waxed paper. Place a wire rack on the bottom of the cake and turn the cake right side up. Serve the coffee cake warm or at room temperature.

maple walnut crumb cake

The classic flavor combination of maple and walnuts turns this coffee cake into something special. Using dark brown sugar will enrich the flavor of this cake. Maple flavoring gives this cake a strong maple taste without adding too much liquid. If you want to use maple syrup instead of maple flavoring, use ⅓ cup Grade B maple syrup and reduce the milk to 7 tablespoons.

MAKES ONE 9-INCH COFFEE CAKE

Unsalted butter or nonstick cooking spray, for the pan

For the Streusel

¾ cup firmly packed brown sugar

⅓ cup Gluten-Free All-Purpose Flour (see p. 11)

¾ cup finely chopped walnuts

¼ cup (4 tablespoons) unsalted butter, cut into pieces

For the Cake

2 cups Gluten-Free All-Purpose Flour (see p. 11)

1½ teaspoons baking powder

½ teaspoon baking soda

½ teaspoon table salt

½ teaspoon xanthan gum

1 cup (2 sticks) unsalted butter, softened

1 cup firmly packed dark brown sugar

2 large eggs

2½ teaspoons maple flavoring

½ teaspoon pure vanilla extract

⅔ cup whole milk

Heat the oven to 350°F. Grease a 9-inch square baking pan with unsalted butter or nonstick cooking spray.

MAKE THE STREUSEL

In a small bowl, whisk together the brown sugar and flour until well blended. Stir in the walnuts. Using a fork or your fingers, work in the butter until evenly combined and the mixture starts to come together. Set aside.

MAKE THE CAKE

1. In a medium bowl, whisk together the flour, baking powder, baking soda, salt, and xanthan gum until well combined. Set aside.

2. In a large bowl, using an electric mixer on medium speed, cream the butter and brown sugar until light and fluffy, about 3 minutes. Scrape down the sides of the bowl. Add the eggs, one at a time, beating well after each addition. Scrape down the sides of the bowl. Stir in the maple flavoring and vanilla extract.

3. Alternately add the flour mixture and milk to the butter-sugar mixture, starting and ending with the flour mixture, stirring between each addition until blended.

4. Spoon half of the batter into the prepared pan. Sprinkle half of the streusel mixture over the batter. Top with the remaining batter and spread smooth. Crumble the remaining streusel over the top of the batter.

5. Bake until golden brown and a wooden pick inserted in the center comes out clean, 40 to 50 minutes. Let the cake cool in the pan on a wire rack for 10 minutes. Invert the cake onto a plate or wire rack lined with waxed paper. Place a wire rack on the bottom of the cake and turn the cake right side up. Serve the coffee cake warm or at room temperature.

raspberry coconut coffee cake

One of my favorite flavor pairings is raspberry and coconut, which makes a terrific coffee cake. I like to chop the flaked coconut before measuring because it gives the cake a smoother texture. For even more coconut flavor, use coconut extract instead of vanilla extract in the icing. Try apricot or seedless blackberry jam in place of the raspberry.

MAKES ONE 9-INCH COFFEE CAKE

Unsalted butter or nonstick cooking spray, for the pan

For the Topping

¾ cup Gluten-Free All-Purpose Flour (see p. 11)

½ cup granulated sugar

⅓ cup flaked coconut, chopped

5 tablespoons unsalted butter, cut into pieces

For the Cake

1¼ cups Gluten-Free All-Purpose Flour (see p. 11)

1½ teaspoons baking powder

¼ teaspoon baking soda

¼ teaspoon table salt

¼ teaspoon xanthan gum

½ cup flaked coconut, finely chopped

⅔ cup (1 stick plus 2⅔ tablespoons) unsalted butter, softened

¾ cup granulated sugar

3 large eggs

1½ teaspoons pure vanilla extract

½ teaspoon coconut extract

⅓ cup buttermilk

¾ cup seedless raspberry jam

For the Icing

½ cup confectioners' sugar

2 teaspoons half-and-half or light cream

¼ teaspoon pure vanilla extract

Heat the oven to 350°F. Grease a 9-inch square baking pan with unsalted butter or nonstick cooking spray.

MAKE THE TOPPING

In a small bowl, whisk together the flour and granulated sugar until well blended. Stir in the coconut. Using a fork or your fingers, work in the butter until evenly combined and the mixture starts to come together. Set aside.

MAKE THE CAKE

1. In a medium bowl, whisk together the flour, baking powder, baking soda, salt, and xanthan gum until well combined. Stir in the coconut. Set aside.

2. In a large bowl, using an electric mixer on medium speed, cream the butter and granulated sugar until light and fluffy, about 3 minutes. Scrape down the sides of the bowl. Add the eggs, one at a time, beating well after each addition. Scrape down the sides of the bowl. Stir in the vanilla and coconut extracts.

3. Alternately add the flour mixture and the buttermilk to the butter-sugar mixture, starting and ending with the flour mixture, stirring between each addition until blended.

4. Spoon two-thirds of the batter into the prepared pan. Drop spoonfuls of raspberry jam over the batter. Top with the remaining batter. Crumble the topping over the top of the batter.

5. Bake until golden brown and a wooden pick inserted in the center comes out clean, 40 to 50 minutes. Let the cake cool in the pan on a wire rack for 10 minutes. Invert the cake onto a plate or wire rack lined with waxed paper. Place a wire rack on the bottom of the cake and turn the cake right side up to cool.

MAKE THE ICING

In a small bowl, combine the confectioners' sugar, cream, and vanilla. Beat until smooth. Drizzle the icing over the cake.

poppy seed coffee cake

This beautiful Bundt cake will dress up any breakfast table. Poppy seeds can turn rancid when stored for a long time so be sure to taste your poppy seeds before adding them to any baked goods.

MAKES ONE 10-INCH COFFEE CAKE

Unsalted butter or nonstick cooking spray, for the pan

For the Cake

3 cups Gluten-Free All-Purpose Flour (see p. 11)

2 teaspoons baking powder

1 teaspoon baking soda

¾ teaspoon xanthan gum

¼ teaspoon table salt

3 tablespoons poppy seeds

1 cup (2 sticks) unsalted butter, softened

1½ cups granulated sugar

4 large eggs

1½ teaspoons almond extract

½ teaspoon pure vanilla extract

1¼ cups buttermilk

For the Icing

1 cup confectioners' sugar

2 tablespoons half-and-half or light cream

1 tablespoon unsalted butter, melted

¼ teaspoon almond extract

1 tablespoon sliced almonds

Heat the oven to 350°F. Grease a 10-inch Bundt pan with unsalted butter or nonstick cooking spray.

MAKE THE CAKE

1. In a medium bowl, whisk together the flour, baking powder, baking soda, xanthan gum, and salt until well combined. Stir in the poppy seeds. Set aside.

2. In a large bowl, using an electric mixer on medium speed, cream the butter and granulated sugar until light and fluffy, about 3 minutes. Scrape down the sides of the bowl. Add the eggs, one at a time, beating well after each addition. Scrape down the sides of the bowl. Stir in the almond and vanilla extracts.

3. Alternately add the flour mixture and buttermilk to the butter-sugar mixture, starting and ending with the flour mixture, stirring between each addition until blended. Mix until smooth, about 30 seconds.

4. Spoon the batter into the prepared pan and spread smooth with lightly greased fingers or the back of a greased spoon.

5. Bake until golden brown and a wooden pick inserted in the center comes out clean, 45 to 55 minutes. Let the cake cool in the pan on a wire rack for 5 minutes. If necessary, gently run a knife blade between the cake and the edge of the pan to loosen. Invert the coffee cake onto a wire rack to cool.

MAKE THE ICING

In a medium bowl, combine the confectioners' sugar, cream, butter, and almond extract. Beat until smooth and spreadable. Spread or drizzle the icing over the cake. Sprinkle the almonds over the top of the icing. Let the icing harden for about 15 minutes before serving the cake.

sour cream coffee cake

Sour cream gives this coffee cake a tender texture and a rich flavor. An abundance of pecans and cinnamon provide layers of delicious streusel, making this cake as attractive as it is tasty.

MAKES ONE 10-INCH COFFEE CAKE

Unsalted butter or nonstick cooking spray, for the pan

For the Streusel

¾ cup Gluten-Free All-Purpose Flour (see p. 11)

½ cup granulated sugar

½ cup firmly packed brown sugar

3 teaspoons ground cinnamon

1½ cups chopped pecans

6 tablespoons (¾ stick) unsalted butter, cut into pieces

For the Cake

3 cups Gluten-Free All-Purpose Flour (see p. 11)

2½ teaspoons baking powder

¾ teaspoon baking soda

¾ teaspoon xanthan gum

½ teaspoon table salt

¾ cup (1½ sticks) unsalted butter, softened

1½ cups granulated sugar

4 large eggs

2½ teaspoons pure vanilla extract

1½ cups sour cream

For the Icing

2 cups confectioners' sugar

2 tablespoons half-and-half or light cream

1 tablespoon unsalted butter, melted

½ teaspoon pure vanilla extract

Heat the oven to 350°F. Grease a 10-inch Bundt pan with unsalted butter or nonstick cooking spray.

MAKE THE STREUSEL

In a small bowl, whisk together the flour, granulated sugar, brown sugar, and cinnamon until well blended. Stir in the pecans. Using a fork or your fingers, work in the butter until evenly combined and the mixture starts to come together. Set aside.

MAKE THE CAKE

1. In a medium bowl, whisk together the flour, baking powder, baking soda, xanthan gum, and salt until well combined. Set aside.

2. In a large bowl, using an electric mixer on medium speed, cream the butter and granulated sugar until light and fluffy, about 3 minutes. Scrape down the sides of the bowl. Add the eggs, one at a time, beating well after each addition. Scrape down the sides of the bowl. Stir in the vanilla.

3. Alternately add the flour mixture and sour cream to the butter-sugar mixture, starting and ending with the flour mixture, stirring between each addition until blended. Mix until smooth, about 30 seconds.

4. Spoon one-quarter of the batter into the prepared pan. Sprinkle half of the streusel mixture over the batter. Top with half of the remaining batter. Crumble the remaining streusel over the top of the batter. Top with the remaining batter and spread smooth with lightly greased fingers or the back of a greased spoon.

5. Bake until golden brown and a wooden pick inserted in the center comes out clean, 50 to 60 minutes. Let the cake cool in the pan on a wire rack for 5 minutes. Gently run a knife blade between the cake and the edge of the pan to loosen. Invert the coffee cake onto a wire rack to cool.

MAKE THE ICING

In a medium bowl, combine the confectioners' sugar, half-and-half, butter, and vanilla. Beat until smooth and spreadable. Spread or drizzle the icing over the cake.

yeast breads *and* sweet rolls

A big challenge in gluten-free baking is making yeast breads. Without gluten to support the structure of the loaves, they can end up very dense. Gluten-free sweet rolls are often either dry or gummy. But this doesn't have to be the case. By using a few simple techniques, you can make gluten-free yeast breads and sweet rolls that you will be proud to serve.

Smaller loaves are better when it comes to baking gluten-free yeast breads. Without gluten, a large loaf is more likely to collapse during baking or fall in the center after coming out of the oven. The larger pan also holds more dough, which makes it harder for the yeast to lift the center of the dough, often resulting in a heavier, denser, underbaked bread loaf.

If you have trouble with a loaf of bread falling or if the bread is gummy in the center, it likely means there is too much liquid in the batter. Try using 2 to 4 tablespoons less liquid the next time you bake the bread. If the bread is cooked through but very moist in the center, try reducing the amount of xanthan gum.

Baking gluten-free yeast bread is not an exact science and can take some practice to master, but it is a lot of fun and the journey is well worth the effort. Once you are experienced with making yeast bread, baking a beautifully risen loaf will become second nature.

Ingredients That Make a Difference

MILK POWDER

I like to add dry milk powder to my gluten-free breads. The milk powder increases the protein content of the dough, helping to improve the structure of the bread. You can omit the milk powder from the recipes if you have dairy allergies. Also, the milk or buttermilk in the recipe may be replaced with almond milk, soy milk, or even coconut milk to accommodate lactose intolerance.

INSTANT YEAST

All of the recipes in this chapter use instant yeast, also known as quick-rising or rapid-rise yeast. Instant yeast does not need to be proofed—the process of activating the yeast in warm water—before being added to the other ingredients. It gets combined in a mixer bowl with part of the flour, and then warm milk or other liquid is added to the bowl.

Because instant yeast is combined with the flour, the temperature of the liquid used to activate instant yeast needs to be higher than that used with regular yeast. The ideal temperature of the liquid added should be between 120°F and 130°F. Use an instant-read thermometer to check the temperature of the liquid before adding it to the yeast and flour mixture. Temperatures over 130°F may weaken or kill the yeast. If the liquid is too warm, let it cool for a minute or two and check the temperature again.

Equipment

LOAF PANS

Loaf pans, also called bread pans or tins, are used for baking loaves of yeast bread. Gluten-free yeast breads bake up best in narrow rectangular metal pans with high sides. Loaf pans made of light-colored aluminum are my preferred choice for gluten-free breads. Shiny or light-colored pans

produce breads with lighter crusts, while pans with a dark finish result in breads with a dark crust. All of the yeast bread recipes in this book are formulated to fit a 4½ x 8½-inch loaf pan.

BAKING PANS

Sturdy, single-walled, light-colored metal round baking pans, preferably made of aluminum, are my favorite choice for baking sweet rolls. Shiny metal pans reflect heat, which slows down the browning process and allows sweet rolls to bake all the way through to the middle without too much browning on the outside. Sweet rolls bake up beautifully in an 8-inch round baking pan, but you can also use an 8-inch square pan if you don't have a round pan.

PASTRY BOARD

A special board reserved just for rolling out gluten-free bread dough, sweet rolls, pie crusts, and other pastries is an important piece of equipment in the gluten-free kitchen. Hardwood, marble, and smooth plastic or acrylic are all good surfaces for rolling doughs.

If you don't have a pastry board, a smooth-surface countertop or kitchen table makes a good rolling surface. Just be sure that the surface is very clean and free of any gluten products or cleaning products that could contaminate your dough.

Working with Yeast Doughs

MIXING THE DOUGHS

Gluten-free yeast breads are easy to mix up in a stand mixer. I don't recommend using a hand-held mixer because the mixing process can put a serious strain on its motor, causing it to burn out. You can also mix gluten-free bread doughs by hand, but this is a long and laborious chore, as the yeast dough is sticky and needs to be thoroughly beaten.

The technique for mixing these yeast bread doughs is simple. First, combine part of the flour, the xanthan gum, and the instant yeast in a large mixer bowl and whisk these ingredients together until well blended. Add the heated liquid ingredients and the eggs and beat with the paddle beater until thoroughly mixed. The remaining flour is then added and the dough is beaten again. The finished dough will be soft and sticky. It will not look the same as a yeast bread dough made from flour that contains gluten.

This two-step process of incorporating the flour into the dough serves two important purposes. By starting with only part of the flour in the mixer bowl, the instant yeast is able to absorb more of the warm milk so it starts to activate faster. Gradually adding the remaining flour after the initial beating creates a smoother texture and helps add structure to the dough.

SHAPING YEAST LOAVES

Gluten-free bread doughs are very sticky, so it is difficult to knead and shape the loaves the same way you would a wheat flour bread loaf. It is easiest to prepare gluten-free bread loaves using the single-rise method. These types of yeast breads are often referred to as batter breads because the mixed dough is not kneaded and has a sticky batterlike texture.

After mixing the dough, spoon it evenly into the greased loaf pan. I recommend using unsalted butter or nonstick cooking spray to grease the pan rather than oil because gluten-free bread doughs tend to absorb the oil into the dough. This can cause the outer edges of the loaf to stay sticky longer and the bread to stick to the pan as it bakes.

Fill the loaf pan about two-thirds full. Too much dough in the pan can cause the loaf to fall during baking. As mentioned, these yeast bread recipes all fit a 4½ x 8½-inch loaf pan.

The top of the dough will be lumpy and bumpy. Smooth it out as best you can with the spoon or spatula used to transfer the dough to the pan.

Then grease your fingers or the back of a clean spoon with unsalted butter or nonstick cooking spray and gently shape the top of the loaf until the surface has a smoother, more even appearance. Homemade gluten-free breads will have a slightly more rustic appearance than breads made with flour containing gluten. I don't recommend using floured hands to smooth the top of the loaf—the dough will quickly absorb the flour and start sticking to your hands. Instead of smoothing out the top of the dough, you will end up with a sticky mess.

PROOFING YEAST DOUGHS

Yeast doughs rise, or proof, best at temperatures between 75°F and 100°F. The optimum rising temperature for yeast is 85°F to 90°F. Cooler temperatures will slow down the rising process and take the dough longer to rise, while warmer temperatures will cause the dough to rise very fast. The faster a dough rises, the more fragile the structure of the loaf. Dough that rises too fast may become unstable and can easily fall when the pan is transferred to the oven.

Place dough being proofed in a warm, draft-free location. Drafts can cause uneven rising, which can result in irregularly shaped loaves or make the dough unstable. To prevent drafts, I create my own bread proofing box by placing a large, rectangular clear plastic food storage container over my loaf pan. Not only does it protect the dough from drafts, but it also creates a warm, slightly moist environment that helps the dough rise up better. An added benefit—I can see through the container to keep an eye on the loaf as it rises. You can also use a box or a large pan as a cover. Just be sure that the cover is tall and wide enough so that it does not come into contact with the dough as it rises.

When the crown of the dough has risen to just above the edge of the loaf pan, it is ready to bake. You don't want the dough to rise too high or double in size because it does not have gluten to support the structure. If the dough rises too much, it will become unstable. When exposed to the heat of the oven, unstable dough will rise rapidly and then collapse. Should you lose track of time and your loaf overproofs, punch down the dough in the pan and turn it out onto a lightly floured board. Knead the dough for a couple of minutes to remove air bubbles and reshape the loaf. Regrease the pan, place the dough in it, and let the loaf rise again. This will work for unfilled loaves or rolls. Overproofed breads or rolls with fillings and toppings cannot be reproofed.

Rising times can vary significantly from one kitchen to another. The temperature of the kitchen, temperature of the liquid ingredients, freshness of the yeast, size of the pan, and even fineness of the flour can all affect rising times. The rising times given in the recipes are an approximate guide; your dough may need more or less time to rise depending on these variables. As you bake more bread, you'll learn how long it takes for your loaves to rise in your kitchen environment.

SHAPING SWEET ROLLS

The process of shaping sweet rolls requires the dough to rise twice. The first rising allows the air bubbles produced by the yeast to expand the dough. This will make the rolls light and tender. The dough is also lightly kneaded to make it easier to handle and to help the sweet rolls maintain their shape. The second rising occurs after the rolls are filled and shaped.

After the sweet roll dough has risen the first time, turn it out onto a pastry board or countertop lightly dusted with gluten-free all-purpose flour (see p. 11). Gently knead the dough by hand for 1 minute to remove the large air bubbles. The dough will be sticky, and you don't want to work in too much flour, which will make the rolls tough and dry. Loosely cover the dough with plastic wrap or

a damp towel and let the dough rest for 5 minutes. This will make it easier to roll.

Use a floured rolling pin to roll the dough out into a 20-inch by 12-inch rectangle of even thickness. Periodically lift the dough to make sure it does not stick to the board. Add only as much flour to the board as needed to prevent sticking. Again, you don't want to work too much flour into the dough. If you have trouble rolling the dough into a rectangle, use your fingers to gently stretch and push it into shape.

Add the filling, leaving a ½-inch border along the long edges of the dough. This will keep the filling from overflowing and allow you to pinch the outer edge of the dough to seal. Starting with one of the long sides, gently roll the dough up jellyroll style, keeping an even thickness. Pinch the seam to seal. Using a sharp knife, cut the rolled log into 18 even slices. If the dough starts sticking to the knife, spray the knife with nonstick cooking spray.

Arrange 9 slices in each prepared pan, as indicated in your recipe. I usually place 1 roll in the center, with 3 rolls around it and 5 rolls in the outer ring. Cover the pans with plastic wrap and let the rolls rise in a warm place until they are nearly doubled in size, about 45 minutes. The rolls will nearly fill the pan.

Baking Bread Loaves and Sweet Rolls

Before heating the oven, position the oven rack in the middle to lower third of the oven. Halfway through the rising time, start heating the oven. Make sure the oven comes up to full temperature before placing the bread in the oven. If the oven is not hot enough, the bread or sweet rolls won't rise enough in the first few minutes of baking and the finished product will be dense and heavy.

YEAST BREAD LOAVES

When the bread loaf is placed in the oven, the heat will cause the trapped air bubbles created by the yeast to rapidly expand. The bread will rise up above the pan and then set as the heat kills the yeast and the air stops expanding.

As the loaf bakes, the top will brown. You may find that it browns too quickly, which is common with gluten-free yeast breads. If this happens, loosely cover the bread with a piece of foil.

The bread is done when the top of the loaf is nicely browned and an instant-read thermometer inserted in the center of the loaf reads 210°F. The loaf will also start to pull away from the sides of the pan and the bread will come out easily when the pan is turned upside down. Remove the loaf from the pan and return the bread to the oven. Let the bread bake on the oven rack for 5 minutes to lightly brown the side and bottom crusts.

Remove the bread from the oven and place the loaf on its side on a wire rack to cool. Placing the bread on its side helps the loaf maintain its shape as it cools. Bread loaves should never be allowed to cool in the pan, as condensation will form in the pan and cause the bottom and sides of the loaf to become soggy.

SWEET ROLLS

Because sweet rolls are baked for a much shorter time than bread loaves, you should not have a problem with the rolls browning too much. However, if your rolls do start to become too brown, loosely cover them with a piece of foil.

The rolls are done when the tops are lightly golden brown and a wooden pick inserted in the center of the dough comes out clean. Be sure to stick the pick down into the dough and not the filling.

Remove the pans from the oven and set on a wire rack. Place a large ovenproof plate over the

top of each pan. Using potholders or oven mitts, immediately invert the pans of rolls onto the plates and carefully remove the hot pans. Let the rolls cool for a few minutes, and then top with icing if desired.

Sweet rolls may be prepared the day before and baked in the morning. After arranging the rolls in the pans, cover tightly with plastic wrap and refrigerate the rolls for up to 24 hours. The rolls will rise slightly in the refrigerator overnight. When ready to bake, remove the pans from the refrigerator and set them on a wire rack in a warm place for about 45 minutes. The rack will allow air to circulate under the pan and help the rolls warm up faster. Bake the rolls as directed in the recipe. You may need to increase the baking time by 5 minutes or more as needed to reach doneness.

Quick Tips
YEAST BREADS AND SWEET ROLLS

- Use yeast before the expiration date, and store bulk yeast in the freezer to preserve its freshness.

- Ingredients such as flour, yeast, and eggs should be at room temperature for best results.

- Eggs provide natural leavening, moisture, protein, and flavor to yeast doughs.

- Too much liquid can cause breads to be soggy.

- Too much xanthan gum can cause the baked bread to be too moist inside.

- When using instant yeast, the temperature of the liquid should be between 120°F and 130°F.

- Temperature, humidity, and altitude all affect how fast yeast dough rises.

- Follow the recipe directions when letting dough rise—allowing the dough to rise too high or too fast can cause the bread to fall during or after baking.

- Let bread loaves rise just until the crown of the dough passes the top of the pan. The bread will rise more in the oven.

- Use an instant-read thermometer to test the internal temperature of gluten-free yeast bread loaves to ensure doneness. Bread loaves are done when the thermometer inserted in the center of the loaf reads 210°F.

- Remove bread loaves from the pan immediately to prevent the bottom of the bread from becoming soggy, and lay loaves on their side on a wire rack to cool.

- When testing sweet rolls for doneness, be sure to insert the wooden pick into the dough and not the filling.

- Immediately remove sweet rolls from the pan to prevent sticking and to keep the rolls from becoming soggy.

white bread

This classic bread is one you'll turn to time and again for many of the recipes in this book. It is also excellent eaten plain, toasted, or used to make grilled cheese sandwiches. Feel free to vary this basic bread by adding different flavorings or herbs, nuts, dried fruit, or cheese.

MAKES ONE 4½ x 8½-INCH LOAF

Nonstick cooking spray or unsalted butter, for the pan

2½ cups Gluten-Free All-Purpose Flour (see p. 11)

2 tablespoons dry milk powder

1 tablespoon instant (quick-rising) active dry yeast

1 teaspoon xanthan gum

1¼ cups whole milk

2 tablespoons granulated sugar

2 tablespoons unsalted butter, cut into large pieces

¾ teaspoon table salt

3 large eggs

1. Grease a 4½ x 8½-inch loaf pan with nonstick cooking spray or unsalted butter. Position the oven rack in the middle to lower third of the oven.

2. In the bowl of a stand mixer, using a wire whisk, combine 1 cup of the flour, the milk powder, yeast, and xanthan gum until well blended. Set aside.

3. In a small saucepan, combine the milk, sugar, butter, and salt. Heat over medium-low heat, stirring constantly, just until the sugar is completely dissolved, the butter is melted, and the mixture reads between 120°F and 130°F on an instant-read thermometer. Add the milk mixture to the flour mixture, then add the eggs.

4. Using an electric stand mixer fitted with the flat paddle beater, beat the mixture on the lowest speed for 30 seconds. Scrape down the sides and bottom of the bowl. Using the next highest speed, beat the mixture for 2 minutes. Scrape down the sides of the bowl. Gradually add the remaining 1½ cups of flour and continue to beat until the flour is incorporated. Beat for an additional 2 minutes. The dough will be sticky.

5. Spoon the dough into the prepared pan. Gently smooth the top of the dough using lightly greased fingers or the back of a greased spoon. Let the bread rise in a warm place until the crown of the loaf rises just above the top of the pan, 40 to 50 minutes. Meanwhile, heat the oven to 375°F.

6. Bake the bread until it is golden brown and an instant-read thermometer inserted in the center of the loaf reads 210°F, 50 to 60 minutes. If necessary, cover the bread with foil partway through baking to prevent the top crust from becoming too dark. Remove the pan from the oven and immediately remove the bread from the pan. Return the bread to the oven, placing the loaf directly on the oven rack, for 5 minutes to brown and crisp the side and bottom crusts. Remove the loaf from the oven and place it on its side on a wire rack to cool.

cinnamon swirl bread

I love the pretty appearance and delightful flavor of this gluten-free version of a childhood favorite. This slightly sweet bread is heavenly when served still warm from the oven. It also makes excellent toast—but be sure the top of the bread is not iced, as the icing will melt and burn in the toaster.

MAKES ONE 4½ x 8½-INCH LOAF

Nonstick cooking spray or unsalted butter, for the pan and bowl

For the Filling

⅔ cup granulated sugar

2½ teaspoons ground cinnamon

¼ cup (4 tablespoons) unsalted butter, melted

For the Bread Dough

2 cups Gluten-Free All-Purpose Flour (see p. 11); more for dusting

2 tablespoons dry milk powder

2½ teaspoons instant (quick-rising) active dry yeast

1 teaspoon xanthan gum

1 cup whole milk

3 tablespoons granulated sugar

3 tablespoons unsalted butter, cut into large pieces

½ teaspoon table salt

2 large eggs

½ teaspoon pure vanilla extract

For the Icing

¾ cup confectioners' sugar

2 teaspoons half-and-half or whole milk

1 teaspoon unsalted butter, melted

¼ teaspoon pure vanilla extract

Grease a 4½ x 8½-inch loaf pan with nonstick cooking spray or unsalted butter. Position the oven rack in the middle to lower third of the oven.

MAKE THE FILLING

In a small bowl, combine the granulated sugar and cinnamon until evenly blended. Set aside.

MAKE THE DOUGH

1. In the bowl of a stand mixer, using a wire whisk, combine 1 cup of the flour, the milk powder, yeast, and xanthan gum until well blended. Set aside.

2. In a small saucepan, combine the milk, granulated sugar, butter, and salt. Heat over medium-low heat, stirring constantly, just until the sugar is completely dissolved, the butter is melted, and the mixture reads between 120°F and 130°F on an instant-read thermometer. Add the milk mixture to the flour mixture, then add the eggs and vanilla.

3. Using an electric stand mixer fitted with the flat paddle beater, beat the mixture on the lowest speed for 30 seconds. Scrape down the sides and bottom of the bowl. Using the next highest speed, beat the mixture for 2 minutes. Scrape down the sides of bowl. Gradually add the remaining 1 cup of flour and continue to beat until the flour is incorporated. Beat for an additional 2 minutes. The dough will be sticky.

4. Scrape the dough into a large bowl greased with nonstick cooking spray or unsalted butter. Cover the bowl with plastic wrap and let the dough rise in a warm place until not quite doubled in bulk, 35 to 45 minutes.

CONTINUED ON PAGE 150

5. Turn the dough out onto a board or other flat surface lightly dusted with gluten-free all-purpose flour. Using lightly greased hands or the back of a greased spoon, gently pat the dough into an 8 x 20-inch rectangle. The dough will be soft and sticky.

6. Brush the dough with 2 tablespoons of the melted butter. Sprinkle the cinnamon sugar evenly over the top of the butter, leaving a 1/2-inch border around all edges. Spoon the remaining melted butter over the top of the filling. Starting with a short edge, roll the dough up jellyroll style. Pinch the ends together to seal. Place the dough, seam side down, in the prepared pan. Using lightly greased fingers or the back of a greased spoon, gently smooth the top of the loaf to remove any large bumps. Let the bread rise in a warm place until the crown of the loaf rises just above the top of the pan, 35 to 45 minutes. Meanwhile, heat the oven to 375°F.

7. Bake the bread until it is golden brown and an instant-read thermometer inserted in the center of the loaf reads 210°F, 45 to 55 minutes. If necessary, cover the bread with foil partway through baking to prevent the top crust from becoming too dark. Remove the pan from the oven and immediately remove the bread from the pan. Be careful as the cinnamon filling will be hot. Return the bread to the oven, placing the loaf directly on the oven rack, for 5 minutes to brown and crisp the side and bottom crusts. Remove the loaf from the oven and place it on its side on a wire rack to cool for 20 minutes.

MAKE THE ICING

In a small bowl, combine the confectioners' sugar, half-and-half, butter, and vanilla. Beat until smooth and spreadable. Spread or drizzle the icing over the warm bread. Let the bread sit for 5 minutes for the icing to harden before slicing.

raisin bread

I like to use a combination of dark raisins and golden raisins in this bread, but you can use either all dark or all golden, if you prefer. If you use all golden, the bread will have a nice sweet bite. Whichever color you choose, be sure the raisins are plump for the best flavor.

MAKES ONE 4½ x 8½-INCH LOAF

Nonstick cooking spray or unsalted butter, for the pan

2½ cups Gluten-Free All-Purpose Flour (see p. 11)

2 tablespoons dry milk powder

1 tablespoon instant (quick-rising) active dry yeast

1 teaspoon xanthan gum

1¼ cups whole milk

3 tablespoons firmly packed brown sugar

3 tablespoons unsalted butter, cut into large pieces

¾ teaspoon table salt

3 large eggs

½ cup dark raisins

½ cup golden raisins

1. Grease a 4½ x 8½-inch loaf pan with nonstick cooking spray or unsalted butter. Position the oven rack in the middle to lower third of the oven.

2. In the bowl of a stand mixer, using a wire whisk, combine 1 cup of the flour, the milk powder, yeast, and xanthan gum until well blended. Set aside.

3. In a small saucepan, combine the milk, brown sugar, butter, and salt. Heat over medium-low heat, stirring constantly, just until the sugar is completely dissolved, the butter is melted, and the mixture reads between 120°F and 130°F on an instant-read thermometer. Add the milk mixture to the flour mixture, then add the eggs.

4. Using an electric stand mixer fitted with the flat paddle beater, beat the mixture on the lowest speed for 30 seconds. Scrape down the sides and bottom of the bowl. Using the next highest speed, beat the mixture for 2 minutes. Scrape down the sides of bowl. Gradually add the remaining 1½ cups of flour and continue to beat until the flour is incorporated. Beat for an additional 2 minutes. The dough will be sticky. By hand, stir in the raisins.

5. Spoon the dough into the prepared pan. Gently smooth the top of the dough using lightly greased fingers or the back of a greased spoon. Let the bread rise in a warm place until the crown of the loaf rises just above the top of the pan, 40 to 50 minutes. Meanwhile, heat the oven to 375°F.

6. Bake the bread until it is golden brown and an instant-read thermometer inserted in the center of the loaf reads 210°F, 50 to 60 minutes. If necessary, cover the bread with foil partway through baking to prevent the top crust from becoming too dark. Remove the pan from the oven and immediately remove the bread from the pan. Return the bread to the oven, placing the loaf directly on the oven rack, for 5 minutes to brown and crisp the side and bottom crusts. Remove the loaf from the oven and place it on its side on a wire rack to cool.

apple cinnamon bread

Cinnamon apples swirled through the loaf make this bread special. I like to use Granny Smith, Gala, or Fuji apples, depending on what is locally available. If you love cinnamon, feel free to increase the amount called for in the recipe to 1½ teaspoons.

MAKES ONE 4½ X 8½-INCH LOAF

Nonstick cooking spray or unsalted butter, for the pan

For the Apple Mixture
¼ cup firmly packed brown sugar

2 tablespoons granulated sugar

1 teaspoon ground cinnamon

1 cup finely chopped peeled apples

For the Bread Dough
2½ cups Gluten-Free All-Purpose Flour (see p. 11)

2 tablespoons dry milk powder

1 tablespoon instant (quick-rising) active dry yeast

1 teaspoon xanthan gum

1¼ cups whole milk

3 tablespoons granulated sugar

3 tablespoons unsalted butter, cut into large pieces

¾ teaspoon table salt

3 large eggs

VARIATION

apple cinnamon raisin bread:
Add ½ cup chopped raisins to the apple mixture.

Grease a 4½ x 8½-inch loaf pan with nonstick cooking spray or unsalted butter. Position the oven rack in the middle to lower third of the oven.

MAKE THE APPLE MIXTURE
In a small bowl, combine the brown sugar, granulated sugar, and cinnamon until evenly blended. Stir in the apples until well combined. Set aside.

MAKE THE DOUGH
1. In the bowl of a stand mixer, using a wire whisk, combine 1 cup of the flour, the milk powder, yeast, and xanthan gum until well blended. Set aside.

2. In a small saucepan, combine the milk, granulated sugar, butter, and salt. Heat over medium-low heat, stirring constantly, just until the sugar is completely dissolved, the butter is melted, and the mixture reads between 120°F and 130°F on an instant-read thermometer. Add the milk mixture to the flour mixture, then add the eggs.

3. Using an electric stand mixer fitted with the flat paddle beater, beat the mixture on the lowest speed for 30 seconds. Scrape down the sides and bottom of the bowl. Using the next highest speed, beat the mixture for 2 minutes. Scrape down the sides of bowl. Gradually add the remaining 1½ cups of flour and continue to beat until the flour is incorporated. Beat for an additional 2 minutes. The dough will be sticky. By hand, fold spoonfuls of the apple mixture into the dough, stirring until nearly combined and giving the dough a swirled appearance.

4. Spoon the dough into the prepared loaf pan. Gently smooth the top of the dough using lightly greased fingers or the back of a greased spoon. Let the bread rise in a warm place until the crown of the loaf rises just above the top of the pan, 40 to 50 minutes. Meanwhile, heat the oven to 375°F.

5. Bake the bread until it is golden brown and an instant-read thermometer inserted in the center of the loaf reads 210°F, 50 to 60 minutes. If necessary, cover the bread with foil partway through baking to prevent the top crust from becoming too dark. Remove the pan from the oven and immediately remove the bread from the pan. Return the bread to the oven, placing the loaf directly on the oven rack, for 5 minutes to brown and crisp the side and bottom crusts. Remove the loaf from the oven and place it on its side on a wire rack to cool.

Make the filling first to give the apples time to release some juice and absorb some of the cinnamon and sugar.

When you add the apple mixture to the dough, don't completely stir it in. You want some streaks of apple and cinnamon to remain in the dough.

ranch bread

Powdered ranch salad dressing mix is added to the dry ingredients of this tasty bread. Serve the bread or rolls (see the variation below) with a hearty stew or roast for a satisfying meal.

MAKES ONE 4½ X 8½-INCH LOAF

Nonstick cooking spray or unsalted butter, for the pan

2½ cups Gluten-Free All-Purpose Flour (see p. 11)

2 tablespoons dry milk powder

1 tablespoon instant (quick-rising) active dry yeast

1 tablespoon gluten-free powdered ranch dressing mix

1 teaspoon xanthan gum

1¼ cups whole milk

2 teaspoons granulated sugar

3 tablespoons unsalted butter, cut into large pieces

¼ teaspoon table salt

3 large eggs

VARIATION

ranch rolls: Grease 18 muffin cups with unsalted butter or nonstick cooking spray. Spoon the prepared dough into the muffin cups, filling them three-quarters full. Let the dough rise in a warm place until the crowns of the rolls rise just above the top of the cups, about 30 minutes. Bake in a 375°F oven until golden brown and a wooden pick inserted in the center comes out clean, 15 to 20 minutes. If necessary, cover the rolls with foil partway through baking to prevent the tops from becoming too dark. Remove the pans from the oven; immediately remove the rolls from the pan and place on a wire rack. Serve warm. Makes 18 rolls.

1. Grease a 4½ x 8½-inch loaf pan with nonstick cooking spray or unsalted butter. Position the oven rack in the middle to lower third of the oven.

2. In the bowl of a stand mixer, using a wire whisk, combine 1 cup of the flour, the milk powder, yeast, ranch dressing mix, and xanthan gum until well blended. Set aside.

3. In a small saucepan, combine the milk, sugar, butter, and salt. Heat over medium-low heat, stirring constantly, just until the sugar is completely dissolved, the butter is melted, and the mixture reads between 120°F and 130°F on an instant-read thermometer. Add the milk mixture to the flour mixture, then add the eggs.

4. Using an electric stand mixer fitted with the flat paddle beater, beat the mixture on the lowest speed for 30 seconds. Scrape down the sides and bottom of the bowl. Using the next highest speed, beat the mixture for 2 minutes. Scrape down the sides of bowl. Gradually add the remaining 1½ cups of flour and continue to beat until the flour is incorporated. Beat for an additional 2 minutes. The dough will be sticky.

5. Spoon the dough into the prepared pan. Gently smooth the top of the dough using lightly greased fingers or the back of a greased spoon. Let the bread rise in a warm place until the crown of the loaf rises just above the top of the pan, 40 to 50 minutes. Meanwhile, heat the oven to 375°F.

6. Bake the bread until it is golden brown and an instant-read thermometer inserted in the center of the loaf reads 210°F, 50 to 60 minutes. If necessary, cover the bread with foil partway through baking to prevent the top crust from becoming too dark. Remove the pan from the oven and immediately remove the bread from the pan. Return the bread to the oven, placing the loaf directly on the oven rack, for 5 minutes to brown and crisp the side and bottom crusts. Remove the loaf from the oven and place it on its side on a wire rack to cool.

buttermilk bread

A rich bread with a pleasant flavor, this loaf makes very good French toast.

MAKES ONE 4½ X 8½-INCH LOAF

Nonstick cooking spray or unsalted butter, for the pan

2½ cups Gluten-Free All-Purpose Flour (see p. 11)

2 tablespoons dry milk powder

1 tablespoon instant (quick-rising) active dry yeast

1 teaspoon xanthan gum

1¼ cups buttermilk

2 tablespoons granulated sugar

2 tablespoons unsalted butter, cut into large pieces

¾ teaspoon table salt

3 large eggs

It's important that the buttermilk mixture reaches a temperature between 115°F and 120°F. Heating above 120°F will cause buttermilk to break down and separate.

1. Grease a 4½ x 8½-inch loaf pan with nonstick cooking spray or unsalted butter. Position the oven rack in the middle to lower third of the oven.

2. In the bowl of a stand mixer, using a wire whisk, combine 1 cup of the flour, the milk powder, yeast, and xanthan gum until well blended. Set aside.

3. In a small saucepan, combine the buttermilk, sugar, butter, and salt. Heat over medium-low heat, stirring constantly, just until the sugar is completely dissolved, the butter is melted, and the mixture reads between 115°F and 120°F on an instant-read thermometer. Add the milk mixture to the flour mixture, then add the eggs.

4. Using an electric stand mixer fitted with the flat paddle beater, beat the mixture on the lowest speed for 30 seconds. Scrape down the sides and bottom of the bowl. Using the next highest speed, beat the mixture for 2 minutes. Scrape down the sides of bowl. Gradually add the remaining 1½ cups of flour and continue to beat until the flour is incorporated. Beat for an additional 2 minutes. The dough will be sticky.

5. Spoon the dough into the prepared pan. Gently smooth the top of the dough using lightly greased fingers or the back of a greased spoon. Let the bread rise in a warm place until the crown of the loaf rises just above the top of the pan, 40 to 50 minutes. Meanwhile, heat the oven to 375°F.

6. Bake the bread until it is golden brown and an instant-read thermometer inserted in the center of the loaf reads 210°F, 50 to 60 minutes. If necessary, cover the bread with foil partway through baking to prevent the top crust from becoming too dark. Remove the pan from the oven and immediately remove the bread from the pan. Return the bread to the oven, placing the loaf directly on the oven rack, for 5 minutes to brown and crisp the side and bottom crusts. Remove the loaf from the oven and place it on its side on a wire rack to cool.

sweet roll dough

This dough is a gluten-free adaptation of one of my favorite sweet dough recipes. It is easy to prepare and perfect for making any of the sweet roll recipes in this book.

MAKES 18 ROLLS

3 cups Gluten-Free All-Purpose Flour (see p. 11); more for dusting

1 tablespoon instant (quick-rising) active dry yeast

1 teaspoon xanthan gum

1¼ cups whole milk

⅓ cup granulated sugar

⅓ cup (5⅓ tablespoons) unsalted butter, cut into large pieces; more for greasing the bowl

¼ teaspoon table salt

3 large eggs

1 teaspoon pure vanilla extract

1. In the bowl of a stand mixer, using a wire whisk, combine 1 cup of the flour, the yeast, and xanthan gum until well blended. Set aside.

2. In a small saucepan, combine the milk, sugar, butter, and salt. Heat over medium-low heat, stirring constantly, just until the sugar is completely dissolved, the butter is melted, and the temperature of the mixture reads between 120°F and 130°F on an instant-read thermometer. Add the milk mixture to the flour mixture, then add the eggs and vanilla.

3. Using an electric stand mixer fitted with the flat paddle beater, beat the mixture on the lowest speed for 30 seconds. Scrape down the sides and bottom of the bowl. Using the next highest speed, beat the mixture for 2 minutes. Scrape down the sides of the bowl. Gradually add the remaining 2 cups of flour and beat until the flour is fully incorporated. Beat for an additional 2 minutes. The dough will be sticky.

4. Turn the dough out onto a board moderately dusted with gluten-free all-purpose flour and knead by hand for 1 minute. Shape the dough into a ball and place in a large greased bowl and turn over to coat all sides of the dough. Cover the bowl with plastic wrap or a damp towel and let rise in a warm place for 1 hour, or until nearly doubled in bulk.

5. Turn the dough out onto a board or other flat surface lightly dusted with gluten-free all-purpose flour and knead by hand for 1 minute to remove the large air bubbles. Loosely cover the dough with plastic wrap or a damp towel and let the dough rest for 5 minutes.

6. Use the dough in the desired sweet roll recipe.

caramel nut rolls

These nutty sweet rolls are very versatile. Try making them with almonds, hazelnuts, peanuts, macadamia nuts, or even cashews. A mix is fine, but choose no more than two types of nuts.

MAKES 18 ROLLS

Unsalted butter, for the pans

1 recipe Sweet Roll Dough (see p. 157)

Gluten-Free All-Purpose Flour (see p. 11), for rolling

For the Topping

½ cup (1 stick) unsalted butter

1 cup firmly packed brown sugar

2 tablespoons light corn syrup

1 cup chopped pecans or walnuts

For the Filling

¾ cup firmly packed brown sugar

3 tablespoons granulated sugar

¾ cup finely chopped pecans or walnuts

⅓ cup (5⅓ tablespoons) unsalted butter, melted

Prepare the Sweet Roll Dough as directed on p. 157. Grease two 8-inch round baking pans with unsalted butter. Set aside.

MAKE THE TOPPING

1. In a small saucepan, over medium-low heat, melt the butter. Stir in the brown sugar and corn syrup. Cook and stir until the brown sugar is dissolved, 1 minute.

2. Divide the syrup equally between two 8-inch round baking pans, and spread to cover the bottoms of the pans.

3. Sprinkle the pecans or walnuts evenly over the syrup. Set aside.

MAKE THE FILLING

In a small bowl, combine the brown sugar and granulated sugar until evenly blended. Stir in the pecans or walnuts. Set aside.

MAKE THE ROLLS

1. On a flat surface lightly dusted with gluten-free all-purpose flour, roll the risen Sweet Roll Dough into a 12 x 20-inch rectangle.

2. Brush the dough with half of the melted butter. Sprinkle the filling evenly over the butter, leaving a ½-inch border along the long edges of the dough. Drizzle the remaining melted butter over the filling. Starting with one of the long sides, roll up the dough jellyroll style. Pinch the seam together to seal.

3. Cut the roll into 18 even slices, and arrange 9 slices in each prepared pan on top of the topping. Cover the pans with plastic wrap and let rise in a warm place until the rolls are nearly doubled in size, about 45 minutes. Meanwhile, heat the oven to 350°F.

4. Bake the rolls until they're lightly golden brown and a wooden pick inserted in the dough in the center of the pan comes out clean, 20 to 25 minutes (be sure to insert the pick into the dough, not the filling). Immediately invert the pans onto heatproof serving plates and remove the pans. Be careful—the pans and rolls will be very hot. Let cool for 5 to 10 minutes.

cinnamon sweet rolls

With a delightful cinnamon filling and creamy icing, these heavenly sweet rolls are a wonderful treat for breakfast, brunch, or even dessert. They are easy to master, so you'll find yourself turning to them as a staple.

MAKES 18 ROLLS

Unsalted butter, for the pans

1 recipe Sweet Roll Dough (see p. 157)

Gluten-Free All-Purpose Flour (see p. 11), for rolling

For the Filling

½ cup granulated sugar

½ cup firmly packed dark brown sugar

2 teaspoons ground cinnamon

⅓ cup (5⅓ tablespoons) unsalted butter, melted

For the Icing

2 cups confectioners' sugar

2 tablespoons half-and-half or whole milk

1 tablespoon unsalted butter, melted

½ teaspoon pure vanilla extract

Prepare the Sweet Roll Dough as directed on p. 157. Grease two 8-inch round baking pans with unsalted butter. Set aside.

MAKE THE FILLING

In a medium bowl, combine the granulated sugar, brown sugar, and cinnamon until evenly blended. Set aside.

MAKE THE ROLLS

1. On a board or other flat surface lightly dusted with gluten-free all-purpose flour, roll the risen Sweet Roll Dough into a 12 x 20-inch rectangle.

2. Brush the dough with half of the melted butter. Sprinkle the filling evenly over the butter, leaving a ½-inch border along the long edges of the dough. Drizzle the remaining melted butter over the filling. Starting with one of the long sides, roll up the dough jellyroll style. Pinch the seam together to seal.

3. Cut the roll into 18 even slices and arrange 9 slices in each prepared pan. Cover the pans with plastic wrap and let rise in a warm place until the rolls are nearly doubled in size, about 45 minutes. Meanwhile, heat the oven to 350°F.

4. Bake the rolls until they're lightly golden brown and a wooden pick inserted in the dough in the center of the pan comes out clean, 20 to 25 minutes (be sure to insert the pick into the dough, not the filling). Immediately invert the pans onto heatproof serving plates and remove the pans. Be careful—the pans and rolls will be very hot. Let cool for 5 to 10 minutes.

MAKE THE ICING

In a medium bowl, combine the confectioners' sugar, half-and-half, butter, and vanilla. Beat until smooth and spreadable. Spread or drizzle the icing over the warm rolls. Serve warm.

pumpkin sweet rolls

Thanks to canned pumpkin purée, you can bring the taste of fall to the breakfast table any day of the year.

MAKES 18 ROLLS

Unsalted butter, for the pans
1 recipe Sweet Roll Dough (see p. 157)
Gluten-Free All-Purpose Flour (see p. 11), for rolling

For the Filling
¼ cup firmly packed brown sugar
½ teaspoon ground cinnamon
⅛ teaspoon grated nutmeg
Pinch ground ginger
¾ cup canned pumpkin purée
1 tablespoon unsalted butter, melted
½ teaspoon pure vanilla extract
½ cup finely chopped walnuts

For the Icing
1 cup confectioners' sugar
1 tablespoon half-and-half or whole milk
1½ teaspoons unsalted butter, melted
¼ teaspoon pure vanilla extract

Prepare the Sweet Roll Dough as directed on p. 157. Grease two 8-inch round baking pans with unsalted butter. Set aside.

MAKE THE FILLING

1. In a small bowl, combine the brown sugar, cinnamon, nutmeg, and ginger until evenly blended.

2. In a medium bowl, combine the pumpkin purée, melted butter, and vanilla until well blended.

3. Stir in the sugar mixture until well combined. Set aside.

MAKE THE ROLLS

1. On a board or other flat surface lightly dusted with gluten-free all-purpose flour, roll the risen Sweet Roll Dough into a 12 x 20-inch rectangle.

2. Spoon the pumpkin filling over the dough and spread evenly, leaving a ½-inch border along the long edges of the dough. Sprinkle the walnuts over top of the filling. Starting with one of the long sides, roll up the dough jellyroll style. Pinch the seam together to seal.

3. Cut the roll into 18 even slices, and arrange 9 slices in each prepared pan. Cover the pans with plastic wrap and let rise in a warm place until the rolls are nearly doubled in size, about 45 minutes. Meanwhile, heat the oven to 350°F.

4. Bake the rolls until they're lightly golden brown and a wooden pick inserted in the dough in the center of the pan comes out clean, 20 to 25 minutes (be sure to insert the pick into the dough, not the filling). Immediately invert the pans onto heatproof serving plates and remove the pans. Be careful—the pans and rolls will be very hot. Let cool for 5 to 10 minutes.

MAKE THE ICING

In a medium bowl, combine the confectioners' sugar, half-and-half, butter, and vanilla. Beat until smooth and spreadable. Spread or drizzle the icing over the warm rolls. Serve warm.

cranberry walnut sweet rolls

While finely chopped dried cranberries and walnuts make a delicious filling, the orange-flavored icing elevates these sweet rolls to must-have status.

MAKES 18 ROLLS

Unsalted butter, for the pans

1 recipe Sweet Roll Dough (see p. 157)

Gluten-Free All-Purpose Flour (see p. 11), for rolling

For the Filling

¼ cup granulated sugar

½ cup firmly packed brown sugar

⅔ cup finely chopped dried cranberries

½ cup finely chopped walnuts

2 teaspoons finely grated orange zest

¼ cup (4 tablespoons) unsalted butter, melted

For the Icing

1 cup confectioners' sugar

1½ tablespoons fresh orange juice

1½ teaspoons unsalted butter, melted

1 teaspoon finely grated orange zest

Prepare the Sweet Roll Dough as directed on p. 157. Grease two 8-inch round baking pans with unsalted butter. Set aside.

MAKE THE FILLING

In a medium bowl, combine the granulated sugar and brown sugar until evenly blended. Stir in the dried cranberries, walnuts, and orange zest. Set aside.

MAKE THE ROLLS

1. On a board or other flat surface lightly dusted with gluten-free all-purpose flour, roll the risen Sweet Roll Dough into a 12 x 20-inch rectangle.

2. Brush the dough with half of the melted butter. Sprinkle the filling evenly over the butter, leaving a ½-inch border along the long edges of the dough. Drizzle the remaining melted butter over the filling. Starting with one of the long sides, roll up the dough jellyroll style. Pinch the seam together to seal.

3. Cut the roll into 18 even slices, and arrange 9 slices in each prepared pan. Cover the pans with plastic wrap and let rise in a warm place until the rolls are nearly doubled in size, about 45 minutes. Meanwhile, heat the oven to 350°F.

4. Bake the rolls until they're lightly golden brown and a wooden pick inserted in the dough in the center of the pan comes out clean, 20 to 25 minutes (be sure to insert the pick into the dough, not the filling). Immediately invert the pans onto heatproof serving plates and remove the pans. Be careful—the pans and rolls will be very hot. Let cool for 5 to 10 minutes.

MAKE THE ICING

In a medium bowl, combine the confectioner's sugar, orange juice, butter, and orange zest. Beat until smooth and spreadable. Spread or drizzle the icing over the warm rolls. Serve warm.

almond sweet rolls

These tantalizing rolls are perfect to serve on holidays or special occasions, or any day you want to be special.

MAKES 18 ROLLS

Unsalted butter, for the pans

1 recipe Sweet Roll Dough (see p. 157)

Gluten-Free All-Purpose Flour (see p. 11), for rolling

For the Filling

3 tablespoons unsalted butter, softened

¼ cup granulated sugar

2 large egg whites

One 8-ounce package almond paste, crumbled

⅛ teaspoon almond extract

⅔ cup finely chopped sliced almonds

For the Icing

1 cup confectioners' sugar

1 tablespoon half-and-half or whole milk

1½ teaspoons unsalted butter, melted

⅛ teaspoon almond extract

¼ cup coarsely chopped sliced almonds

Prepare the Sweet Roll Dough as directed on p. 157. Grease two 8-inch round baking pans with unsalted butter. Set aside.

MAKE THE FILLING

1. In the bowl of a stand mixer, using an electric mixer on medium speed, cream the butter and granulated sugar until light and fluffy.

2. Add the egg whites, one at a time, beating well after each addition. Scrape down the sides of the bowl.

3. Add the crumbled almond paste, 1 tablespoon at a time, beating until smooth after each addition. Stir in the almond extract. Set aside.

MAKE THE ROLLS

1. On a board or other flat surface lightly dusted with gluten-free all-purpose flour, roll the risen Sweet Roll Dough into a 12 x 20-inch rectangle.

2. Spoon the almond filling over the dough and spread evenly, leaving a ½-inch border along the long edges of the dough. Sprinkle the almonds over the top of the filling. Starting with one of the long sides, roll up the dough jellyroll style. Pinch the seam together to seal.

3. Cut the roll into 18 even slices, and arrange 9 slices in each prepared pan. Cover the pans with plastic wrap and let rise in a warm place until the rolls are nearly doubled in size, about 45 minutes. Meanwhile, heat the oven to 350°F.

4. Bake the rolls until they're lightly golden brown and a wooden pick inserted in the dough in the center of the pan comes out clean, 20 to 25 minutes (be sure to insert the pick into the dough, not the filling). Immediately invert the pans onto heatproof serving plates and remove the pans (the pans and rolls will be hot). Let cool for 10 minutes.

MAKE THE ICING

In a medium bowl, combine the confectioners' sugar, half-and-half, butter, and almond extract. Beat until smooth and spreadable. Spread or drizzle the icing over the rolls, then sprinkle the chopped almonds over the top. Serve warm.

french rolls

Light and fluffy muffin-shaped French rolls make a great accompaniment for any meal. Serve them fresh and hot from the oven for the best flavor and texture.

MAKES 12 ROLLS

Unsalted butter, for the pan

2 cups Gluten-Free All-Purpose Flour (see p. 11)

2 tablespoons dry milk powder

2½ teaspoons instant (quick-rising) active dry yeast

1 teaspoon xanthan gum

1 cup whole milk

½ teaspoon table salt

2 large egg whites

1. Grease a 12-cup muffin pan with unsalted butter.

2. In the bowl of a stand mixer, using a wire whisk, combine 1 cup of the flour, the milk powder, yeast, and xanthan gum until well blended. Set aside.

3. In a small saucepan, combine the milk and salt. Heat over medium-low heat, stirring constantly, just until the butter is melted and the mixture reads between 120°F and 130°F on an instant-read thermometer. Add the milk mixture to the flour mixture, then add the egg whites.

4. Using an electric stand mixer fitted with the flat paddle beater, beat the mixture on the lowest speed for 30 seconds. Scrape down the sides and bottom of the bowl. Using the next highest speed, beat the mixture for 2 minutes. Scrape down the sides of the bowl. Gradually add the remaining 1 cup of flour and continue to beat until the flour is incorporated. Beat for an additional 2 minutes. The dough will be sticky.

5. Spoon the dough into the prepared pan. Let the rolls rise in a warm place until the crowns of the rolls rise just above the top of the pan, 30 to 40 minutes. Meanwhile, heat the oven to 375°F.

6. Bake the rolls until they are golden brown and a wooden pick inserted in the center comes out clean, 15 to 17 minutes. Remove the pan from the oven and immediately remove the rolls from the pan. Transfer to a wire rack.

frittatas
and
omelets

Eggs are versatile in all kinds of cooking, but they can be your best friend if you eat gluten-free. They are the foundation for delicious frittatas and omelets, creating a meal for any time of day. I've included here some of my favorite egg recipes for frittatas and oven omelets, but variations—and other combinations—abound since all kinds of proteins, vegetables, and fruits pair nicely with eggs and work well in both frittatas and omelets.

A frittata is essentially an Italian version of an omelet with the filling ingredients mixed into the eggs instead of placed in the middle of the folded omelet. Think of frittatas as quiches without a crust. They make excellent entrées for any meal and can also be cut into small pieces for party appetizers—wedges, squares, and diamonds are attractive options. Frittatas can be served hot or at room temperature.

Oven omelets are fast and easy to assemble. Once the ingredients are in the pan, you pop it into the oven and then let the mixture bake into a puffy omelet. Omelets baked in the oven have a lighter, fluffier texture than classic omelets cooked on the stovetop. They also give you the freedom to get the rest of the meal ready while your main dish bakes. Oven omelets are great for any meal. Some are hearty enough on their own or can be served alongside other breakfast foods when hosting a brunch; a side salad or fresh fruit pairs nicely for lunch or dinner.

Baking Dishes and Ovenproof Pans

BAKING DISHES

Baking dishes are usually made of glass, ceramic, or porcelain and come in different shapes, such as square, rectangular, round, and oval. The baked frittata recipes in this chapter call for the most common size, a 9-inch square pan. These recipes will also fit in a 10-inch round baking dish.

OVENPROOF PANS

Stainless-steel frying pans, omelet pans, and cast-iron skillets all work well for preparing frittatas. Stainless-steel frying pans and omelet pans are good choices for making oven omelets, but a cast-iron skillet will also work. You can even use a small paella pan for baking oven omelets. Whichever you choose, make sure that all parts of the skillet or pan, including the handle, are ovenproof.

Mixing Frittatas and Omelets

Be careful not to overmix the eggs when you whisk the egg mixture and then add in the other ingredients. You want to whisk the eggs just until the yolks and whites are thoroughly combined. A wire whisk is a great tool for lightly beating eggs. Using a light hand will produce more tender, fluffier frittatas and oven omelets. Overbeating the eggs can make them tough and also can cause the eggs to release liquid while cooking, known as weeping.

Frittatas cook best when the vegetables and other filling ingredients are cooked or partially cooked before being added to the egg mixture. Precooking the vegetables also ensures their texture in the frittata is just right. Adding sour cream to the egg mixture makes baked frittatas creamier and fluffier. If you prefer a denser frittata, you can omit the sour cream.

Cooking and Baking Frittatas and Oven Omelets

The key to successful frittatas and oven omelets is to not overcook the eggs. When eggs are cooked, the proteins coagulate and clot, causing the eggs to thicken. If eggs are overcooked, the protein network contracts and forces out some of the liquid from the egg. If you've ever had weepy scrambled eggs sitting in a puddle of liquid, you've seen this overcooking process in action.

There are two basic methods for cooking frittatas. The classic method is to cook the frittata on the stovetop in a frying pan just until set and then finish it off under the broiler to brown the top. The second method is to pour all of the ingredients into a baking dish, pop it into the oven, and let the frittata bake until done. I have included recipes for both types so you can try them out and decide which you like best.

Many recipes for frittatas cooked on top of the stove call for cooking the vegetables and meats in the frying pan and then adding the egg mixture directly to the pan. I have found that frittatas tend to stick to the bottom and sides of the pan with this method. Instead, I add the filling ingredients to the bowl containing the egg mixture, wipe the pan clean, add a good amount of butter to the pan, and then pour in the entire frittata mixture. This significantly reduces the chances of the frittata sticking to the pan and produces a tasty, nicely browned frittata.

Be sure to cook stovetop frittatas over low heat without stirring, and cover the frying pan while the frittata cooks. This will keep the heat in the pan and let the egg mixture cook slowly. When you cook your first couple of stovetop frittatas, keep an eye on the egg mixture to figure out exactly how long it should cook. You want the center of the frittata to set without overcooking the outer edges. This slow cooking process will take about 10 minutes over low heat.

For oven omelets, the frying pan is heated on the stovetop until hot and the butter melts. Half of the egg mixture is added to the pan, the cheese is sprinkled over top, and then the remaining egg mixture is added. The pan is then carefully transferred to the oven so the omelet can bake up light and fluffy.

Quick Tips
FRITTATAS AND OMELETS

- Do not use cracked or chipped eggs as they may be contaminated with salmonella bacteria.

- Lightly beat the eggs with a whisk just until the yolks and whites are thoroughly combined.

- Cast-iron skillets are great for cooking stovetop frittatas. They hold heat well and produce nicely browned sides.

- Be sure you cook stovetop frittatas on low heat for the specified time in the recipe. Eggs can overcook quickly, becoming very firm, tough, and dry.

- Position the oven rack in the center of the oven for baking omelets and frittatas.

- Position the oven rack about 5 inches from the broiler element for finishing stovetop frittatas to give the top a nice golden brown color.

- Use potholders or oven mitts to remove the pans from the oven; the handles will be very hot!

- Cut baked frittatas into small square or diamond shapes to serve as party appetizers.

- Buy a block of cheese and grate it just before using in your recipe. Freshly grated cheese has more flavor than packaged grated cheese.

cheese frittata

This classic frittata can be made with any combination of cheeses. Any cheese that will grate or crumble is a good choice to use in a frittata. Soft cheeses like mascarpone, Brie, and cream cheese can add too much moisture and affect the way the frittata cooks. To make a cheese and herb frittata, add 1 tablespoon of mixed minced fresh herbs along with the parsley.

SERVES 2 TO 4

6 large eggs

¼ cup whole milk or half-and-half

1 tablespoon chopped fresh
   flat-leaf parsley

⅛ teaspoon table salt

⅛ teaspoon freshly ground black pepper

⅓ cup grated Cheddar cheese

⅓ cup grated Monterey Jack cheese

¼ cup grated Parmesan cheese

2 tablespoons unsalted butter

1. Position an oven rack about 5 inches from the broiler element and heat the broiler.

2. In a large bowl, using a wire whisk, lightly beat the eggs just until the yolks and whites are fully combined. Add the milk and whisk until well combined. Stir in the parsley, salt, and pepper. Add the Cheddar and Jack cheeses, plus 2 tablespoons of the Parmesan to the egg mixture and stir gently until combined.

3. In a 10-inch ovenproof frying pan or omelet pan, melt the butter over medium heat. Add the egg mixture to the pan; do not stir. Reduce the heat to low, cover, and cook until the edges are golden brown and the egg mixture is just set in the center but not dry, about 10 minutes. Uncover and remove the pan from the heat. Sprinkle the remaining Parmesan over the top.

4. Place the pan under the broiler and broil until the top is golden brown, about 2 minutes. Remove the pan from the oven. Serve hot.

VARIATIONS

This cheese frittata is very versatile. You can create flavorful variations by using different cheeses and herbs. Here are some ideas to spark your creativity.

CHEESE COMBINATIONS	HERBS
Cheddar and Monterey Jack	Thyme
Fontina and Gruyère	Rosemary
Mozzarella and Parmesan	Sage
Feta and Monterey Jack	Tarragon
Provolone and Gruyère	Dill
Swiss and Cheddar	Parsley
Gorgonzola, Stilton, or Blue and	Basil
Monterey Jack	Chervil
Gruyère and Parmesan	
Asiago and Cheddar	

zucchini frittata

This easy vegetable frittata can be made with all zucchini or part zucchini and part yellow squash. I use young zucchini and yellow squash that are about 1 inch in diameter. These smaller squash contain less moisture than larger zucchini, hold their shape better, and make a pretty frittata.

SERVES 4 TO 6

Nonstick cooking spray, for the pan

1 tablespoon unsalted butter

1½ teaspoons minced garlic

1½ cups thinly sliced small zucchini (2 to 3)

8 large eggs

⅓ cup sour cream

¼ cup whole milk or half-and-half

⅛ teaspoon table salt

⅛ teaspoon freshly ground black pepper

⅔ cup grated Gruyère cheese

⅓ cup grated Parmesan cheese

1. Heat the oven to 350°F. Spray a 9-inch square or 10-inch round baking dish with nonstick cooking spray.

2. In a large frying pan, over medium heat, melt the butter. Add the garlic and sauté until tender, about 2 minutes. Add the zucchini to the pan, stir to combine, and cook for 1 minute. Remove the pan from the heat and set aside.

3. In a large bowl, using a wire whisk, lightly beat the eggs just until the yolks and whites are fully combined. Add the sour cream and whisk until smooth and well combined. Gradually whisk in the milk. Stir in the salt and pepper. Add the zucchini mixture and the Gruyère and Parmesan cheeses to the egg mixture and stir gently until combined. Pour into the prepared baking dish.

4. Bake for 25 to 30 minutes, or until the edges are puffed up and golden brown and the center is set. Remove the pan from the oven and cool on a wire rack for 5 minutes before cutting and serving.

mushroom frittata

I like to use small portabella mushrooms, also called Italian brown mushrooms or baby bellas, for this recipe because they add a lot of flavor. Regular white button mushrooms will also work well in this dish. Substitute grated Swiss or Cheddar for the feta, if you prefer.

SERVES 4 TO 6

Nonstick cooking spray, for the pan
1 tablespoon unsalted butter
1½ cups sliced mushrooms
¼ cup finely chopped onions
1½ teaspoons minced garlic
8 large eggs
⅓ cup sour cream
¼ cup whole milk or half-and-half
⅛ teaspoon table salt
⅛ teaspoon freshly ground black pepper
½ cup crumbled feta cheese
½ cup grated Monterey Jack cheese

1. Heat the oven to 350°F. Spray a 9-inch square or 10-inch round baking dish with nonstick cooking spray.

2. In a large frying pan, over medium heat, melt the butter. Add the mushrooms, onions, and garlic and sauté until the mushrooms are tender and the onions are translucent, about 5 minutes. Remove the pan from the heat and set aside.

3. In a large bowl, using a wire whisk, lightly beat the eggs just until the yolks and whites are fully combined. Add the sour cream and whisk until smooth and well combined. Gradually whisk in the milk. Stir in the salt and pepper. Add the mushroom mixture and feta and Jack cheeses to the egg mixture and stir gently until combined. Pour into the prepared baking dish.

4. Bake for 25 to 30 minutes, or until the edges are puffed up and golden brown and the center is set. Remove the pan from the oven and cool on a wire rack for 5 minutes before cutting and serving.

chicken frittata

This delicious frittata is a great way to use up leftover roast chicken. Don't use grilled chicken, though; it is too crispy for the texture of the eggs.

SERVES 4 TO 6

Nonstick cooking spray, for the pan

1 tablespoon unsalted butter

2 tablespoons minced shallots or onions

2 teaspoons minced garlic

1½ cups shredded or cubed cooked chicken, at room temperature

8 large eggs

⅓ cup sour cream

¼ cup whole milk or half-and-half

1 tablespoon finely chopped fresh flat-leaf parsley

1½ teaspoons finely chopped fresh sage or oregano

⅛ teaspoon table salt

⅛ teaspoon freshly ground black pepper

½ cup grated Cheddar cheese

½ cup grated Monterey Jack cheese

1. Heat the oven to 350°F. Spray a 9-inch square or 10-inch round baking dish with nonstick cooking spray.

2. In a large frying pan, over medium heat, melt the butter. Add the shallots and garlic and sauté until tender, about 3 minutes. Add the chicken to the pan and stir to combine (the chicken will absorb the flavors in the pan). Remove the pan from the heat and set aside.

3. In a large bowl, using a wire whisk, lightly beat the eggs just until the yolks and whites are fully combined. Add the sour cream and whisk until smooth and well combined. Gradually whisk in the milk. Stir in the parsley, sage, salt, and pepper. Add the chicken mixture and Cheddar and Jack cheeses to the egg mixture and stir gently until combined. Pour into the prepared baking dish.

4. Bake for 25 to 30 minutes, or until the edges are puffed up and golden brown and the center is set. Remove the pan from the oven and cool on a wire rack for 5 minutes before cutting and serving.

VARIATION

day after thanksgiving frittata: Substitute shredded cooked turkey for the chicken. Add about ½ cup diced cooked sweet potatoes. Serve with cranberry sauce alongside.

southwest frittata

Serve this dish topped with a dollop of sour cream and a spoonful of fresh salsa. Eliminate the chicken if you'd like to make this a vegetarian entrée.

SERVES 2 TO 4

3 tablespoons unsalted butter

1 small red or green bell pepper, seeded and chopped

¼ cup finely chopped onions

1 tablespoon minced seeded jalapeño peppers

¾ cup shredded or cubed cooked chicken, at room temperature

6 large eggs

¼ cup whole milk or half-and-half

2 teaspoons finely chopped fresh cilantro or flat-leaf parsley

2 teaspoons finely chopped fresh oregano

⅛ teaspoon table salt

⅛ teaspoon freshly ground black pepper

⅔ cup grated Monterey Jack cheese

2 tablespoons grated Parmesan cheese

1. Position an oven rack about 5 inches from the broiler element and heat the broiler.

2. In a 10-inch ovenproof frying pan or omelet pan, over medium heat, melt 1 tablespoon of butter. Add the bell peppers, onions, and jalapeños and sauté until tender, 2 to 3 minutes. Add the chicken to the pan and stir to combine. Remove the pan from the heat and set aside.

3. In a large bowl, using a wire whisk, lightly beat the eggs just until the yolks and whites are fully combined. Add the milk and whisk until well combined. Stir in the cilantro, oregano, salt, and pepper. Add the chicken mixture and the Jack cheese to the egg mixture and stir gently until combined.

4. Wipe the frying pan clean. Add the remaining 2 tablespoons butter and melt over medium heat. Add the egg mixture to the pan. Reduce the heat to low, cover, and cook until the edges are golden brown and the egg mixture is just set in the center but not dry, about 10 minutes. Uncover and remove the pan from the heat. Sprinkle the Parmesan cheese over the top.

5. Place the pan under the broiler and broil until the top is golden brown, about 2 minutes. Remove the pan from the oven. Serve hot.

Use a mix of brightly colored peppers to give the frittata an eye-catching appearance.

italian sausage frittata

This frittata is an excellent entrée for breakfast or dinner. I like to use fragrant, spicy Italian sausage, but you can use any flavor of gluten-free sausage to make this recipe. Serve homemade marinara sauce and grated Parmesan at the table if you'd like.

SERVES 2 TO 4

2 tablespoons plus 1 teaspoon
    unsalted butter

¼ cup finely chopped onions

12 ounces bulk gluten-free Italian
    sausage

6 large eggs

¼ cup whole milk or half-and-half

1 tablespoon chopped fresh
    flat-leaf parsley

⅛ teaspoon table salt

⅛ teaspoon freshly ground black pepper

½ cup grated Cheddar cheese

½ cup grated Monterey Jack cheese

1. Position an oven rack about 5 inches from the broiler element and heat the broiler.

2. In a 10-inch ovenproof frying pan, or omelet pan over medium heat, melt 1 teaspoon of butter. Add the onions and sauté until tender, about 3 minutes. Transfer to a small bowl and set aside.

3. Increase the heat to medium high. Add the sausage to the pan, breaking it up into small pieces. Cook until lightly browned and cooked all the way through, 4 to 5 minutes. Drain the sausage well on a paper-towel-lined plate.

4. In a large bowl, using a wire whisk, lightly beat the eggs just until the yolks and whites are fully combined. Add the milk and whisk until well combined. Stir in the parsley, salt, and pepper. Add the onions and sausage, the Cheddar cheese, and ⅓ cup of the Jack cheese to the egg mixture and stir gently until combined.

5. Wipe the frying pan clean. Add the remaining 2 tablespoons of butter and melt over medium heat. Add the egg mixture to the pan. Reduce the heat to low, cover, and cook until the edges are golden brown and the egg mixture is just set in the center but not dry, about 10 minutes. Uncover and remove the pan from the heat. Sprinkle the remaining Jack cheese over the top.

6. Place the pan under the broiler and broil until the top is golden brown, about 2 minutes. Remove the pan from the oven. Serve hot.

Many health-food stores and some specialty-food stores and meat markets carry gluten-free sausage.

broccoli cheddar frittata

I love the combination of broccoli and Cheddar, but you can also use Monterey Jack, Swiss, or Gruyère. Instead of sautéing the broccoli, roast it in the oven with a little olive oil and garlic to bring out its nutty flavor.

SERVES 4 TO 6

Nonstick cooking spray, for the pan
1 tablespoon unsalted butter
1⅓ cups small fresh broccoli florets
1 teaspoon minced garlic
8 large eggs
⅓ cup sour cream
¼ cup whole milk or half-and-half
⅛ teaspoon table salt
⅛ teaspoon freshly ground black pepper
1¼ cups grated Cheddar cheese

1. Heat the oven to 350°F. Spray a 9-inch square or 10-inch round baking dish with nonstick cooking spray. Set aside.

2. In a large frying pan, over medium heat, melt the butter. Add the broccoli florets and garlic and sauté until the broccoli starts to soften, 4 to 5 minutes. Remove the pan from the heat and set aside.

3. In a large bowl, using a wire whisk, lightly beat the eggs just until the yolks and whites are fully combined. Add the sour cream and whisk until smooth and well combined. Gradually whisk in the milk. Stir in the salt and pepper. Add the broccoli mixture and Cheddar cheese to the egg mixture and stir gently until combined. Pour into the prepared baking dish.

4. Bake for 25 to 30 minutes, or until the edges are puffed up and golden brown and the center is set. Remove the pan from the oven and cool on a wire rack for 5 minutes before cutting and serving.

VARIATION

cauliflower frittata: **Substitute small fresh cauliflower florets for the broccoli florets.**

cheese omelet

You probably have most of the ingredients for this omelet in your pantry and fridge, making this a good last-minute supper or busy-morning meal. Substitute any cheese for the Gruyère and add fresh parsley if you don't have chives.

SERVES 2 TO 4

5 large eggs
⅓ cup whole milk
1 tablespoon minced fresh chives
Pinch of table salt
1 tablespoon unsalted butter
¾ cup Gruyère cheese

1. Heat the oven to 375°F.

2. In a medium bowl, using a wire whisk, lightly beat the eggs just until the yolks and whites are fully combined. Gradually whisk in the milk. Stir in the chives and salt. Set aside.

3. In an 8-inch ovenproof frying pan or omelet pan, over medium-low heat, melt the butter. As the butter melts, tilt the pan to evenly coat the bottom and sides. Spoon half of the egg mixture into the pan. Evenly sprinkle the Gruyère cheese over top of the egg mixture. Gently spoon on the remaining egg mixture. Transfer the pan to the hot oven.

4. Bake until the omelet is puffed up and the eggs are set in the center, 18 to 22 minutes. Remove the pan from the oven and invert the omelet onto a serving plate. Serve immediately.

spinach omelet

If you like spanakopita, the Greek pastry filled with spinach, feta, and onions, then you're going to love this omelet. Don't substitute frozen or canned spinach for the fresh— any leftover moisture, even after draining, will cause the omelet to be runny and not set up properly.

SERVES 2 TO 4

5 large eggs

⅓ cup whole milk

1¼ cups small or coarsely chopped large fresh spinach leaves

1 tablespoon unsalted butter

⅔ cup crumbled feta cheese

1. Heat the oven to 375°F.

2. In a medium bowl, using a wire whisk, lightly beat the eggs just until the yolks and whites are fully combined. Gradually whisk in the milk. Add the spinach and stir until well distributed. Set aside.

3. In an 8-inch ovenproof frying pan or omelet pan, over medium-low heat, melt the butter. As the butter melts, tilt the pan to evenly coat the bottom and sides. Spoon half of the egg mixture into the pan. Evenly sprinkle the feta over top of the egg mixture. Gently spoon on the remaining egg mixture. Transfer the pan to the hot oven.

4. Bake until the omelet is puffed up and the eggs are set in the center, 18 to 22 minutes. Remove the pan from the oven and invert the omelet onto a serving plate. Serve immediately.

Not a feta cheese fan? You can use Swiss, Monterey Jack, Cheddar, or even goat cheese in place of the feta.

mushroom herb omelet

I make this delicious mushroom omelet with one of my favorite herb blends—parsley, thyme, and tarragon. Feel free to use any combination of herbs that you like with mushrooms. A combination of button and Italian brown mushrooms makes a tasty omelet, or you can use all of one kind. If you like lots of mushrooms, sauté up some more to serve alongside the omelet.

SERVES 2 TO 4

2 tablespoons unsalted butter

1 cup thinly sliced mushrooms

2 tablespoons minced red onions

5 large eggs

⅓ cup whole milk

1½ teaspoons finely chopped fresh
   flat-leaf parsley

¾ teaspoon finely chopped fresh
   thyme leaves

¾ teaspoon finely chopped fresh tarragon

Pinch of table salt

⅔ cup Swiss cheese

1. Heat the oven to 375°F.

2. In a medium frying pan, over medium heat, melt 1 tablespoon of butter. Add the mushrooms and red onions and sauté until the mushrooms are tender and the onions are translucent, 3 to 4 minutes. Set aside.

3. In a medium bowl, using a wire whisk, lightly beat the eggs just until the yolks and whites are fully combined. Gradually whisk in the milk. Stir in the parsley, thyme, tarragon, and salt. Add the mushroom mixture and stir until well distributed. Set aside.

4. In an 8-inch ovenproof frying pan or omelet pan, over medium-low heat, melt the remaining 1 tablespoon butter. As the butter melts, tilt the pan to evenly coat the bottom and sides. Spoon half of the egg mixture into the pan. Evenly sprinkle the Swiss cheese over top of the egg mixture. Gently spoon on the remaining egg mixture. Transfer the pan to the hot oven.

5. Bake until the omelet is puffed up and the eggs are set in the center, 18 to 22 minutes. Remove the pan from the oven and invert the omelet onto a serving plate. Serve immediately.

CHAPTER NINE

quiches

A quiche is a pie made with a pastry crust and filled with an egg and cheese custard. Meat and vegetables can be added to a quiche base to create a variety of fillings. The filling flavor can be adapted easily by changing the ingredients and is limited only by your imagination. Quiches make satisfying entrees to serve for any meal, from morning to night.

I recommend using whole milk in the egg custard base that binds the quiche together. You can make a richer custard by using half-and-half or even light cream in place of all or part of the milk. To set properly, the custard needs to contain a moderate level of milk fat. Lowfat and nonfat milks contain less milk fat and have a higher water content than whole milk. This increased water content can prevent the custard from setting up and also can cause the quiche to weep after baking.

About Pie Pans

Deep-dish pie pans are the best choice for making quiches. They allow plenty of room for the quiche filling to puff up as it bakes without overflowing the dish. The pan can be glass, ceramic, or shiny metal; however, I recommend glass pans for baking gluten-free crusts. Glass pans conduct heat better and this will help the crust bake more thoroughly and produce a crispier bottom crust.

Making Quiche Crusts

The key to making a great pastry crust is to cut the butter and shortening into the flour mixture without melting the fat. Using cold butter and shortening along with ice water when mixing the crust helps make a flakier crust. The cold fats surround and separate the flour particles as you work the fat into the dough. Also, when the cold fat particles melt as the quiche bakes, they release

steam and create small air pockets. These air pockets set during baking and help create a flaky texture.

I like to use a pastry blender to cut the fat into the flour. It is a simple hand-held tool made of a set of U-shape wires attached to a handle that fits snugly into the palm of your hand. If you don't have a pastry blender, you can use two knives drawn together in a scissorlike motion or a large sturdy fork to cut the fat into the flour mixture. I don't like to use a food processor to make pastry because it's easy to overwork the dough mixture, which can result in a dense, heavy crust.

The fat should be cut into the flour until the mixture resembles coarse crumbs. Size matters: If the fat pieces are too large, they could form small holes in the bottom or sides of the crust as they melt. These holes will allow the filling to escape, which can make the crust soggy and cause the quiche to stick to the pan.

The amount of water needed to hold the crust together can vary from one day to the next and from kitchen to kitchen. Depending on the weather, humidity, and the amount of moisture in the flour, you may need to increase or decrease the amount of water called for in the recipe. Always add water a tablespoon at a time so that you don't overmoisten the dough.

The dough will be easier to handle if you let it chill in the refrigerator for a bit before rolling it out. Roughly shape the prepared dough into a flat disk, wrap tightly in plastic wrap, and chill for 20 minutes. Chilling the crust will firm up the butter and shortening, which will produce a more tender, flakier crust. You should also chill the crust shell before filling and baking. This will allow the flour to evenly absorb the water and help the crust hold its shape as it bakes.

Because gluten is what gives baked goods their structure, gluten-free pie crusts should be handled with care. While overhandling the dough

won't make the crust tough, because you won't be developing the gluten, it can make the dough dense, which will yield a heavy crust. Always use a light touch when handling any pastry dough.

ROLLING THE CRUST

Gluten-free quiche crusts are fragile and tend to tear when transferred from a pastry board to the pie pan. To make the process easier and reduce the amount of tearing and patching, roll the dough out between two sheets of waxed paper placed on a flat surface, such as a countertop.

If you have trouble with the dough sticking to the waxed paper, try lightly dusting the bottom piece of waxed paper with gluten-free flour. Place the chilled dough disk on top and lightly dust it with flour. Cover with the second sheet of waxed paper and roll out the dough. Halfway through the rolling, lift and reposition the waxed paper to prevent sticking. You can add a little more flour if needed, but be careful not to add too much as it will make the crust drier and more prone to tearing.

To transfer the dough to the pie pan, carefully remove the top sheet of waxed paper. Center the pie pan upside down on top of the dough. Gently slide one hand under the bottom sheet of waxed paper. Place your other hand on top of the pie pan. In one quick motion, invert the pan and dough. Loosely settle the dough into the pan and slowly remove the waxed paper. Gently fit the dough into the pan, patching any tears.

I like to trim the dough ½ inch beyond the edge of the pan and then fold the cut edge under the dough on the rim of the pan to create a raised edge. The edge can then be finished in a decorative manner, such as crimping it between your thumb and fingers. This raised edge is not only pretty, but it also will keep the filling from overflowing the pan as the quiche bakes.

BAKING THE QUICHE

Position the oven rack in the lower third of the oven before preheating the oven. This will help the bottom crust cook through and prevent it from underbaking and becoming soggy. Nothing ruins a quiche more than an underdone crust. If you have trouble with your quiche crusts being underbaked, try partially prebaking the crust before adding the filling (for more on this see the sidebar on p. 186). If the crust overbakes because your oven has a hot spot in the bottom of the oven, then place a piece of foil on the bottom rack below the pie pan or position the upper rack in the middle of the oven.

The quiche will be done when the top is golden brown, the filling is set, and a knife blade or wooden pick inserted in the center comes out clean. If the crust starts to brown too much before the quiche is done, cover the crust edge with a thin strip of foil for the remainder of the baking time.

HOW TO PREBAKE A QUICHE CRUST

1. After fitting the crust into the pan, chill the crust in the refrigerator for 30 minutes.

2. Heat the oven to 350°F.

3. Prick the bottom of the crust with a fork in several places. Line the crust with a piece of foil and add a layer of ceramic pie weights, dried beans, or rice to the pan.

4. Bake the crust for 10 minutes. Remove the pan from the oven and carefully remove the foil and weights. Return the crust to the oven for 5 minutes. Remove the pan from the oven and cool on a wire rack for 10 to 15 minutes while you prepare the filling. Add the filling to the warm crust and bake as instructed in the recipe.

Quick Tips
QUICHES

- Adding an egg to the dough helps bind a gluten-free crust together, gives it more flavor, and makes it easier to handle.

- Use ice water (not just cold tap water) in the pastry dough to help keep the butter cold, which yields a tender quiche crust.

- Grease the pie pan with unsalted butter to make it easier to fit the dough into the pan and also help the bottom of the crust bake up crispier.

- Glass pie pans will produce a crispier crust than metal pie pans.

- Roll the pastry crust from the center of the dough toward the outer edges, applying even pressure and maintaining a uniform thickness.

- If you have trouble rolling out the dough or keeping it from tearing when transferring it to the pan, you can dump the mixture into the pan and gently press the crust into the bottom and up the sides of the pan instead of rolling.

- If the crust tears while transferring it to the pie pan, moisten both edges of the tear with water and press them back together to seal.

- Position the rack in the lower third of the oven to help prevent underdone crusts.

- If the edges of the crust start to brown too much, cover them with a strip of foil.

- You can change the type of cheese used in most recipes to suit your taste. See the recipes for suggestions.

- Feel free to experiment with herbs and seasonings in the fillings.

- You can give a little heat to a quiche by adding a few dashes of hot sauce to the egg custard.

quiche crust

This recipe makes a wonderful pastry crust that can be used with any quiche or pie recipe. When making a gluten-free crust, I like to use a combination of butter and shortening because it gives the crust a rich flavor and a nice flaky texture, but you may use all butter, if you prefer. The touch of baking powder in the dough also helps create a light, tender crust.

MAKES ONE 9-INCH QUICHE CRUST

2 cups Gluten-Free All-Purpose Flour (see p. 11)

½ teaspoon table salt

½ teaspoon xanthan gum

¼ teaspoon baking powder

⅓ cup (5⅓ tablespoons) cold unsalted butter, cut into pieces; more for the pan

⅓ cup cold vegetable shortening, cut into pieces

1 large egg

4 to 5 tablespoons ice water

VARIATIONS

cheese quiche crust: For a savory crust with a light, tangy cheese flavor, stir ⅓ cup of freshly grated Parmesan cheese into the flour mixture before cutting in the butter and shortening. You may need to add a little extra water to the crust. This crust works well with any of the quiche recipes in this chapter.

herb quiche crust: For a savory crust, stir 1½ teaspoons of very finely minced fresh herbs into the flour mixture before cutting in the butter and shortening. Fresh thyme, rosemary, parsley, or a combination of herbs are all good choices.

1. Grease a 9-inch pie pan with unsalted butter.

2. In a large bowl, whisk together the flour, salt, xanthan gum, and baking powder until well combined. Using a pastry blender, two knives, or a fork, cut in the butter and shortening until the mixture resembles coarse crumbs.

3. In a small bowl, whisk together the egg and 1 tablespoon of the water until well blended. Sprinkle over the flour mixture and toss with a fork until evenly combined. Add the remaining water, 1 tablespoon at a time, stirring until the mixture pulls away from the sides of the bowl and starts to come together into a ball. Shape the dough into a flat disk. Tightly wrap in plastic wrap and chill for 20 minutes.

4. Unwrap the dough and center it on a piece of waxed paper. Place another piece of waxed paper on top. Using a rolling pin, start in the center of the dough and roll toward the outer edges. Roll out the dough to a uniform ⅛-inch thickness. Remove the top piece of waxed paper. Slide one hand under the bottom piece of waxed paper and center the pie pan over the top of the dough. In one motion, quickly invert the pan and dough. Carefully remove the top piece of waxed paper.

5. Gently fit the dough into the pan, patching any tears. Trim the dough ½ inch larger than the pan rim. Fold the edge of the dough under to create a raised edge and crimp in a decorative pattern.

6. Chill the crust for 30 minutes before using. Fill and bake as directed in the quiche recipe.

almond quiche crust

Almond flour, which can be found in many specialty markets and health-food stores, creates a tender crust that adds a nutty flavor to savory quiches. This crust does not hold together well when rolled out and transferred to the pie pan, so simply press the dough mixture into the pan.

MAKES ONE 9-INCH QUICHE CRUST

1½ cups almond flour

¼ teaspoon table salt

½ teaspoon xanthan gum

⅛ teaspoon baking powder

⅓ cup (5⅓ tablespoons) unsalted butter, melted, or vegetable oil; more butter for the pan

3 to 4 tablespoons ice water

1. Grease a 9-inch pie pan with unsalted butter.

2. In a large bowl, whisk together the almond flour, salt, xanthan gum, and baking powder until well combined. Drizzle the melted butter over the flour mixture. Using a fork, toss until the butter is evenly distributed and the mixture resembles coarse crumbs. Gradually add the water, 1 tablespoon at a time, stirring until the mixture pulls away from the sides of the bowl and starts to come together into a ball.

3. Transfer the dough to the prepared pie pan. Form the quiche crust by gently pressing the dough evenly across the bottom, up the sides, and onto the rim of the pan. The dough should be of uniform thickness on the bottom and sides of the crust.

4. Chill the crust for 30 minutes before using. Fill and bake as directed in the quiche recipe.

quiche lorraine

Originally created in the Alsace-Lorraine region of France, Quiche Lorraine is the classic recipe most people think of when quiche comes to mind. This recipe is a variation of the original.

SERVES 6

1 chilled, unbaked, 9-inch Quiche Crust (see p. 187) or Almond Quiche Crust (see the facing page)

4 large eggs

1 cup whole milk

1 tablespoon finely chopped fresh flat-leaf parsley

¼ teaspoon table salt

⅛ teaspoon ground black pepper

8 slices gluten-free bacon, cooked and crumbled

¼ cup thinly sliced scallions (white and light green parts)

1½ cups grated Gruyère cheese

1. Prepare the quiche crust of your choice.

2. Position the oven rack in the lower third of the oven and heat the oven to 350°F.

3. In a medium bowl, using a wire whisk, lightly beat the eggs. Gradually whisk in the milk until well combined. Stir in the parsley, salt, and pepper.

4. Layer the bacon and scallions in the bottom of the chilled quiche crust. Sprinkle the cheese over the top. Pour the egg mixture into the crust, filling nearly to the top.

5. Bake until the top of the crust is golden brown, the filling is set, and a knife inserted in the center comes out clean, 40 to 50 minutes. Place the pan on a wire rack and cool for 10 minutes before cutting. Serve warm.

VARIATION

ham and cheese quiche: Substitute 1 cup of ¼-inch-cubed gluten-free ham for the bacon. Use Cheddar cheese in place of the Gruyère.

asparagus quiche

Young, tender asparagus works best in this recipe and gives the quiche lots of flavor.

SERVES 6

1 chilled, unbaked, 9-inch Quiche Crust (see p. 187) or Almond Quiche Crust (see p. 188)

2 tablespoons unsalted butter

2 tablespoons finely chopped shallots or onions

1 tablespoon minced garlic

2 cups 1-inch-pieces fresh asparagus

4 large eggs

1 cup whole milk

1 tablespoon finely chopped fresh flat-leaf parsley

¼ teaspoon table salt

⅛ teaspoon ground black pepper

1 cup grated Gruyère cheese

¼ cup grated Parmesan cheese

1. Prepare the quiche crust of your choice.

2. Position the oven rack in the lower third of the oven and heat the oven to 350°F.

3. In a medium frying pan over medium heat, melt the butter. Stir in the shallots and garlic. Add the asparagus and sauté, stirring frequently, just until the asparagus is tender but still crisp, 3 to 5 minutes. Remove the pan from the heat and set aside.

4. In a medium bowl, using a wire whisk, lightly beat the eggs. Gradually whisk in the milk until well combined. Stir in the parsley, salt, and pepper.

5. Spread the asparagus mixture evenly into the bottom of the chilled quiche crust. Sprinkle the cheeses over the top. Pour the egg mixture into the crust, filling nearly to the top.

6. Bake until the top of the crust is golden brown, the filling is set, and a knife inserted in the center comes out clean, 40 to 50 minutes. Place the pan on a wire rack and cool for 10 minutes before cutting. Serve warm.

sausage and onion quiche

Use your favorite gluten-free sausage in this versatile recipe. Regular sausage, Italian sausage, or even a hot and spicy sausage, if you want to add some heat, all make a great quiche. Fresh sage blends nicely with sausage, but if you are using a sage sausage, other flavored sausage, or a hot sausage, use fresh parsley instead of the sage called for here.

SERVES 6

1 chilled, unbaked, 9-inch Quiche Crust (see p. 187) or Almond Quiche Crust (see p. 188)

Nonstick cooking spray

12 ounces bulk gluten-free sausage

⅔ cup chopped onions

4 large eggs

1 cup whole milk

1 tablespoon finely chopped fresh sage or flat-leaf parsley

¼ teaspoon table salt

⅛ teaspoon ground black pepper

1½ cups grated Swiss cheese

1. Prepare the quiche crust of your choice.

2. Position the oven rack in the lower third of the oven and heat the oven to 350°F.

3. Spray a large frying pan with nonstick cooking spray. Over medium heat, crumble the sausage into the pan and cook, stirring frequently, until the sausage is cooked through. Remove the sausage from the pan and drain well, reserving 1 tablespoon of fat in the pan. Add the onions to the pan and sauté until tender, 3 to 5 minutes. Drain the onions and set aside.

4. In a medium bowl, using a wire whisk, lightly beat the eggs. Gradually whisk in the milk until well combined. Stir in the sage, salt, and pepper.

5. Layer the cooked sausage and onions in the bottom of the chilled quiche crust. Sprinkle the cheese over the top. Pour the egg mixture into the crust, filling nearly to the top.

6. Bake until the top of the crust is golden brown, the filling is set, and a knife inserted in the center comes out clean, 40 to 50 minutes. Place the pan on a wire rack and cool for 10 minutes before cutting. Serve warm.

I like the flavor blend of sausage and Swiss cheese, but feel free to change the type of cheese, or use a combination of cheeses, if you are not a Swiss fan.

cheese and chive quiche

This recipe is an example of one where a few ingredients add up to a flavor-packed dish. I like an aged French blue cheese in this quiche, but feel free to use your favorite blue-veined cheese. Roquefort, American or Danish blue, and Stilton are all good choices.

SERVES 6

1 chilled, unbaked, 9-inch Quiche Crust (see p. 187) or Almond Quiche Crust (see p. 188)

4 large eggs

1 cup whole milk

¼ cup finely chopped fresh chives

¼ teaspoon table salt

⅛ teaspoon ground black pepper

1¾ cups grated Gruyère cheese

¾ cup crumbled blue cheese

1. Prepare the quiche crust of your choice.

2. Position the oven rack in the lower third of the oven and heat the oven to 350°F.

3. In a medium bowl, using a wire whisk, lightly beat the eggs. Gradually whisk in the milk until well combined. Stir in the chives, salt, and pepper.

4. Layer the Gruyère and blue cheeses in the bottom of the chilled quiche crust. Pour the egg mixture into the crust, filling nearly to the top.

5. Bake until the top of the crust is golden brown, the filling is set, and a knife inserted in the center comes out clean, 40 to 50 minutes. Place the pan on a wire rack and cool for 10 minutes before cutting. Serve warm.

tomato basil quiche

Ripe tomatoes and fresh basil give this savory quiche a Mediterranean flavor. Use a firm variety of tomato that does not contain a lot of juice, such as Roma, to prevent the quiche from being too watery.

SERVES 6

1 chilled, unbaked, 9-inch Quiche Crust (see p. 187) or Almond Quiche Crust (see p. 188)

4 large eggs

1 cup whole milk

¼ teaspoon table salt

⅛ teaspoon ground black pepper

2 cups diced, peeled, and seeded Roma tomatoes

1½ cups grated Gruyère cheese

3 tablespoons finely chopped fresh basil

1. Prepare the quiche crust of your choice.

2. Position the oven rack in the lower third of the oven and heat the oven to 350°F.

3. In a medium bowl, using a wire whisk, lightly beat the eggs. Gradually whisk in the milk until well combined. Stir in the salt and pepper.

4. Layer half of the tomatoes, half of the cheese, and half of the basil in the bottom of the chilled quiche crust. Top with another layer of tomatoes, cheese, and basil. Pour the egg mixture into the crust, filling nearly to the top.

5. Bake until the top of the crust is golden brown, the filling is set, and a knife inserted in the center comes out clean, 40 to 50 minutes. Place the pan on a wire rack and cool for 10 minutes before cutting. Serve warm.

Roma tomatoes are the best choice for use in this recipe. They are firmer and contain less juice than salad or slicing tomatoes, which can make the quiche watery and keep the custard from setting. Also avoid using very ripe tomatoes, which contain more juice.

For a dramatic presentation, use peeled sliced tomatoes instead of diced tomatoes.

broccoli quiche

Loaded with broccoli and Cheddar cheese, this delightful quiche makes a wonderful entrée for brunch or dinner. If you use very small florets, there's no need to cook them first. For larger florets, steam or boil the broccoli until crisp-tender, 3 to 4 minutes. You can also roast the broccoli in the oven to lightly caramelize and bring out its nutty flavor.

SERVES 6

1 chilled, unbaked, 9-inch Quiche Crust (see p. 187) or Almond Quiche Crust (see p. 188)

4 large eggs

1 cup whole milk

2 tablespoons finely chopped shallots or onions

1 tablespoon finely chopped fresh flat-leaf parsley

¼ teaspoon table salt

⅛ teaspoon ground black pepper

2 cups small broccoli florets

1½ cups grated Cheddar cheese

1. Prepare the quiche crust of your choice.

2. Position the oven rack in the lower third of the oven and heat the oven to 350°F.

3. In a medium bowl, using a wire whisk, lightly beat the eggs. Gradually whisk in the milk until well combined. Stir in the shallots, parsley, salt, and pepper.

4. Spread the broccoli florets in the bottom of the chilled quiche crust. Sprinkle the cheese over the top. Pour the egg mixture into the crust, filling nearly to the top.

5. Bake until the top of the crust is golden brown, the filling is set, and a knife inserted in the center comes out clean, 40 to 50 minutes. Place the pan on a wire rack and cool for 10 minutes before cutting. Serve warm.

VARIATION

cauliflower quiche: **Substitute small cauliflower florets for the broccoli. Steam or boil the cauliflower for a few minutes until it is partially cooked, rinse with cool water, and then drain well before adding it to the quiche crust.**

turkey mushroom quiche

This satisfying quiche is a good way to use up leftover turkey. Button mushrooms or small Italian brown mushrooms both are great with turkey, or try a combination of your favorite varieties. Add some cooked broccoli or green beans to make a one-dish meal. You can also use Swiss or Cheddar cheese instead of Gruyère, if you prefer.

SERVES 6

1 chilled, unbaked, 9-inch Quiche Crust
   (see p. 187) or Almond Quiche Crust
   (see p. 188)
1 tablespoon unsalted butter
1 cup thinly sliced mushrooms
2 tablespoons finely chopped shallots
   or onions
4 large eggs
1 cup whole milk
1 tablespoon finely chopped fresh
   flat-leaf parsley
¼ teaspoon table salt
⅛ teaspoon ground black pepper
1½ cups shredded or diced cooked turkey
1½ cups grated Gruyère cheese

1. Prepare the quiche crust of your choice.

2. Position the oven rack in the lower third of the oven and heat the oven to 350°F.

3. In a medium frying pan over medium heat, melt the butter. Add the mushrooms and shallots and sauté until tender, 3 to 5 minutes. Remove the pan from the heat and set aside.

4. In a medium bowl, using a wire whisk, lightly beat the eggs. Gradually whisk in the milk until well combined. Stir in the parsley, salt, and pepper.

5. Layer the turkey and the mushroom mixture in the bottom of the chilled quiche crust. Sprinkle the cheese over the top. Pour the egg mixture into the crust, filling nearly to the top.

6. Bake until the top of the crust is golden brown, the filling is set, and a knife inserted in the center comes out clean, 40 to 50 minutes. Place the pan on a wire rack and cool for 10 minutes before cutting. Serve warm.

chicken and cheese quiche

Tarragon makes a nice pairing with chicken, but you could use sage, thyme, rosemary, or parsley instead.

SERVES 6

1 chilled, unbaked, 9-inch Quiche Crust (see p. 187) or Almond Quiche Crust (see p. 188)
4 large eggs
1 cup whole milk
2 teaspoons finely chopped fresh tarragon
¼ teaspoon table salt
⅛ teaspoon ground black pepper
1½ cups shredded or diced cooked chicken
1½ cups grated Swiss cheese

1. Prepare the quiche crust of your choice.

2. Position the oven rack in the lower third of the oven and heat the oven to 350°F.

3. In a medium bowl, using a wire whisk, lightly beat the eggs. Gradually whisk in the milk until well combined. Stir in the tarragon, salt, and pepper.

4. Layer the chicken and cheese in the bottom of the chilled quiche crust. Pour the egg mixture into the crust, filling nearly to the top.

5. Bake until the top of the crust is golden brown, the filling is set, and a knife inserted in the center comes out clean, 40 to 50 minutes. Place the pan on a wire rack and cool for 10 minutes before cutting. Serve warm.

zucchini parmesan quiche

Overwhelmed with zucchini from a bumper summer harvest? This quiche is a tasty way to use some of it up. Small zucchini work best in this recipe. If you only have large zucchini, cut the slices in half or in quarters and remove the seeds before measuring.

SERVES 6

1 chilled, unbaked, 9-inch Quiche Crust (see p. 187) or Almond Quiche Crust (see p. 188)

4 large eggs

1 cup whole milk

2 tablespoons minced shallots or onions

1½ teaspoons finely chopped fresh thyme leaves

¼ teaspoon table salt

⅛ teaspoon ground black pepper

1½ cups thinly sliced, unpeeled small zucchini

1 cup grated Parmesan cheese

VARIATION

Use thinly sliced yellow crookneck squash instead of zucchini, or use a combination of yellow squash and zucchini.

1. Prepare the quiche crust of your choice.

2. Position the oven rack in the lower third of the oven and heat the oven to 350°F.

3. In a medium bowl, using a wire whisk, lightly beat the eggs. Gradually whisk in the milk until well combined. Stir in the shallots, thyme, salt, and pepper.

4. Layer the zucchini and Parmesan cheese in the bottom of the chilled quiche crust. Pour the egg mixture into the crust, filling nearly to the top.

5. Bake until the top of the crust is golden brown, the filling is set, and a knife inserted in the center comes out clean, 40 to 50 minutes. Place the pan on a wire rack and cool for 10 minutes before cutting. Serve warm.

You can grate the Parmesan cheese yourself or use prepackaged grated Parmesan found in the cheese section of most major grocery stores. Do not use the canned cheese product found near the dried pasta as it will significantly alter the taste and texture of the quiche.

herb quiche

You can use your favorite combination of fresh herbs and cheeses in this quiche. Sage, tarragon, dill, and basil are all good choices.

SERVES 6

1 chilled, unbaked, 9-inch Quiche Crust (see p. 187) or Almond Quiche Crust (see p. 188)

4 large eggs

1 cup whole milk

¼ cup finely chopped fresh chives

2 tablespoons finely chopped fresh flat-leaf parsley

1 tablespoon finely chopped fresh thyme

1 tablespoon finely chopped fresh rosemary

¼ teaspoon table salt

⅛ teaspoon ground black pepper

1½ cups grated Gruyère cheese

1 cup grated Cheddar cheese

1. Prepare the quiche crust of your choice.

2. Position the oven rack in the lower third of the oven and heat the oven to 350°F.

3. In a medium bowl, using a wire whisk, lightly beat the eggs. Gradually whisk in the milk until well combined. Stir in the chives, parsley, thyme, rosemary, salt, and pepper.

4. Layer the Gruyère and Cheddar cheeses in the bottom of the chilled quiche crust. Pour the egg mixture into the crust, filling nearly to the top.

5. Bake until the top of the crust is golden brown, the filling is set, and a knife inserted in the center comes out clean, 40 to 50 minutes. Place the pan on a wire rack and cool for 10 minutes before cutting. Serve warm.

crab quiche

Fresh cooked crabmeat or defrosted frozen cooked crabmeat has a much better flavor and texture than canned crabmeat and will make a much tastier quiche. For a spicier quiche, add a dash or two of cayenne pepper or Old Bay® seasoning.

SERVES 6

1 chilled, unbaked, 9-inch Quiche Crust
(see p. 187) or Almond Quiche Crust
(see p. 188)

4 large eggs

1 cup whole milk

2 tablespoons finely chopped shallots
or onions

1 tablespoon finely chopped fresh
flat-leaf parsley

1 teaspoon finely chopped fresh dill

¼ teaspoon table salt

⅛ teaspoon ground black pepper

1½ cups flaked crabmeat

1 cup grated Gruyère cheese

1. Prepare the quiche crust of your choice.

2. Position the oven rack in the lower third of the oven and heat the oven to 350°F.

3. In a medium bowl, using a wire whisk, lightly beat the eggs. Gradually whisk in the milk until well combined. Stir in the shallots, parsley, dill, salt, and pepper.

4. Layer the crabmeat and Gruyère cheese in the bottom of the chilled quiche crust. Pour the egg mixture into the crust, filling nearly to the top.

5. Bake until the top of the crust is golden brown, the filling is set, and a knife inserted in the center comes out clean, 40 to 50 minutes. Place the pan on a wire rack and cool for 10 minutes before cutting. Serve warm.

VARIATION

shrimp quiche: Substitute 1½ cups chopped cooked, peeled, and deveined medium or large shrimp for the crabmeat.

spinach feta quiche

Fresh spinach with feta cheese is a classic combination. Feta is salty, so there's no need to add salt to the quiche custard.

SERVES 6

1 chilled, unbaked, 9-inch Quiche Crust (see p. 187) or Almond Quiche Crust (see p. 188)

1 tablespoon unsalted butter

2 tablespoons finely chopped shallots or onions

2 teaspoons minced garlic

3 cups stemmed and chopped fresh spinach leaves (about 1 large bunch or a 12-ounce bag)

4 large eggs

1 cup whole milk

1½ teaspoons finely chopped fresh basil

⅛ teaspoon ground black pepper

1¼ cups crumbled feta cheese

¼ cup grated Parmesan cheese

1. Prepare the quiche crust of your choice.

2. Position the oven rack in the lower third of the oven and heat the oven to 350°F.

3. In a medium frying pan over medium heat, melt the butter. Stir in the shallots and garlic and sauté, stirring frequently, until tender, about 3 minutes. Add the spinach and stir to combine. Cover the pan and cook just until the spinach is wilted, about 1 minute. Uncover, remove the pan from the heat, and set aside.

4. In a medium bowl, using a wire whisk, lightly beat the eggs. Gradually whisk in the milk until well combined. Stir in the basil and pepper.

5. Layer half of the spinach mixture in the bottom of the chilled quiche crust. Evenly sprinkle the cheeses over the spinach. Top with the remaining spinach mixture. Pour the egg mixture into the crust, filling nearly to the top.

6. Bake until the top of the crust is golden brown, the filling is set, and a knife inserted in the center comes out clean, 40 to 50 minutes. Place the pan on a wire rack and cool for 10 minutes before cutting. Serve warm.

CHAPTER TEN

savory
stratas

A perfect meal to serve any time of day, stratas are casseroles made with bread, an egg custard, and a variety of savory ingredients, such as cooked meats and vegetables. Fresh herbs are frequently added to enhance the flavor of these dishes. Stratas can be assembled during the day for an easy evening meal or put together the night before and baked the next day for a stress-free brunch entrée.

Stratas turn out best when made with a lighter weight bread rather than a heavy multigrain bread. Lighter breads will absorb more of the egg mixture and produce a more fluffy texture, while heavier breads will produce a dense-textured strata. Drier bread should be used for making stratas (day old is perfect) because it will absorb more of the egg custard than fresh-made bread.

You may remove the crust from the bread before cubing it or leave the crust on; stratas cooked with the crust are a bit heartier than those that use crustless bread. Regardless of whether you leave the crust on the bread or not, be sure to cut the bread into cubes about ½ inch to 1 inch in size so that the entire dish has the same texture.

Any raw meats should be thoroughly cooked before combining them with other ingredients. Cruciferous vegetables, such as broccoli and cauliflower, which are high in insoluble fiber, should be cooked until crisp-tender before adding them to the strata mixture. If left raw, these vegetables may not cook all the way through as the dish bakes.

Stratas should be refrigerated for at least 4 hours or overnight to allow the bread to soak up the egg custard. Before baking, remove the strata from the refrigerator, place on a wire rack, and allow to sit for 30 minutes to come to room temperature.

Quick Tips
STRATAS

- Cut the bread into uniform-size pieces to give the strata a nice texture.
- Toss the bread and filling ingredients together until everything is evenly distributed.
- Spread the bread filling in a lightly greased baking dish in an even layer.
- Refrigerate the strata for several hours or overnight to allow the bread to soak up the egg custard.
- Remove the strata from the refrigerator 30 minutes before baking.
- If the top of the strata starts to brown too quickly while baking, cover it loosely with aluminum foil.

broccoli cauliflower strata

This dish is a great way to use up extra broccoli or cauliflower. Feel free to add more of one than the other, though you'll need to use a total of 3 cups in the recipe. A bit of chopped carrots will add color as well. While this strata is a meal in itself, it's also tasty alongside grilled chicken or pork.

SERVES 6 TO 8

Nonstick cooking spray, for the pan

1½ cups small broccoli florets

1½ cups small cauliflower florets

6 cups cubed day-old gluten-free bread
(homemade or store-bought)

1⅓ cups grated Cheddar cheese

⅔ cup grated Parmesan cheese

¼ cup thinly sliced scallions
(white and light green parts)

12 large eggs

3 cups whole milk

2 tablespoons finely chopped fresh
flat-leaf parsley

¼ teaspoon table salt

⅛ teaspoon ground black pepper

1. Grease a 13 x 9 x 2-inch baking pan with nonstick cooking spray. Set aside.

2. Steam or boil the broccoli and cauliflower just until tender, but still crisp, 3 to 4 minutes. Rinse in cool water to stop the cooking process and drain well.

3. In a large bowl, combine the bread, broccoli, cauliflower, Cheddar and Parmesan cheeses, and scallions and toss until well blended. Spread evenly in the bottom of the prepared pan.

4. In a large bowl, using a wire whisk, beat the eggs until foamy. Gradually whisk in the milk until well blended. Stir in the parsley, salt, and pepper. Pour the custard evenly over the top of the bread mixture. Cover the pan with plastic wrap and refrigerate for at least 4 hours or overnight.

5. Remove the pan from the refrigerator and let stand at room temperature for 30 minutes.

6. Heat the oven to 350°F.

7. Bake the strata, uncovered, until the top is puffed and golden brown, 45 to 55 minutes. If the top starts to brown too quickly, cover loosely with a piece of foil. Remove the pan from the oven and place on a wire rack. Let cool for 5 minutes. Cut the strata into squares or spoon from the pan to serve home-style. Serve hot.

VARIATIONS

broccoli strata: **Use all broccoli in place of the cauliflower.**

cauliflower strata: **Use all cauliflower in place of the broccoli.**

ham broccoli strata: **Add 2 cups ¼-inch-cubed gluten-free ham in place of the cauliflower. Use all Cheddar cheese, if desired.**

vegetable strata

Before making the strata, press the grated zucchini between layers of paper towels to squeeze out some of the liquid. This will keep the strata from being too watery.

SERVES 6 TO 8

Nonstick cooking spray, for the pan

2 tablespoons unsalted butter

½ cup finely chopped red onions

2 teaspoons minced garlic

1½ cups grated zucchini

1½ cups grated carrots

6 cups cubed day-old gluten-free bread (homemade or store-bought)

1¼ cups grated Gruyère cheese

¾ cup grated Parmesan cheese

12 large eggs

3 cups whole milk

3 tablespoons finely chopped fresh flat-leaf parsley

2 teaspoons finely chopped fresh thyme leaves

¼ teaspoon table salt

⅛ teaspoon ground black pepper

1. Grease a 13 x 9 x 2-inch baking pan with nonstick cooking spray. Set aside.

2. In a large frying pan, over medium heat, melt the butter. Stir in the onions and garlic and sauté, stirring frequently, until tender, about 3 minutes. Add the zucchini and carrots and stir to combine. Cook, stirring frequently, for 3 minutes.

3. In a large bowl, combine the bread, zucchini and carrot mixture, and Gruyère and Parmesan cheeses and toss until well blended. Spread evenly in the bottom of the prepared pan.

4. In a large bowl, using a wire whisk, beat the eggs until foamy. Gradually whisk in the milk until well blended. Stir in the parsley, thyme, salt, and pepper. Pour the custard evenly over the top of the bread mixture. Cover the pan with plastic wrap and refrigerate for at least 4 hours or overnight.

5. Remove the pan from the refrigerator and let stand at room temperature for 30 minutes.

6. Heat the oven to 350°F.

7. Bake the strata, uncovered, until the top is puffed and golden brown, 45 to 55 minutes. If the top starts to brown too quickly, cover loosely with a piece of foil. Remove the pan from the oven and place on a wire rack. Let cool for 5 minutes. Cut the strata into squares or spoon from the pan to serve home-style. Serve hot.

spinach strata

Gruyère is a traditional cheese in egg dishes, but you can use a variety of cheeses in this strata. Try Swiss, Monterey Jack, Cheddar, or feta. A small salad makes the perfect accompaniment when serving this strata for brunch, lunch, or dinner.

SERVES 6 TO 8

Nonstick cooking spray, for the pan

1 tablespoon unsalted butter

2 tablespoons finely chopped shallots or onions

2 teaspoons minced garlic

6 cups cubed day-old gluten-free bread (homemade or store bought)

3 cups stemmed and chopped fresh spinach (about 1 bunch or one 12-ounce package)

2 cups grated Gruyère cheese

12 large eggs

3 cups whole milk

¼ teaspoon table salt

⅛ teaspoon ground black pepper

1. Grease a 13 x 9 x 2-inch baking pan with nonstick cooking spray. Set aside.

2. In a small frying pan, over medium heat, melt the butter. Stir in the shallots and garlic and sauté, stirring frequently, until tender, about 3 minutes.

3. In a large bowl, combine the bread, spinach, cheese, and the sautéed shallots and garlic and toss until well blended. Spread evenly in the bottom of the prepared pan.

4. In a large bowl, using a wire whisk, beat the eggs until foamy. Gradually whisk in the milk until well blended. Stir in the salt and pepper. Pour the custard evenly over the top of the bread mixture. Cover the pan with plastic wrap and refrigerate for at least 4 hours or overnight.

5. Remove the pan from the refrigerator and let stand at room temperature for 30 minutes.

6. Heat the oven to 350°F.

7. Bake the strata, uncovered, until the top is puffed and golden brown, 45 to 55 minutes. If the top starts to brown too quickly, cover loosely with foil. Remove the pan from the oven and place on a wire rack. Let cool for 5 minutes. Cut the strata into squares or spoon from the pan to serve home-style. Serve hot.

VARIATION

bacon spinach strata: Cook 8 to 10 slices of gluten-free bacon until crisp; drain, then crumble and add to the bread mixture.

cheddar chicken strata

Simple yet delicious, this strata makes a great lunch or evening meal. If you like, you can give it a little zing by adding 3 tablespoons of finely chopped seeded jalapeño peppers to the bread mixture and a couple dashes of hot sauce to the egg custard. This dish is a great way to use up leftover roast chicken or a store-bought rotisserie chicken.

SERVES 6 TO 8

Nonstick cooking spray, for the pan

6 cups cubed day-old gluten-free bread
   (homemade or store-bought)

3 cups shredded or chopped
   cooked chicken

2 cups grated Cheddar cheese

¼ cup thinly sliced scallions
   (white and light green parts)

12 large eggs

3 cups whole milk

¼ teaspoon table salt

⅛ teaspoon ground black pepper

1. Grease a 13 x 9 x 2-inch baking pan with nonstick cooking spray. Set aside.

2. In a large bowl, combine the bread, chicken, cheese, and scallions and toss until well blended. Spread evenly in the bottom of the prepared pan.

3. In a large bowl, using a wire whisk, beat the eggs until foamy. Gradually whisk in the milk until well blended. Stir in the salt and pepper. Pour the custard evenly over the top of the bread mixture. Cover the pan with plastic wrap and refrigerate for at least 4 hours or overnight.

4. Remove the pan from the refrigerator and let stand at room temperature for 30 minutes.

5. Heat the oven to 350°F.

6. Bake the strata, uncovered, until the top is puffed and golden brown, 45 to 55 minutes. If the top starts to brown too quickly, cover loosely with foil. Remove the pan from the oven and place on a wire rack. Let cool for 5 minutes. Cut the strata into squares or spoon from the pan to serve home-style. Serve hot.

VARIATION

chicken broccoli strata: **Add 1½ cups cooked fresh small broccoli florets to the bread mixture. Cook the broccoli just until crisp-tender, 3 to 4 minutes. You can also use thawed and drained, but not cooked, frozen broccoli florets.**

ham and cheese strata

If you're looking for a way to use up leftovers after a holiday meal, then this recipe is perfect. For an extra punch of cheese flavor, use all Cheddar instead of a combination of Cheddar and Monterey Jack.

SERVES 6 TO 8

Nonstick cooking spray, for the pan

6 cups cubed day-old gluten-free bread (homemade or store-bought)

3 cups ¼-inch cubes gluten-free ham

1 cup grated Cheddar cheese

1 cup grated Monterey Jack cheese

¼ cup thinly sliced scallions (white and light green parts)

12 large eggs

2 teaspoons Dijon mustard

3 cups whole milk

1 tablespoon finely chopped fresh flat-leaf parsley

¼ teaspoon table salt

⅛ teaspoon ground black pepper

1. Grease a 13 x 9 x 2-inch baking pan with nonstick cooking spray. Set aside.

2. In a large bowl, combine the bread, ham, Cheddar and Monterey Jack cheeses, and scallions and toss until well blended. Spread evenly in the bottom of the prepared pan.

3. In a large bowl, using a wire whisk, beat the eggs until foamy. Stir in the mustard. Gradually whisk in the milk until well blended. Stir in the parsley, salt, and pepper. Pour the custard evenly over the top of the bread mixture. Cover the pan with plastic wrap and refrigerate for at least 4 hours or overnight.

4. Remove the pan from the refrigerator and let stand at room temperature for 30 minutes.

5. Heat the oven to 350°F.

6. Bake the strata, uncovered, until the top is puffed and golden brown, 45 to 55 minutes. If the top starts to brown too quickly, cover loosely with a piece of foil. Remove the pan from the oven and place on a wire rack. Let cool for 5 minutes. Cut the strata into squares or spoon from the pan to serve home-style. Serve hot.

turkey strata

This comforting dish is especially good served with cranberry sauce on the side. Although I call for Swiss cheese here, turkey strata is also very good made with Cheddar.

SERVES 6 TO 8

Nonstick cooking spray, for the pan

6 cups cubed day-old gluten-free bread (homemade or store-bought)

3 cups shredded or chopped cooked turkey

2 cups grated Swiss cheese

¾ cup thinly sliced celery

3 tablespoons thinly sliced scallions (white and light green parts)

12 large eggs

3 cups whole milk

1½ tablespoons finely chopped fresh sage

¼ teaspoon table salt

⅛ teaspoon ground black pepper

1. Grease a 13 x 9 x 2-inch baking pan with nonstick cooking spray. Set aside.

2. In a large bowl, combine the bread, turkey, cheese, celery, and scallions and toss until well blended. Spread evenly in the bottom of the prepared pan.

3. In a large bowl, using a wire whisk, beat the eggs until foamy. Gradually whisk in the milk until well blended. Stir in the sage, salt, and pepper. Pour the custard evenly over the top of the bread mixture. Cover the pan with plastic wrap and refrigerate for at least 4 hours or overnight.

4. Remove the pan from the refrigerator and let stand at room temperature for 30 minutes.

5. Heat the oven to 350°F.

6. Bake the strata, uncovered, until the top is puffed and golden brown, 45 to 55 minutes. If the top starts to brown too quickly, cover loosely with a piece of foil. Remove the pan from the oven and place on a wire rack. Let cool for 5 minutes. Cut the strata into squares or spoon from the pan to serve home-style. Serve hot.

VARIATION

turkey asparagus strata: Add 1½ cups cooked 1-inch slices of fresh asparagus to the bread mixture.

italian sausage strata

Sweet or spicy Italian sausage works well in this recipe, or try a combination of both. You can also make it with regular gluten-free sausage. I like to use Monterey Jack cheese in this recipe, but Mozzarella or Gruyère also gives it a nice flavor.

SERVES 6 TO 8

Nonstick cooking spray, for the pan

2 tablespoons unsalted butter

1 cup sliced mushrooms

½ cup finely chopped onions

2 teaspoons minced garlic

6 cups cubed day-old gluten-free bread (homemade or store-bought)

1 pound bulk gluten-free Italian sausage, cooked and drained

2 cups grated Monterey Jack cheese

12 large eggs

3 cups whole milk

1 tablespoon finely chopped fresh flat-leaf parsley

1 tablespoon finely chopped fresh oregano

¼ teaspoon table salt

⅛ teaspoon ground black pepper

1. Grease a 13 x 9 x 2-inch baking pan with nonstick cooking spray. Set aside.

2. In a medium frying pan, over medium heat, melt the butter. Stir in the mushrooms, onions, and garlic and sauté, stirring frequently, until tender, 3 to 5 minutes.

3. In a large bowl, combine the bread, sausage, mushroom mixture, and cheese and toss until well blended. Spread evenly in the bottom of the prepared pan.

4. In a large bowl, using a wire whisk, beat the eggs until foamy. Gradually whisk in the milk until well blended. Stir in the parsley, oregano, salt, and pepper. Pour the custard evenly over the top of the bread mixture. Cover the pan with plastic wrap and refrigerate for at least 4 hours or overnight.

5. Remove the pan from the refrigerator and let stand at room temperature for 30 minutes.

6. Heat the oven to 350°F.

7. Bake the strata, uncovered, until the top is puffed and golden brown, 45 to 55 minutes. If the top starts to brown too quickly, cover loosely with a piece of foil. Remove the pan from the oven and place on a wire rack. Let cool for 5 minutes. Cut the strata into squares or spoon from the pan to serve home-style. Serve hot.

shrimp strata

Be sure to use medium to large shrimp, which have more flavor and a better texture than the tiny bay shrimp, often called salad or cocktail shrimp. Sold by size, it takes 31 to 35 medium shrimp to make a pound, and large shrimp come 21 to 30 to the pound. You will need 1 to 1½ pounds of shrimp for this recipe.

SERVES 6 TO 8

Nonstick cooking spray, for the pan

6 cups cubed day-old gluten-free bread (homemade or store-bought)

3 cups coarsely chopped cooked, peeled, and deveined medium to large shrimp

1¼ cups grated Gruyère cheese

¾ cup grated Parmesan cheese

¼ cup thinly sliced scallions (white and light green parts)

12 large eggs

3 cups whole milk

3 tablespoons finely chopped fresh flat-leaf parsley

¼ teaspoon table salt

⅛ teaspoon ground black pepper

1. Grease a 13 x 9 x 2-inch baking pan with nonstick cooking spray. Set aside.

2. In a large bowl, combine the bread, shrimp, Gruyère and Parmesan cheeses, and scallions and toss until well blended. Spread evenly in the bottom of the prepared pan.

3. In a large bowl, using a wire whisk, beat the eggs until foamy. Gradually whisk in the milk until well blended. Stir in the parsley, salt, and pepper. Pour the custard evenly over the top of the bread mixture. Cover the pan with plastic wrap and refrigerate for at least 4 hours or overnight.

4. Remove the pan from the refrigerator and let stand at room temperature for 30 minutes.

5. Heat the oven to 350°F.

6. Bake the strata, uncovered, until the top is puffed and golden brown, 45 to 55 minutes. If the top starts to brown too quickly, cover loosely with a piece of foil. Remove the pan from the oven and place on a wire rack. Let cool for 5 minutes. Cut the strata into squares or spoon from the pan to serve home-style. Serve hot.

VARIATION

seafood strata: Instead of all shrimp, use a combination of cooked shrimp, crab, scallops, and lobster.

crab strata

A wonderful dish to serve for brunch or dinner, this strata makes any meal a special occasion. Fresh cooked crabmeat or defrosted frozen lump crabmeat will make a tastier strata than canned. You may omit the wine and use a total of 3 cups milk, if preferred.

SERVES 6 TO 8

Nonstick cooking spray, for the pan

1 tablespoon unsalted butter

¼ cup finely chopped shallots or onions

6 cups cubed day-old gluten-free bread (homemade or store-bought)

2 cups flaked or chopped cooked crabmeat

2 cups grated Swiss cheese

12 large eggs

2 cups whole milk

1 cup dry white wine

2 tablespoons finely chopped fresh flat-leaf parsley

2 teaspoons grated lemon zest

¼ teaspoon table salt

⅛ teaspoon ground black pepper

1. Grease a 13 x 9 x 2-inch baking pan with nonstick cooking spray. Set aside.

2. In a small frying pan, over medium heat, melt the butter. Stir in the shallots and sauté, stirring frequently, until tender, about 3 minutes.

3. In a large bowl, combine the bread, crabmeat, cheese, and sautéed shallots and toss until well blended. Spread evenly in the bottom of the prepared pan.

4. In a large bowl, using a wire whisk, beat the eggs until foamy. Gradually whisk in the milk until well blended, then whisk in the wine. Stir in the parsley, lemon zest, salt, and pepper. Pour the custard evenly over the top of the bread mixture. Cover the pan with plastic wrap and refrigerate for at least 4 hours or overnight.

5. Remove the pan from the refrigerator and let stand at room temperature for 30 minutes.

6. Heat the oven to 350°F.

7. Bake the strata, uncovered, until the top is puffed and golden brown, 45 to 55 minutes. If the top starts to brown too quickly, cover loosely with foil. Remove the pan from the oven and place on a wire rack. Let cool for 5 minutes. Cut the strata into squares or spoon from the pan to serve home-style. Serve hot.

mexican chicken strata

You can use mild, medium, or hot salsa in this strata to suit your family's heat preference. For extra heat, add 2 tablespoons or more of finely chopped seeded jalapeño peppers to the chicken mixture. Garnish the top with chopped fresh cilantro, or add a tablespoon or two of finely chopped cilantro to the egg mixture, if you prefer. A spoonful of sour cream and some diced avocado make a flavorful garnish.

SERVES 6 TO 8

Nonstick cooking spray, for the pan

3 cups shredded or chopped cooked chicken

One 12-ounce jar chunky salsa

6 cups cubed day-old gluten-free bread (homemade or store-bought)

1 cup grated Monterey Jack cheese

1 cup grated Cheddar cheese

12 large eggs

3 cups whole milk

¼ teaspoon table salt

⅛ teaspoon ground black pepper

Sour cream (optional)

Diced avocado (optional)

1. Grease a 13 x 9 x 2-inch baking pan with nonstick cooking spray. Set aside.

2. In a medium bowl, combine the chicken and salsa until well blended.

3. In a large bowl, combine the bread, chicken mixture, and Monterey Jack and Cheddar cheeses and toss until well blended. Spread evenly in the bottom of the prepared pan.

4. In a large bowl, using a wire whisk, beat the eggs until foamy. Gradually whisk in the milk until well blended. Stir in the salt and pepper. Pour the custard evenly over the top of the bread mixture. Cover the pan with plastic wrap and refrigerate for at least 4 hours or overnight.

5. Remove the pan from the refrigerator and let stand at room temperature for 30 minutes.

6. Heat the oven to 350°F.

7. Bake the strata, uncovered, until the top is puffed and golden brown, 45 to 55 minutes. If the top starts to brown too quickly, cover loosely with a piece of foil. Remove the pan from the oven and place on a wire rack. Let cool for 5 minutes. Cut the strata into squares or spoon from the pan to serve home-style. Serve hot, with sour cream and avocado on the side, if desired.

asparagus strata

This is a great dish to make in spring, when young, tender fresh asparagus is plentiful. I prefer to use green asparagus because it has a stronger flavor and more vibrant color than white asparagus. If your asparagus spears are large, peel the lower section of the stalk to remove the woody outer layer.

SERVES 6 TO 8

Nonstick cooking spray, for the pan

2 tablespoons unsalted butter

2 tablespoons finely chopped shallots or onions

1 tablespoon minced garlic

3 cups 1-inch slices fresh asparagus

6 cups cubed day-old gluten-free bread (homemade or store-bought)

2 cups grated Gruyère cheese

12 large eggs

3 cups whole milk

2 tablespoon finely chopped fresh flat-leaf parsley

¼ teaspoon table salt

⅛ teaspoon ground black pepper

1. Grease a 13 x 9 x 2-inch baking pan with nonstick cooking spray. Set aside.

2. In a large frying pan, over medium heat, melt the butter. Stir in the shallots and garlic. Add the asparagus and sauté, stirring frequently, just until the asparagus is tender but still crisp, 2 to 4 minutes. Remove the pan from the heat and set aside.

3. In a large bowl, combine the bread, asparagus mixture, and cheese and toss until well blended. Spread evenly in the bottom of the prepared pan.

4. In a large bowl, using a wire whisk, beat the eggs until foamy. Gradually whisk in the milk until well blended. Stir in the parsley, salt, and pepper. Pour the custard evenly over the top of the bread mixture. Cover the pan with plastic wrap and refrigerate for at least 4 hours or overnight.

5. Remove the pan from the refrigerator and let stand at room temperature for 30 minutes.

6. Heat the oven to 350°F.

7. Bake the strata, uncovered, until the top is puffed and golden brown, 45 to 55 minutes. If the top starts to brown too quickly, cover loosely with a piece of foil. Remove the pan from the oven and place on a wire rack. Let cool for 5 minutes. Cut the strata into squares or spoon from the pan to serve home-style. Serve hot.

tomato strata

Roma tomatoes, also known as plum tomatoes, are more firm than regular slicing tomatoes, so use that variety in this strata. They will hold their shape better without making the custard too watery.

SERVES 6 TO 8

Nonstick cooking spray, for the pan

2 tablespoons unsalted butter

½ cup finely chopped onions

2 teaspoons minced garlic

6 cups cubed day-old gluten-free bread (homemade or store-bought)

3 cups chopped, peeled, and seeded Roma tomatoes

1⅓ cups grated Gruyère cheese

⅔ cup grated Parmesan cheese

⅔ cup coarsely chopped fresh basil leaves

12 large eggs

3 cups whole milk

1 tablespoon finely chopped fresh oregano

¼ teaspoon table salt

⅛ teaspoon ground black pepper

1. Grease a 13 x 9 x 2-inch baking pan with nonstick cooking spray. Set aside.

2. In a small frying pan, over medium heat, melt the butter. Stir in the onions and garlic and sauté, stirring frequently, until tender, about 3 minutes.

3. In a large bowl, combine the bread, tomatoes, Gruyère and Parmesan cheeses, basil, and onion mixture and toss until well blended. Spread evenly in the bottom of the prepared pan.

4. In a large bowl, using a wire whisk, beat the eggs until foamy. Gradually whisk in the milk until well blended. Stir in the oregano, salt, and pepper. Pour the custard evenly over the top of the bread mixture. Cover the pan with plastic wrap and refrigerate for at least 4 hours or overnight.

5. Remove the pan from the refrigerator and let stand at room temperature for 30 minutes.

6. Heat the oven to 350°F.

7. Bake the strata, uncovered, until the top is puffed and golden brown, 45 to 55 minutes. If the top starts to brown too quickly, cover loosely with a piece of foil. Remove the pan from the oven and place on a wire rack. Let cool for 5 minutes. Cut the strata into squares or spoon from the pan to serve home-style. Serve hot.

To quickly seed the tomatoes, cut them lengthwise into quarters and use a small spoon or a grapefruit spoon to scoop out the seeds and juicy part surrounding them.

gluten-free
ingredients

Grains and Starches

Amaranth
Arrowroot
Bean flours
Brown rice
Buckwheat flour
   (labeled gluten-free)
Chickpea (garbanzo bean) flour
Coconut flour
Corn
Corn flour
Cornmeal
Cornstarch
Cream of tartar
Flax
Garfava
Grits
Guar gum
Hominy
Maize
Masa
Masa harina
Mesquite
Millet
Montina
Oats (labeled gluten-free)
Polenta
Potato flour
Potato starch
Quinoa
Rice
Rice flour
Sago
Sorghum flour

Soy (not soy sauce)
Sweet rice (glutinous rice)
Tapioca
Taro root
Teff
Wild rice
Xanthan gum

Other Gluten-Free Ingredients

These foods are usually considered gluten-free. Be sure to select plain, unseasoned, unprocessed products without additives and double-check the labels.

Alcohol (distilled only)
Almond milk
Beans
Brown sugar (most brands)
Butter
Buttermilk
Chocolate (check labels)
Citric acid
Cocoa powder
Coconut milk
Confectioners' sugar
Cow's milk
Dried fruit (check label)
Eggs
Fish
Flavoring extracts
   (U.S.-made only)

Fresh fruit
Fresh vegetables
Granulated sugar
Legumes
Margarine (check label)
Meat
Nuts
Poultry
Rice milk
Seafood
Sour cream
Soy milk (check label)
Tofu
Vanilla beans
Vanilla extract (U.S.-made only)
Vinegar (except malt vinegar)
Wine
Yeast (except brewer's yeast)
Yogurt (check label)

ingredients that contain gluten

Grains

Wheat, rye, and barley all contain gluten, as do any grains related to these three. All of the grains in the list below contain gluten.

Barley
Barley malt
Bran
Bulgur
Couscous
Durum
Farina
Farro
Graham
Kamut
Malt
Matzo flour/meal
Orzo
Rye
Seitan
Semolina
Spelt
Tabbouleh
Triticale
Udon
Wheat
Wheat bran/germ

Other Ingredients and Foods that Contain Gluten

Gluten can hide in the foods and ingredients listed here. While there are gluten-free versions available for some of these items, carefully check the labels and confirm the ingredients with the manufacturer of any product not labeled as gluten-free.

Ale (also lager and stout)
Bacon (look for gluten-free)
Beer
Bouillon
Breadcrumbs
Brewer's yeast
Broth
Brown-rice syrup
Candy (check label)
Commercial baked goods
    (unless certified gluten-free)
Communion wafers
Cornbread
Deli meats
Energy bars
Flavored teas
Flavors and natural flavorings
Gravies
Ice cream (check label)
Imitation crab

Imitation seafood
Licorice
Malt vinegar
Malted milk
Maltodextrin
Marinades
Panko breadcrumbs
Pasta
Pickles and relishes (check label)
Processed meats
Salad dressings
Sauces
Sausage (look for gluten-free)
Seasonings and spice blends
Soup
Soup mixes
Soy sauce
Stabilizers

convert your favorite recipes to
gluten-free

Now that you have baked some gluten-free breakfast treats, you may be wondering how to convert your favorite wheat-flour recipes to gluten-free. Many recipes containing wheat flour can be changed to gluten-free by substituting Gluten-Free All-Purpose Flour (see p. 11) for all-purpose wheat flour, adjusting the amounts of a few ingredients, and adding an ingredient or two to improve the texture of the finished recipe.

There is no exact science or formula to converting regular baked goods recipes to gluten-free. Each will require a little experimenting and may take a try—or two or three—to get the results you are looking for. If a recipe doesn't turn out exactly the way you want it the first time, be patient, make a few adjustments, and give it another try. Once you get a feel for the changes you need to make to get the desired results, converting similar recipes will be much easier and faster.

Gluten-free breads and cakes bake up better in smaller pans—it's hard to get the center done without overbaking and drying out the edges in larger pans—so you may need to adjust the volume of the recipe to fit a smaller pan to get the best results. Because there's no gluten for support, bread or cake baked in a large pan is less likely to rise, may fall or shrink after baking, and is more likely to be heavy and dense.

The baking temperature for a gluten-free converted recipe will be the same as in the original recipe, and the baking time will generally be about the same as well. Some gluten-free baked goods may take a little longer to bake, though, so keep a close eye on the time the first time you bake and check a little early just to be sure. Make note of how long the item takes to bake.

Gluten-free baked goods can be a little bland. To improve the flavor, try increasing the amount of extracts, spices, salt, herbs, nuts, or dried fruit called for in the recipe. If these ingredients are not present in the original recipe, add them to help boost the flavor.

Here are some general guidelines to help you adapt recipes to gluten free.

Flour

The general rule in gluten-free baking is that you can replace all-purpose wheat flour with an equal amount of rice flour-based, all-purpose, gluten-free flour in most recipes. If you use a bean flour, nut flour, or other type of gluten-free flour, you may need to experiment with the substitution amount to find out what ratio works best in the specific recipe. The Gluten-Free All-Purpose Flour recipe provided on p. 11 can be used to replace all-purpose wheat flour in many types of recipes.

Eggs

Eggs are very important in gluten-free baking because they provide protein, moisture, and structure, and help improve the texture and flavor of gluten-free baked goods. If your recipe calls for eggs, try increasing the quantity by one egg

when you convert a standard recipe to gluten-free. The extra egg will bind the ingredients together and replace some of the support that is lost by removing the gluten.

Using egg substitutes in place of eggs can cause problems with some gluten-free breads and baked goods. The finished item may have a gummy texture or be too wet in the middle. If you use an egg substitute, you may need to do some experimentation with the amount of liquid in the recipe to achieve the desired results.

Liquid Ingredients

Because gluten-free flours are drier than all-purpose wheat flour, you may need to increase the milk or other liquid amount called for in the recipe slightly to keep batters from being too stiff. But gluten-free flours can absorb a lot of liquid, so don't add too much or the finished baked goods may be gummy (see the Dairy Ingredient Substitution Guide on p. 226 for suggested substitutions). Expect the batter to be thicker than a wheat flour batter; yeast bread doughs will be softer and stickier than bread doughs made with wheat flour.

Leaveners

To give gluten-free baked goods a lift and help them rise in the oven, you may need to increase the amount of leavener in the recipe by 25% to 50%. If the recipe already contains a high leavener-to-flour ratio, you may not need to add much more.

Adding ¼ teaspoon to ½ teaspoon of baking soda to a recipe leavened only with baking powder can help boost the leavening power and lighten gluten-free baked goods. Be careful not to add too much leavener as it can make the batter unstable or cause peaks in the center of muffins, quick breads, and cakes.

Additional Adjustments for Gluten-Free Recipes

Both altitude and weather can have an influence on gluten-free baked goods, so you may need to make some adjustments to your recipe. When making gluten-free baked goods at elevations above 3,000 feet, you may need to increase the amount of liquid called for in the recipe; otherwise, the baked goods may not rise as well and the finished item may be dry.

Humidity can also have a significant impact on gluten-free baking. Both the outside weather and the humidity in your kitchen can affect the amount of liquid needed in a recipe. When the humidity is low, you may need to add more liquid to the recipe. If the humidity is high, you should be able to use about the same amount of liquid, or maybe a little less, than is called for in the recipe.

XANTHAN GUM AND GUAR GUM

Adding xanthan gum or guar gum to the recipe can make gluten-free baked goods moister and help prevent them from drying out and crumbling as they cool. I recommend using xanthan gum in gluten-free recipes because guar gum can cause digestive issues for some people. As a general rule, add ¼ teaspoon to ½ teaspoon xanthan gum per 1 cup of flour in the recipe. After experimenting with a variety of recipes, I developed the following formula for adding xanthan gum to gluten-free recipes.

BISCUITS AND SCONES
¾ teaspoon xanthan gum per batch of 8 to
    14 biscuits or scones

COFFEE CAKES AND OTHER CAKES
¼ teaspoon xanthan gum for a 1½-cup flour recipe
½ teaspoon xanthan gum for a 2-cup flour recipe
¾ teaspoon xanthan gum for a 3-cup flour recipe

MUFFINS
¾ teaspoon xanthan gum per batch of 12 muffins

PANCAKES
½ teaspoon xanthan gum per recipe

QUICK BREADS
¾ teaspoon xanthan gum per 4½ x 8½-inch loaf

SWEET ROLL DOUGH
1 teaspoon xanthan gum per batch of 18 rolls

WAFFLES
¼ teaspoon xanthan gum per recipe

YEAST BREADS
1 teaspoon xanthan gum per 4½ x 8½-inch loaf

DAIRY INGREDIENT SUBSTITUTION GUIDE

If you are allergic to dairy ingredients made from cow's milk, you can use the following suggestions to make ingredient substitutions in the recipes to suit your needs.

MILK
Replace cow's milk with an equal amount of one of the following:

Rice milk (unsweetened)
Almond milk (unsweetened)
Coconut milk
Soy milk (plain)
Goat's milk (if tolerated)

BUTTERMILK
Replace 1 cup of buttermilk with the following:

Pour 2 teaspoons lemon juice or distilled white vinegar into a measuring cup. Add enough rice milk, almond milk, or soy milk to measure 1 cup. Stir until well combined and wait 5 minutes before using.

SOUR CREAM
Replace dairy sour cream with an equal amount of one of the following:

Soy sour cream
Soy yogurt
Coconut yogurt

BUTTER
Replace unsalted butter with an equal amount of one of the following:

Unsalted margarine (stick form only)
Vegetable shortening
Organic shortening

gluten-free
ingredient sources

In many parts of the country, large grocery stores and specialty markets now carry a wide selection of gluten-free flours and ingredients. But in some regions, these ingredients are not readily available at the local market, and some specific ingredients are still difficult to find. Below is a list of stores and Internet sources that carry gluten-free products.

Specialty Markets

In addition to carrying packaged products, some specialty markets also carry bulk foods, such as rice flour and tapioca flour, in large bins at lower prices. However, these bulk foods are not certified as gluten-free because they are sold in open bins that can be exposed to other foods containing gluten. While these flours, starches, and other ingredients might be a good cost-conscious choice for people who are choosing gluten-free as a lifestyle change, they should not be used by those with celiac disease or a gluten sensitivity.

You can find packaged products at the following markets:

Trader Joe's
Wild Oats
Whole Foods
WinCo Foods
Henry's Marketplace/Sprouts Farmers Market
Baron's Market

Internet Sources

Many of these brands and products are carried by large retailers and may be available at stores in your local area.

Arrowhead Mills
www.arrowheadmills.com
(800) 434-4246

Bob's Red Mill Natural Foods
Has a large selection of gluten-free flours and other gluten-free ingredients.
www.bobsredmill.com
(800) 349-2173

Davis Baking Powder (Clabber Girl Corporation)
www.clabbergirl.com
(812) 232-9446

Ener-G Foods, Inc.
Gluten-free egg substitute
www.ener-g.com
(800) 331-5222

King Arthur Flour Company
Has a large selection of gluten-free flours, starches, yeast, extracts, and other gluten-free ingredients. Also offers a wide selection of baking pans and dishes, bread pans, muffin tins, cake pans, and other baking equipment.
www.kingarthurflour.com/shop
(800) 827-6836

Red Star Yeast
www.redstaryeast.com
(877) 677-7000

metric equivalents

LIQUID/DRY MEASURES

U.S.	METRIC
¼ teaspoon	1.25 milliliters
½ teaspoon	2.5 milliliters
1 teaspoon	5 milliliters
1 tablespoon (3 teaspoons)	15 milliliters
1 fluid ounce (2 tablespoons)	30 milliliters
¼ cup	60 milliliters
⅓ cup	80 milliliters
½ cup	120 milliliters
1 cup	240 milliliters
1 pint (2 cups)	480 milliliters
1 quart (4 cups; 32 ounces)	960 milliliters
1 gallon (4 quarts)	3.84 liters
1 ounce (by weight)	28 grams
1 pound	454 grams
2.2 pounds	1 kilogram

OVEN TEMPERATURES

°F	GAS MARK	°C
250	½	120
275	1	140
300	2	150
325	3	165
350	4	180
375	5	190
400	6	200
425	7	220
450	8	230
475	9	240
500	10	260
550	Broil	290

index

If you like this book, you'll love *Fine Cooking*.

Read *Fine Cooking* Magazine:

Get six idea-filled issues including FREE digital access. Every issue is packed with triple-tested recipes, expert advice, step-by-step techniques – everything for people who love to cook!

Subscribe today at:
FineCooking.com/4Sub

Discover our *Fine Cooking* Online Store:

It's your destination for premium resources from America's best cookbook writers, chefs, and bakers: cookbooks, DVDs, videos, special interest publications, and more.

Visit today at:
FineCooking.com/4More

Get our FREE *Fine Cooking* eNewsletter:

Our *Make It Tonight* weekday email supplies you with no-fail recipes for quick, wholesome meals; our weekly eNewsletter inspires with seasonal recipes, holiday menus, and more.

Sign up, it's free:
FineCooking.com/4Newsletter

Become a CooksClub member

Join to enjoy unlimited online access to member-only content and exclusive benefits, including: recipes, menus, techniques, and videos; our Test Kitchen Hotline; digital issues; monthly giveaways, contests, and special offers.

Discover more information online:
FineCooking.com/4Join